*The Best of*
# ORGANIC
# GARDENING ®

*Over 50 Years*
*of Organic Advice*
*and Reader-Proven*
*Techniques from*
*America's Best-Loved*
*Gardening Magazine*

**Edited by Mike McGrath**
**Contributing Editors: Vicki Mattern and Jill Jesiolowski**

Rodale Press, Emmaus, Pennsylvania

**Distributed in the book trade by St. Martin's Press**

2 4 6 8 10 9 7 5 3 1 hardcover

**The Best of Organic Gardening Editorial Staff:**

*Editor-in-Chief,* Organic Gardening *magazine:* Mike McGrath

*Managing Editor,* Organic Gardening *magazine:* Vicki Mattern

*Senior Editor,* Organic Gardening *magazine:* Jill Jesiolowski

*Project Editor:* Deborah L. Martin

*Cover and Interior Designer:* Karen Coughlin

*Front and Back Cover Photographer:* Rob Cardillo

*Book Layout:* Barbara Snyder

*Interior Photographers:* John Hamel (page 20), Ed Landrock (pages vi and 23), and RSI (pages 2, 11, 47, 68, 292, 299, and 300)

*Illustrators:* Frank Fretz, Tom Quirk, and Elayne Sears

*Technical Illustrator:* Randall Sauchuck

*Copy Editor:* Patricia E. Boyd

*Indexer:* Lynn Hutchinski

*Editorial Assistance:* Stephanie Wenner

*Manufacturing Coordinator:* Patrick T. Smith

**Rodale Home and Garden Books**

*Vice President and Editorial Director:* Margaret Lydic Balitas

*Managing Editor, Garden Books:* Ellen Phillips

*Art Director:* Michael Mandarano

*Copy Director:* Dolores Plikaitis

*Office Manager:* Karen Earl-Braymer

*If you have any questions or comments concerning this book, please write to:*

Rodale Press, Inc.
Book Readers' Service
33 East Minor Street
Emmaus, PA 18098

**Library of Congress Cataloging-in-Publication Data**

The best of Organic gardening : over 50 years of organic advice and reader-proven techniques from America's best-loved gardening magazine / edited by Mike McGrath and the editors of Organic gardening magazine.
    p.   cm.
Includes index.
ISBN 0–87596–646–2 (hardcover : alk. paper)
   1. Organic gardening. I. McGrath, Mike. II. Organic gardening.
SB453.5.B475   1995
635'.0484—dc20         95–30428

# Contents

# Introduction

## Mike McGrath

Hi, I'm Mike McGrath, and you're not.

Sorry folks, but once I typed out those first four words, the other three came charging out of the keyboard and jumped up onto the page, knocking me out of the way, kicking sand in my face, and taking my wallet—pretty much the same way slugs act when they first notice that you have planted potatoes and lettuce for them again this year.

But enough foolishness (and if you believe that, I have land to sell you in addition to this book).

Ahem...cough, cough...Step right up! Ladles, germs, chittlins of all ages! Welcome to a very special book! Why is it special, brother? Why, I'm glad you asked (but interrupt me again, and I'll yell "Hey Rube!")! It is special because the material herein all comes from a *very* special "book": *Organic Gardening* magazine!

In a tip o' the hat to my comic book past (as a comics "pro," I had two short cups of coffee working as a writer/editor in Marvel Comics' old Madison Avenue offices, but as a "fanboy" [a non-gender-specific term used to describe people who know *way* too much about the characters in those comics (Green Arrow's secret identity? A cinch! The name of the tiny European nation under Dr. Doom's dictatorial heel? *Super* easy. I even [and yes, I *am* somewhat ashamed to admit this] know Aquaman's real name and all five or six [it depends on how you count silver] colors of kryptonite)]), I like to refer to *OG* as "The World's Greatest Gardening Magazine!" (and yes, that ! is essential!), but I would also like to note that way back in the old original *Whole Earth Catalog* days, Stuart Brand gave *OG* a wonderful nickname and paid it a tremendous compliment at the same time when he called it "the most subversive magazine published in America."

And just who am I? Why I'm the person who strives to keep the spirit of both those monikers alive in *OG*'s current incarnation—a free-swinging, easy-to-hold, fun-to-read, yet scrupulously fact-checked and researched hands-in-the-dirt gardening magazine that also happens to contain more alliteration per page than the average Dr. Suess book.

Maybe you're a subscriber and already knew that. Maybe you remember the *OG* of an earlier era—a smaller size magazine, printed on what more than one reader has described as "potato-colored paper" that was filled with advice and tips from readers—and wonder what I'm talking about when I describe the *OG* of today. And maybe you're a current subscriber who *is* familiar with "today's *OG*" and *still* wonder what I'm talking about most (OK, all) of the time. (Note to those in category 3: Be

assured that few would ascribe the blame for any such cornfusion entirely to you.) And maybe you're just wondering when this guy is going to begin writing something that the average relatively sane person might mistake for a book introduction. (This last group, by the way, includes this reporter as a charter member.)

Well, whatever you are, you are almost certainly holding in your hands at this very moment a really nifty book, containing some of the absolute best stories ever published in this venerable magazine. How venerable are we? Well, I'm starting to notice that I have more gray hair than brown these days, and that what there is of *any* color is also starting to shy away from the front where maybe the light's too bright and...Oh, you mean the *magazine*?! Sheesh—that thing's been around forever—since Mel Bartholomew was tending square-*inch* gardens!

Actually, the first issue appeared in May 1942, the magazine has been published continuously ever since, and today (or at least on the day I spent pounding these words into my poor helpless keyboard, in a manner not unlike that of a carpenter driving nails into unyielding wood), I am very proud to point out *OG* has the largest paid circulation of any gardening magazine in the world! That's some pretty hot compost, eh? And I firmly believe that *OG* is number one *because* we're organic, not despite it.

Yes, a lot of things have changed over the years—the magazine's pages are physically larger now, the paper quality is better, there are lots of lush color photos and helpful illustrations, and there's this guy in charge who seems to need to have his medication adjusted. But one thing that has remained unchanged over the years is our unyielding commitment to the organic philosophy. Fifty-plus years of pointing out that maybe it isn't the best possible idea to spray poison all over your food before you eat it.

That's the basic thought process that got J. I. Rodale going back in the late thirties. J. I. (officially Jerome Irving, but either J. I. or Jerry to his friends, family, and employees [a trio of circles that are often interconnected]) had long been concerned that food grown with toxic and/or artificial chemicals was not as nourishing as food grown the way nature grows it. And then Sir Albert Howard, a British nobleman who had been sent to India to modernize their system of agriculture but instead embraced the Indian way, solidified everything that J. I. had been thinking in his 1940 book, *An Agricultural Testament.*

J. I. was in England when the book was published there and got to read it long before it was available in the States. When he got back to America and his fledgling "gentleman's publishing company" (like a "gentleman's farm," it had not a prayer of making money), he was so inspired by Sir Albert that he produced a special issue of his most successful magazine, *Fact Digest.*

Previously, *Fact Digest* had been essentially a *Reader's Digest* knockoff: interesting articles picked up from newspapers and magazines with their titles listed in tiny type on the cover so it looked as if there were a lot inside. But the February 1942 issue was a different animal indeed: A *wonderfully* garish green and purple cover was dominated by the single giant headline: "Present Day Crops Unfit for Human Consumption!" Boom—this issue, unlike its predecessors, flew off the racks and resulted in a deluge of letters calling for more such articles.

J. I. did them one better—he closed down *Fact Digest* and began publishing *Organic Farming and Gardening* in its place a scant three months later, with Sir Albert hisself as one of the editors! (And this was not an honorary title—Sir Albert actually worked for the magazine and continued in his position until his death some years later.) J. I. soon lured his son, Bob, into the business, and "OG," now titled *Organic Gardening and Farming* (some of our readers still refer to the current mag as "OGF" out of habit; I do the same thing with Shibe Park), really began to blossom.

One of my favorite discoveries in going through all the old *OGs* was the first real "anniversary issue" in 1962. *OGF* was then 20 years old, and many of the articles traced the magazine's two-decade history. But Editor Bob Rodale still found space in this celebratory issue to recommend a new book to his readers. It was written by a woman whose work they might already be familiar with, Bob wrote, as her previous book about the world's oceans had been very popular. The name of this new book by Rachel Carson was *Silent Spring*, and Bob felt that *OGF* readers would greatly enjoy it.

That's the perspective I always try to keep: This magazine was already 20 years old when *Silent Spring* was published.

It just shows to go ya—you stake out a radical position that receives no backing whatsoever from the scientific community but that is based on common sense (i.e., if the forests, plains, fields of wildflowers, etc., flourished so well before agricultural chemicals were invented, maybe the chemicals weren't *absolutely* necessary) and hold fast to it for four or five decades, you will wake up one morning and find that you have suddenly become mainstream.

J. I. Rodale passed away in 1971 at the age of 73. That may not sound like much of an "aging achievement" unless you know that all of the other men (and many of the women) in his immediate family had died—of heart disease mostly—in their fifties. J. I.'s "crackpot" ideas on health had added a good 20 years to his life.

And Bob Rodale was the youngest 60-year-old in the world when he was tragically killed in 1990 in an auto accident in Moscow while developing a magazine that would help Russian farmers restore their battered agricultural system. And yes, that magazine *is* being published today.

Soon after Bob's death, I was given the gift of editing the national treasure that is *Organic Gardening* magazine. As you'll see from the wonderful stories that we found, all I had to do was not screw it up. The pattern was perfect and the template so sound that it should continue to last for a long, long time.

"We," by the way, are three people (not counting my various multiple personalities, clones, imperfect duplicates, and/or dopplegangers created by exposure to Red Kryptonite [which current *OG* readers know always affects me in a unique and unpredictable manner]).

*OG* Senior Editor Jill Jesiolowski and *OG* Managing Editor Vicki Mattern performed the hard work of going through the 600-plus existing issues (mostly zeroing in on the '40s through the '70s) to locate the treasures herein (my personal favorite being "Rex Stout Tells Ruth How to Garden"!), and I helped a lot (OK, so mostly I tried not to get in their way too much; I think that still makes my original statement true).

They did a great job. And like I said, I didn't get in the way too much.

Enjoy this book—it's packed! And I'll see you in the next ish of *OG!*

*Mike McG*

# Chapter 1

# Openings

# "What Does Organic Mean?"

*J. I. Rodale*

*J. I. Rodale*

The genuine organiculturist is not merely an organic gardener or farmer, he lives his whole life in the organic manner. The organic principles must be felt deep in one's heart, and in everything one does. . . .

What good would it be if a man eats a dinner grown completely by the organic method, and then arises from the table to do an unkindness to a neighbor?

The organic way is the golden-rule way. It means that we must be kind to the soil, to ourselves, and to our fellowman. Organic means goodness. A heart that is full of benevolence will create in the body a spirit of physical and mental well-being that will enable it to better absorb all the nutritional elements from organically grown food.

## "Drought and Floods" 1955

This water problem is going to become increasingly acute as the years go on, if agriculture continues to be blind to the simple logic that water and chemicals do not mix. . . .

The handwriting is on the wall. Scientists see a future in which there will not be enough water to go around, so they are working on processes to make it from seawater. But there is no substitute for the natural rainwater that God makes fall upon us. There is much scientific evidence to show that irrigated crops have a lower nutritional quality. When will people begin to learn that man's survival depends on remaining close to natural principles, that life is a cycle in which water, food and man are automatically regulated, but that if man becomes a brigand and despoils the soil for the sake of a mess of cash pottage, his water supplies will suffer? Any bird knows how to keep its nest clean of its droppings, but man? . . .

## Excerpts from *Pay Dirt*, 1945

Where any one item in nature's cycle is disturbed, it will be found that others are automatically affected. Nature consists of a chain of interrelated and interlocking life cycles. Remove any one factor and you will find that nature cannot do her work effectively.

This back-to-the-land movement is one of the healthiest signs of a progressive people. Civilizations that get too far from the land are bound to decay. Town and farm complement each other, need each other, and must understand each other's problems and ideals. If not, society and civilization decay through ignorance, antagonism, exploitation, and the artificiality that is their product.

I believe that a whole new era of agricultural research is in the making—one that will benefit our country at large far more than all the research of the past has done, one that will more nearly help to create a healthy society and keep it in close touch with the land from which it gets its strength and sweetness—a country without city or rural slums, a country of homes and gardens, parks and forests, a country of prosperous farms and a healthy, vigorous people creating a fine, new community life "in the pursuit of happiness."

## "How Should Towns Handle Garbage?" 1947

Very little has been done in this country in the way of municipal projects for composting town wastes, but good progress seems to have been made in New Zealand, South Africa, and England. Recently I have received letters asking for information about plans to devise methods for converting such household refuse into humus. I recall communications from Toledo and Middletown, Ohio. However, there is practically no information or experience available. A movement could be set on foot to get the U.S. government to start an experimental project going.

The handling of town wastes or garbage should not be confused with the making of sludge from sewage. Household wastes in the average town in Pennsylvania are picked up by truck and in many cases are brought out to farmers who feed it to pigs. It would be better if it could be composted in some manner. In the nearby city of Allentown, whose population is about one hundred thousand, the garbage is burned in a municipal incinerator at a high cost to the city. No thought is given to the irreparable loss to the land of this valuable organic matter, to the benefit of the health of the inhabitants if it were composted and returned to the soil.

## "The Organic Creed" 1956

The organiculturist must realize that in him is placed a sacred trust, the task of producing food that will impart health to the people who consume it. As a patriotic duty he assumes an obligation to preserve fertility of the soil, a precious heritage that he must pass on, undefiled and even enriched, to subsequent generations.

## What Is Organic Gardening?

Very briefly, organic gardening or farming is a system whereby a fertile soil is maintained by applying nature's own law of replenishing it—that is, the addition and preservation of humus, the use of organic matter in-

stead of chemical fertilizers, and, of course, the making of a compost pile and mulching. Organiculture is a vigorous and growing movement, one that is destined to alter our concepts of the garden and the farm and to revolutionize our methods of operating them in order to secure for ourselves more abundant and more perfect food. The seed sown by Sir Albert Howard, the great pioneer in organic farming, is beginning to bloom lustily and with such vim that it is already thriving and propagating by its own strength. Composters by the thousands are telling their neighbors of the wonders of this new, yet in reality age-old, method, and they in turn are listening and beginning to follow. Compost heaps are becoming an integral part of the farm, the garden, and the landscape. Organiculture is here to stay. When it is possible to see astounding results obtained by one's own hand, a quick good-bye is said to groping and artificial test-tube methods.

## Economic Aspects versus Health Aspects

One newspaper states that a certain spray will save the nation's farmers millions of dollars' worth of crops a year; but, I might add, it could cause the people who eat foods raised by it tens of millions of dollars in medical and hospital costs. Business is in the form of a monetary equation, and we must not fail to study that formula in its every aspect, paying attention to both sides. The agricultural press wildly acclaims a new product, mouthing the prepared statements of the manufacturers to the effect that the product is not dangerous to human beings in the quantity present in the harvested crop. But if it is added to all the food preservatives, all the germ killers, the benzoates of soda, the chlorine and alum in water, the sodium nitrite in frankfurters, the chemicals in bread and in every item of food on the daily menu, what then would be the cumulative effect? I am sure such a test has not been made.

This is a situation that calls for immediate action. The public must speak out boldly and at once. It must write to congressmen, senators, newspapers, agricultural colleges, and the Pure Food and Drug Administration [now the Food and Drug Administration], asking that an unqualified ban be placed on this type of insecticide, even for ornamental plants, because there are too many uneducated farmers and truck gardeners who will be tempted to use it on food crops if they can purchase it for ornamental use. This subject must be brought up for discussion in public forums and at parent-teacher meetings. The public has an inalienable right to eat unpoisoned food, and industry must learn to make profits without infringing upon that right.

*September 1971*

## Briefly Quoted
## February 1954

"The most important of the earth's resources is a fertile soil, because on this depends the food supply of mankind both now and in the future. It follows therefore that soil fertility occupies a place apart and must be regarded as a trust: Each generation may make the fullest use of it, but each generation must hand it on unimpaired for those who follow. If, on the other hand, we allow this precious heritage to be exploited for the profit of some individual or group, we condone profiteering at the expense of posterity—one of the meanest forms of banditry."

*Sir Albert Howard, C.I.E.*

# Why I Started Organic Gardening

*J. I. Rodale*

Editor J. I. Rodale recalls the events that launched the organic idea in America—and begins his own exciting crusade.

People often ask how I became interested in the organic idea. "Why did you ever start a publication like *Organic Gardening*?" is one way the question is frequently put to me. Sometimes it's not phrased quite so politely—as when someone inquires, "What in the world made you take up such a crazy notion?"

Well, no matter which attitude shows itself in the inquirer's tone, I'm glad to explain the evolution of the organic concept—and hope to bring a measure of understanding and benefits to anyone who is seeking to learn.

On a worldwide level, the organic movement had its inception in the researches and experiments of Sir Albert Howard in India, over a period of 40 years, culminating in the publishing of his outstanding findings in 1940. Sir Albert was a British government agronomist whose mind integrated itself with what his eyes saw.

Howard's basic theory was not to wait until the plant got sick, not to use the artificial method of spraying poisons to prevent disease organisms from taking hold in the plant, but to endow the plant with such strength that it could resist disease.

He had an instinctive feeling that the use of chemical fertilizers was doing more harm than good, that it was destroying the life, the vitality, of the topsoil, that it was merely a "shot-in-the-arm" that gave you a momentary spurt in yield, but struck back in bringing about conditions that actually invited pests and disease.

Around the 75-acre experimental farm that he stubbornly insisted the government provide him without restrictions on its use, Sir Albert kept a close watch on the methods of the natives. He saw how careful they were that all animal and plant residues were returned to the soil. Every blade of grass that could be salvaged, all leaves that fell, all weeds that were cut down found their way back into the soil, there to decompose and take what was their proper place in nature's balance sheet.

Sir Albert wasn't surprised when he observed a gradual lessening of disease. He was amazed, however, that when his oxen rubbed noses with other cattle that had the dreaded hoof-and-mouth disease they did not contract it, although they had not been inoculated. Their bodies had become strengthened and could fight off dangerous disease organisms because their food came from a soil rich in living humus matter, which had not been defiled with dead chemicals. Sir Albert summed up his work with the classic statement, "Artificial fertilizers lead to artificial nutrition, artificial animals and finally to artificial men and women."

## Health Idea "Hit Me Like a Ton of Bricks"

I had read about Sir Albert Howard's work in a British health magazine, and his idea hit me like a ton of bricks. Up to this time, in reading many books, I found that no one had ever questioned how a vegetable was raised as far as its nutritional quality was concerned. Whether a carrot was grown in a highly fertile soil or in a cinder bank seemed to make no difference to nutritionists who made up tables of the nutritional contents of carrots, obtaining the vegetables from one source and sometimes from another.

What really got me excited in that original article that introduced me to Sir Albert Howard was a description of a feeding experiment in a boys' boarding school in New Zealand, where the students ate foods raised with compost made by Howard's method, a method that had taken him 30 years to perfect. Formerly, in the days when artificial fertilizers were used on the school's farm, cases of colds, measles, and scarlet fever used to run through the school. Now they tended to be confined to the single case imported from the outside. The number of colds was reduced tremendously. Further, the taste and quality of the vegetables definitely improved.

Reports on the school's findings appeared in the British medical journal, the *Lancet,* and the *N. Y. Times* of June 30, 1940. Identifying it as the Mount Albert Grammar School, the

*Times* said, "Dr. Chapman (of the Physical and Mental Welfare Society of New Zealand) advised that a change should be made from vegetables and fruits grown in soil fertilized by chemicals, to produce raised on soil treated only with humus. The results were startling. Catarrh, colds and influenza were greatly reduced and in the 1938 epidemic of measles, the boys had only mild attacks whereas new admissions succumbed readily."

## "We Must Get a Farm"

Then I found that Sir Albert had written a book called *An Agricultural Testament,* published by Oxford University Press. I obtained a copy and read it with great enthusiasm. It changed my whole way of life. I decided that we must get a farm at once and raise as much of our family's food by the organic method as possible.

We bought a 60-acre farm halfway between Allentown and Emmaus, Pennsylvania. I made contact with Sir Albert, and we had an interesting correspondence in which he answered many questions.

The farm we bought was a most miserable piece of land—we chose it on account of its location. It was greatly run-down because of the poverty of the tenant farmer who had run it. There were many dead chickens, which had been thrown under the corn cribs. We inherited a small amount of corn in the cribs— small, gnarled, disease-ridden speci-

mens. A government farm agency told me later that they had turned down a request for a loan to this farmer because they couldn't see how he could make a living on this farm.

I had difficulty getting a farmhand, but at last got what you might call an "unemployable." Together we began to farm organically—making plenty of mistakes. Compost was made by piling up animal manures mixed with leaves, weeds, spoiled hay, and any other organic refuse we could find. We used no so-called chemical fertilizers or insecticidal sprays of any kind. The results, for a couple of amateurs, were simply remarkable. At harvesttime wagonload upon wagonload of long, golden, healthy corn came into our cribs.

When I saw this I felt I had to share this information with the rest of the country. I started publishing and editing a magazine called *Organic Farming and Gardening* in 1942, with Sir Albert Howard as my associate editor. Little did I realize what I was touching off—that I would be the one to introduce this great movement into the United States.

Our first issue came out in May 1942, a slim thing with a self-cover and 16 pages of coarse newsprint. What did I know about farming or gardening? Practically nothing. But I began to read and practice.

I was surprised by how much fertilizer material we could get from our own farm. We cut weeds from out-of-the-way places. We used the corncobs instead of burning them up as other farmers did. We gathered up leaves and grass clippings. We found that the table garbage amounted to a sizable amount at the end of a year of eating. Every bit of it was placed in the compost heaps, and in about four months, after turning the heap twice, it turned into a fine, brown, woodsy-looking substance that made my mouth water merely to look at. We used the litter from our chickenhouse and the bedded manure of our steers.

In the city we found places where the municipality had dumped leaves for years, feed mills that had accumulated chaff, wholesale poultry establishments that had barrels of valuable cuttings every day, breweries with spent hops, and shoe repairers with leather dust (which is living organic matter). In the country we hauled the spoiled hay of lazy farmers who did not know that it is a wonderful fertilizer. When we told them that they should use it themselves for this purpose, they thought we were crazy.

In the second issue there was an article by Sir Albert Howard ("The Good Earth"), and he did not miss an issue for many years. I loved his writing. He was a literary man and used phrases like "soil banditry . . . the depletion and recuperation of a fertile soil . . . they are a part of Creation . . . Nature is the supreme farmer . . . Mother Earth . . . to transgress Nature's immutable laws . . . " and so on.

Meanwhile, I went from book to book and from farm to farm, trying to squeeze into days what should have gone into years. The publication of a magazine furnished a wonderful means for farmers and gardeners to pool their cumulative experiences.

I printed about 14,000 copies of our first issue and sent them out free to farmers, soliciting their subscriptions. The price was ten cents a copy or one dollar a year. We received 12 subscriptions from this campaign, and our prospects looked bleak. I reduced the number of copies printed and started working by means of circular letters. This began to show better results, and soon I became more encouraged when our list of subscribers began to grow.

In those days we were held up by war-time paper quotas and could not do a real job of building circulation until about 1946. When the restrictions were removed, our list of subscribers began to soar until we hit the hundred thousand mark. Later, in 1948, we began publishing the *Organic Farmer,* for the large-scale growers, then recombined it with *Organic Gardening* in 1954.

Unfortunately, with respect to our country, *Organic Gardening and Farming*'s evolution took place in a period of too-rapid growth and inflation, in the years of war and turbu-

---

**Briefly Quoted
February 1954**

For what things a man shall sow, those also shall he reap.

*Galatians 6:7*

lence and strife. Our voices have sometimes been blotted out, but we have accomplished a great deal in this preparatory period and are satisfied.

We came on the scene just in time to be a deterring force against the reckless misuse of our lands. Never before in the history of our country has there been a 25-year period in which there has been so much soil erosion, so much drought and flooding, so much spraying of insecticide and fungicide poisons, so much chemical fertilizer used, and so much plant and animal disease. In fact, never before in the history of our country has there been so much human chronic disease.

During this period we unearthed much evidence indicating there is a relationship between a chemicalized soil and the increasing amount of human degenerative disease, and we gathered among our readers hundreds of physicians who also did not fear to express the same opinion. Among our readers, thousands upon thousands began to raise their own vegetables organically, and many of them have written to us expressing the improvement of their health in glowing words. Many have also written to their local newspapers, describing how the organic method has produced fabulously bountiful growth in their vegetables and flowers, and thus the knowledge of the method has spread to every part of our country.

## "Greater Progress Ahead"

And the number of people who are doing more than just growing organic vegetables is increasing. I mean the people who are buying places with a little acreage and who are raising chickens, pigs, sheep, rabbits, and so on. Also, the number of larger farms that are adopting the organic method is growing rapidly. It is becoming a way of life for more and more people. It is giving character to people who have taken up the cudgels for an important issue—and that, too, is why I started *Organic Gardening!*

I am confident and determined that *Organic Gardening and Farming* will bring more people into our ranks, to make them more health-conscious, to teach them the philosophy and desirability of producing our food organically, to cause them to batter at the doors of our halls of legislation so that a better conception of nutrition may be reflected in the future laws of our country.

The next 25 years will mean even greater progress ahead, I'm convinced. It's a lot of years to do things in. Let's keep our chins up and help toward bringing America to an organic consciousness!

*September 1971*

# Organic Soil Keeps the Insects Away

*Robert Rodale*

The most controversial of all organic claims is that plants grown on rich organic soil, without use of chemical fertilizers, and without being sprayed, will not be attacked by insects because insects won't like their tastes. Down through the decades, organic gardeners and farmers have made that claim because they saw with their own eyes that their plants often enjoyed an almost mysterious immunity to insect attack. Neighboring growers would have to spray several times a season, while organic gardeners and farmers could keep insects well under control by using a few biological controls plus some old-fashioned hand-picking of beetles and insect egg clusters.

Needless to say, that kind of belief in the power of organic fertilizer raised the hackles of many orthodox garden experts, who put far more confidence in poison sprays than in the ability of healthy plants to send out "keep off" signals to bugs. How well I remember one time, about ten years ago, when the famous horticulturist Norman Taylor visited the Organic Gardening Experimental Farm to gather information to update the "organic" entry in his popular *Encyclopedia of Gardening*.

*Robert Rodale*

"I am impressed by what you people are doing," he told me, "but I don't believe that there is any truth to your claim that plants grown on organically fertilized soil will resist insects."

Even the evidence of a thriving, unsprayed garden didn't convince him, but I do give Mr. Taylor credit for at least coming to look, at a time when organic gardeners were widely thought to be slightly weird or downright eccentric. Many of the more vocal critics of organic methods just sneered, without bothering to check on the evidence they said didn't exist.

## Evidence Supports Organic Claims

Organic gardeners began saying that their plants repelled bugs because of what they saw with their own eyes, not because they read about it in books. In the early days, there were only practical results to show doubters, not laboratory evidence. However, in 1950 positive evidence was found that certain kinds of insect pests could taste the difference between healthy plants and sick plants. And they preferred the sick plants! Leonard Haseman, a professor of entomology at the University of Missouri, began to publish results of experiments showing that insects thrived on a different nutritional mix than people—hardly surprising, yet revolutionary. Here are Professor Haseman's own words:

"It is a well-established fact that man and the higher animals, in order to escape the ill effects of 'hidden hunger' and nutritional deficiency diseases, generally require a well-balanced diet rich in minerals, vitamins and other factors protecting health. Such a diet calls for vegetables, fruits, grains and other plant products grown on fertile soil, and meat and dairy products from animals fed well-enriched crops. On the other hand, not all insects require or can utilize well-balanced diets of this type. Some of them, we find, thrive and reproduce better on unbalanced or inferior diets as we think of them. Such being the case, it is but natural that these types of insect pests should thrive and increase as depletion of soil fertility requires the growing of less nutritious and less bountiful crops."

You would think an idea like that would arouse interest and spur discussion and investigation. The Haseman statements, though, were greeted with loud silence by the orthodox pest control community, which was hell-bent on a search for ever more powerful pesticide poisons. Most entomologists were not interested in what bugs like to eat, but only in what chemicals would kill insects most effectively.

Today, Professor Haseman's ideas are far more likely to be given wide consideration. Let's read more of what he had to say back in 1950, writing in the *Organic Farmer*:

"In nature there are abundant illustrations of insect pests choosing and breeding more abundantly on weak and undernourished plants or crops and livestock. Take for instance lice on calves. It is the weak, underfed, and undernourished, rough-coated, weaned calves and not those suckling, fat, smooth-coated ones which are often eaten up with lice.

"In like manner weakened trees, due to drought, leaky gas mains or loss of roots due to excavation, will always be more heavily attacked by borers than nearby healthy trees of the same kind. Chinch bugs tend to collect and breed more heavily on corn or wheat up on the eroded slopes rather than down at the foot of the slope where the eroded soil minerals and organic matter pile up. In this case it is the high level of nitrogen in the vigorous crop at the foot of the slope that the bug is unable to take. As is well known, the chinch bug never attacks the legumes, and soybeans planted with corn may even help to protect the corn crop from attack by the pest. To prove that high levels of nitrogen in the soil and taken up by plants will protect corn from chinch bugs, we here at the Missouri Agricultural Experiment Station have reared the pest on seedling corn plants grown on low and high levels of nitrogen, and have found that they thrive, breed better and live longer on a diet low in nitrogen. What then is more simple in dealing with this pest than to keep soil fertility high with plenty of nitrogen supplied with legume green-manures supplemented in other ways?"

## Other Research Points to Soil-Pest Connection

Professor Haseman is not by any means completely alone among scientists in following a natural approach to insect control and in pointing out that insects like to eat plants that have wrong nutritional balance. The American Association for the Advancement of Science held a seminar in 1957 on biological control of plant and animal pests, and the report of that meeting contains an article on the very subject we are talking about. "Nutrition of the Host and Reaction to Pests" by Professor J. G. Rodriguez of the University of Kentucky is loaded with evidence that the condition of the soil can make plants either more or less attractive to pests.

First, Professor Rodriguez says there is a strong possibility pesticides actually make plants taste better to insects. There is no question, he says, that plants take up pesticide chemicals in their leaves, because there is proof that sometimes plants are actually stimulated by small applications of DDT, for example, or are stunted by larger amounts. Therefore, although spraying kills insects, it works against the grower in the long run by making the plants more attractive to insects.

Lack of water can have a similar effect. During a dry spell, says Professor Rodriguez, some plants take up nitrates much more quickly than the drought-stricken foliage can reduce them. The imbalance can attract mites, which "develop in high numbers in orchards and fields under drought conditions." How does the organic method help in that case? Ample humus in the soil is one of the best protections against drought because humus is a perfect reservoir to balance soil moisture reserves. Humus soaks up moisture during rains, and meters it out slowly in dry spells.

The research reported in the Rodriguez article covers insect appetite for plants that have been grown in different artificial nutrient solutions. Such hydroponic soil media are in fact an exact opposite of organic methods. Yet there is some usefulness to this kind of research because it shows that when plants grow in a medium that is imbalanced, with too much or too little of certain nutrients, insect attack tends to increase.

## Nutrient Imbalances Favor Mites and Aphids

Mites seem particularly sensitive to differences in plant quality caused by fertilizer imbalances, which incidentally are very common in chemical gardening or farming situations. For example, Professor Rodriguez says that when concentrations of all the major elements were doubled in solutions used to grow tomatoes, the mite population doubled, too. Haven't you known of a chemical gardener who put on twice as much fertilizer as recommended "to be sure that the plants are well fed," then saw his

plants getting eaten up by pests?

Putting too much of one particular nutrient on soil can also cause trouble, by creating imbalances of other nutrients. Potassium is one of the major nutrients for plants, and is present in all mixed chemical fertilizers in varying amounts. But too much potassium in the soil can block uptake of magnesium, a very important element that is not usually present in mixed fertilizers. Professor Rodriguez reported that mites thrived when potassium was high and magnesium and calcium were low. In a good organic garden, that situation is not likely to happen, because potassium and magnesium are supplied as natural rock powders, whose nutrients are made available to plants slowly, over a period of years.

Of interest in the Rodriguez article is a report from Russian scientists that "the introduction of high rates of mineral fertilizer can increase the osmotic pressure of plant sap two to three times that of normal, and also increase populations of *T. urticae*," which is a kind of mite. "This introduces the interesting possibility," says Professor Rodriguez, "that mites not only obtain more favorable nutrients with increased fertilization, but also may have the feeding process facilitated."

Next we move on to aphids. The article "Nutrition of Host and Reaction to Pests" says that "aphids respond positively to increased elements, particularly nitrogen." In other words, put more nitrogen fertilizer on your soil and you will make aphids happier.

Professor Rodriguez reports that extra nitrogen pleases the bean aphid, the cabbage aphid, the cotton aphid, and the pea aphid. That's a lot of aphids.

Professor Rodriguez sums up his review article by making a few basic points. First, he says, "because of the complex interrelationships between elements in the plant, the exact mineral requirements of a particular pest are difficult if not impossible to determine." In other words, when we talk about plants having a natural ability to repel pests, we are speaking of something that is far from an exact science. The environment of plants—soil, nutrients, light, temperature, and water—vary almost indescribably. One part of a field is different from another part, and one plant responds to a certain situation differently than does another plant. The chemical growers' answer to this variability is to rebel against it, to fight with chemicals for a uniform, scorched-earth policy of blasting all pests out of the garden and field.

## Chemical Methods Go against Nature's Logic

Chemical methods are therefore completely at odds with the basic logic of nature. The natural environment is *not* uniform, and it is bound eventually to trip up and disappoint any grower who attempts to garden in a rigid way, following a chemical prescription written by some white-coated dude in a laboratory.

Organic gardeners and farmers, on the other hand, weave the variability of nature into their system, and use it to the fullest. We grow a variety of different plants, rotate crops on different plots each year, and expect something a little different from our gardens every season. The variableness of plants' resistance to insects therefore is not objectionable to us. On the contrary, it is part of the adventure and charm of gardening by nature's way.

The last recommendation made by Professor Rodriguez is an appeal for balance: "There appears to be a good basis for maintaining a conservative fertilization program which is not overbalanced in any one element." The organic grower is able to follow that recommendation better than anyone else, because balance is at the heart of the organic method. Organic matter is the basic balancing agent in the soil, helping to dispense both moisture and nutrients as they are needed by plants. Organic fertilizers do not overwhelm plants with a tremendous amount of one particular nutrient. They feed the soil first, so that the earth can in turn feed plants, animals, and people in a natural way.

And organically grown plants will be eaten by some insects, too, but not as many as chemically grown plants will. For organically grown plants have built-in resistance to insect attack.

*June 1971*

# Soil Is Better Than Gold

## Robert Rodale

I read a story not long ago that made me think about which is a better investment—gold or soil. It was told by an American economist, and happened in Italy about 20 or 30 years ago. I can't remember the name of the economist, or his exact words, but here is roughly how the story went.

"I was working in Italy after the war, and had a very intelligent young Italian man on my staff. He told me that every month he would take part of his pay and buy a small gold coin, which he gave to his wife to keep in a safe place. I told him that was a foolish investment."

"Don't you Americans tell us about gold," the young man snapped back at the American. "If things get bad again, I tell my wife that she can take one of those gold coins to a farmer and get enough food to eat for a month."

That story tells clearly the true appeal of gold. It is the investment of the disaster-minded. Gold does not pay dividends of yield interest, but it increases in value as confidence in paper money declines. And there is always the thought in the back of the gold-hoarder's mind that—especially if the yellow metal is owned in the form of small coins—it can be used as currency in times of economic collapse or war.

Is gold really the *best* disaster investment, though? What about the farmer who grew the food that the young Italian couple were relying on to supply to them when catastrophe struck? When you stop to think about it, the farmer was in a pretty good position, too. His investment, the soil, paid dividends during times of stability and peace, yet he was also there to supply the "good-as-gold" food when regular money couldn't buy anything in the stores.

## Food in the 1980s

We are at the start of a new decade that is going to be a time of big changes in the way we live. There is general agreement about that. But I feel that the changes to come will be more extensive than all but a few people realize. Yes, there is an energy crunch, and the effects of that will ripple throughout all aspects of life. But we are also heading into a soil and food crunch. I am convinced that the days of surplus farm and food production are almost over. My guess is that you haven't heard or read about that possibility anywhere yet, except right here in these pages. But it is bound to happen.

Farm production per acre stopped increasing 10 to 15 years ago and has been flat ever since. Lately, agricultural research has not been able to come up with big breakthroughs that boost production, like the development of hybrid corn, or the introduction of soybeans as a source of protein for animal feed. There is no more new fertile land that can be opened up to farming. Just the opposite. Farm soil is being built over and is washing and blowing away at an astounding rate. If soil destruction is not stopped almost immediately, which is unlikely, farm production of food could begin to *decrease* soon.

I am by nature an optimist, which is probably why up to now I haven't bought any gold coins or ingots. My view is that we have so much slack in our use of energy and so much potential for better use of our soil that our future life is not going to be all that bad. Quite likely we will enjoy life even more after we get over our wasteful ways. But I feel compelled to point out to you that there are a few more reasons why a food crunch is on the horizon.

At one time there was a big stock of surplus cereal in the world. Here in the United States we had a supply that could last for several years. That is now depleted, almost gone. A crop failure could catch us without much food to fall back on. And changes in climate are predicted. We have been through a multiyear period of very favorable weather. While I am not expecting another ice age to start soon, we could find our weather in the 1980s both surprising and disappointing.

Then there is the population situation. The number of people in the world is increasing more rapidly than at any other time in recorded history. True, the birth rate is going down in many countries. But there are so many women of childbearing age that total population is rising. Every day there are about 192,000 additional people in the world. Since agricultural production is increasing much more slowly than population, it is easy to see that avoiding a worsening of the world food situation is going to require some clear thinking, hard work, and a generous dose of good luck.

## Comparing Advantages of Gold versus Soil

The disruption of normal social and economic activities caused by a world-wide food shortage would probably increase the attractiveness of both gold and soil as investments. But I feel that if you compare the relative merits of each, soil is clearly the winner. And because of the shortage of food that is likely to occur within this decade, soil will soon replace gold as the most talked-about and symbolic thing of enduring value.

That is going to happen because people have always put a high value on things that are rare. Gold has always been rare and will remain so, even though more is being mined all the time. But soil has never before been in short supply on a worldwide basis. Erosion and encroachment of deserts have ruined the soil of large

regions, and there have been famines caused by bad weather. But never have people had to contend with the thought that on a global basis there isn't enough soil to go around. Within a few years, that will change. Soil will, for the first time, become rare. And worldwide television and news reports quoting crop production statistics and high food prices will carry that news everywhere.

A new symbolism of soil will develop. Until now, soil has symbolized dirt in the minds of many, especially city people who have little or no feel for the tremendous productive capacity of good soil. I think we are going to see that attitude change rapidly. Access to good earth will become the greatest of all forms of protection against inflation, and a much stronger security blanket than it is at present.

Don't minimize the importance of the idea that the symbolic value of soil can and will increase. The value of gold is mainly symbolic. People think it's money; therefore, it actually is money. They wear it around their necks to show other people their wealth, or keep pieces of it in a safety deposit box and dream of its growing value. For thousands of years gold has worked that mental magic. Soon, soil will begin to have the same appeal.

When you spend gold, it is gone. Soil, properly cared for, is permanent. You can even take land that is poor and build it into rich earth of great productive capacity by planting green manure crops and by adding to it manure, compost, mulch, and natural mineral fertilizers. Especially on a garden scale, you can take land that is not productive now and turn it into black gold by building its fertility. Soon, that regeneration of earth will become one of the most rewarding of all challenges.

Land close to cities could become the most valuable of all, because of the people who live nearby. They are both customers for surplus food and productive workers. The working partnership between people and the land will become a much more important ingredient in the productive capacity of soil in the future. People are needed to make land produce. Farmers substitute for people by using large, energy-guzzling tractors and other machines. Even with that mechanical help, they produce much less food per unit of land than do gardeners working the earth in a more personal way. Land for gardening is already higher-priced than farmland. The difference in value could become even greater.

Isn't all land already overpriced? No. Land here in the United States, where surplus food is still being produced, is much cheaper per acre than in other developed countries that need to import food, such as Japan and most European countries. Land will be needed both as a place for people to live and as a site for the production of food. Both of those real needs, and the new symbolism of land as the ultimate item of value,

could push prices much higher.

I want to make one final point. Suppose you have a hoard of small gold coins at home, and a food shortage develops here in the United States. With luck, the cause will not be war, and it may not even be an absence of food in central storehouses. The shortage could be caused by transportation breakdowns, most likely a lack of fuel to carry food from farms to processing plants to supermarkets.

Where would you take your gold coin to buy food? In postwar Italy, as in this country several decades ago, small, diversified farms could be found near all towns and cities. There were even truck farms within the city limits of New York. All are gone now. Many Americans would have to walk or ride their bicycles for hours to get to a farm, and then likely would find an agribusiness operation with bins of one or two commodities on hand. Spending your coin would present a real challenge.

So the best fallback position is not gold, but a large garden and a pantry full of home-produced food.

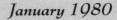

*January 1980*

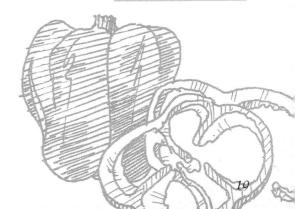

# A Love Story

## Ardie Rodale

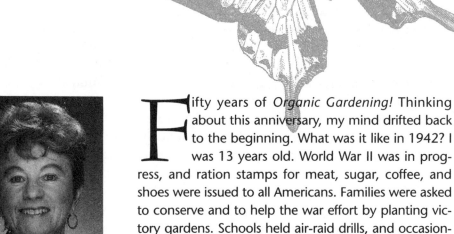

*Ardie Rodale*

Fifty years of *Organic Gardening!* Thinking about this anniversary, my mind drifted back to the beginning. What was it like in 1942? I was 13 years old. World War II was in progress, and ration stamps for meat, sugar, coffee, and shoes were issued to all Americans. Families were asked to conserve and to help the war effort by planting victory gardens. Schools held air-raid drills, and occasionally at night there were blackout practices.

At this time, J. I. Rodale decided to move his family to a farm on the outskirts of Allentown, Pennsylvania, where they planned to grow their own food and raise animals. He had been reading Sir Albert Howard's *Agricultural Testament* and was eager to try out some of the ideas. J. I. was a city man who found his heart and life's work through touching the earth. His son, Robert, who was just 11 years old, worked side by side with retired farmers and masons, working the land and building retaining walls.

One of Bob's first chores was to clean the rocks out of the land so that they could be used to make a "stone garden," in which rows of plants were interspersed between rows of rocks. The sun would heat up the stones, which would heat up the soil, so that vegetables could grow earlier in spring and later in fall. A greenhouse was built, and huge pits were dug in the dark basement where earthworms were bred to later be placed in the soil.

The first issue of *Organic Farming and Gardening* was published in May 1942. In large letters on the front cover were the words: "BACK TO NATURE IN AGRICULTURE." The cover price was ten cents.

Looking over this first issue, I was amazed to read the first article—written by J. I.—about the following experiment: "A few years ago in an English health magazine published in London there appeared a brief account of an experiment in feeding of children which has a tremendous significance in connection with bodily resistance to disease. There were two groups of children. One group was fed on vegetables raised by ordinary methods with liberal use of chemical fertilizers. The second ate vegetables grown by the use of compost fertilizer only, containing no chemicals. The latter children enjoyed a singular immunity to colds whereas the former suffered from the regular, normal conditions as to colds, coughs, etc."

J. I. went on to say that although he had read many health and medical journals, he had never before seen this correlation between how crops were raised and the health of a person.

Another article in that first issue detailed the "Indore method of composting" by Sir Albert Howard. It stated that along with organic wastes—weeds, straw, hedge clippings, leaves, and the like—worn-out clothing, leather, and sacking could also be added to the compost pile after soaking them in water. Then, animal manure could be added, followed by earth, and then the last essential ingredient—water.

That first issue of the magazine was so clearly focused to where we are today. It has been an orchestration of soil and health for 50 years!

## From One Voice to Many

But when I reread that first issue of *Organic Farming and Gardening,* I felt a little sad. It appeared to me that this was a single voice reaching out to the world. The beginning of a dream. A hard road. Then I turned to the latest two issues of *Organic Gardening,* and I felt a bubbling up of excitement as I realized that there are *many* voices now. So many new ideas have been generated over the years! And you, the readers, and the staff and our family have shared so much knowledge! We are all working together to nourish our environment—and each other. It's almost like it has become participatory theater. It's mind-expanding and fun!

J. I. and Anna Rodale and my parents were friends, not through gardening, but because both families were interested in the arts. When J. I.'s name came up, I often remember my father telling people in almost a whisper, "He's a real genius!"

In June 1951, Bob and I were married. I was 22 years old, and he had just turned 21. He was already working for *Organic Gardening*—following in his father's footsteps of publishing information for a better world. Bob never thought of pursuing another career. The land J. I. had purchased for the family was an integral part of their lives.

## Nonstop Ideas

You might wonder what it was like to come into a family like this one. J. I. was a nonstop idea man who was always trying out his new ideas on the family. Often it was hectic, and Anna finally had to make a decree: "J. I., I need 24 hours' notice on any change you expect us to carry out." Mealtime was always invigorating. We ate our homegrown organic food and ingested ideas and dreams as well.

J. I. and Bob were gardeners of the soil and planters of the mind. As our family grew, the land, the dreams, and the work continued to be an integrated whole in all our lives.

When J. I. died in 1971 of a massive heart attack while taping a guest appearance on the *Dick Cavett Show*, his ideas were beginning to be accepted after 29 years of spreading the organic mission. The dream was becoming a reality.

Bob carried the dream even further. He was able to bring wide vision and credibility to J. I.'s ideas, and while he may have appeared shy, he loved people. He worked hard to find out what people needed and then helped them find solutions. And as he reached out to help others, it filled him with the energy to keep going.

He reached out to farmers and gardeners, starting projects first in our country and then in developing nations to provide better food and a better way of life for the people. He gave his life in Russia while working on a project to help improve the Russian food supply and gardening methods—in a car accident on September 20, 1990, en route to the airport on his way home.

The last few years of his life, Bob spent a lot of time in contemplation—listening to nature through walks in the fields, riding his bicycle investigating back roads, sitting quietly. He looked for untouched nature. Nature can't speak to you if you don't listen.

He listened with his inner soul. After he was gone, about 40 books that he had ordered came to the office. Over half of them dealt with the inner being. Perhaps we could add to the original concept of the magazine and call it Soil, Health and Spirit!

To me, *Organic Gardening* is a love story. A dream for a healthier way of life that is more important for our world now than when it began.

And I thank you, dear friend, for being part of that dream.

*May/June 1992*

# Why We Grow

*Mike McGrath*

S urveys tell us that the vast majority of gardeners now identify themselves as organic or heading there. Every year a smaller percentage of gardeners admit to using insecticides, herbicides, and chemical fertilizers.

So we don't talk about chemicals much. Everyone knows that chemicals are bad.

Still, there is the occasional letter. "My neighbor sprays everything in sight and just laughs at me when I tell him how wrong he is," goes one version. "Please explain again *why* we avoid chemicals, so that I know what to say."

And then there are the people who have been confused by those members of the scientific community who have sold their white coat along with their soul and turned their back on morality and scientific method.

"I read in the paper that you get sick from organically grown food," or "My neighbor showed me a newspaper clipping in which a researcher says that a switch to organic food would raise every family's food bill $400 a week and that we'd all starve to death without chemicals."

Then another editor here at Rodale received a

*Mike McGrath*

very thoughtful letter from a friend who had just begun to garden and was confused about the "war" between organic gardeners and those who use chemicals. Another gardening magazine had announced that it was going to seek the middle ground, to try to be objective about chemicals rather than just reject them outright. He urged me to do the same, to "end the shouting" and say that some chemicals were safe and that it was okay to use them if you were careful.

## A War Worth Fighting

That letter helped put things in perspective for me. When I attended Temple University a couple of decades ago, I took a lot of documentary film courses and I was shocked to learn that one of my all-time favorite directors, Frank Capra (*It's a Wonderful Life, Mr. Smith Goes to Washington,* etc.), had produced a series of short "Why We Fight" films during the war years. I had never *dreamed* that the American people needed to be convinced that World War II was worth fighting. I had grown up believing that WWII was universally popular. But of course, nothing is universal or obvious, and there is no shame in needing to be reminded why we fight.

Or why we grow. Organically.

The World Health Organization quantifies the public health impact of pesticides. Their most recent tally (1990): 3 million "severe, acute" poi-

sonings that year, 735,000 chronic defects caused, and 220,000 deaths. This, they add, is about half of the actual total, because of the large number of incidents that go unreported.

Here in America, agricultural chemicals are the single biggest cause of surface water pollution. Most of the nation's *underground* water supplies are also contaminated by insecticides, herbicides, and chemical fertilizers. And, unfortunately, the filtration systems that treat public drinking water can't get all the chemicals out. In Ohio and Iowa, for example, 82 percent of the *treated* public drinking water still contained residues of two or more pesticides. Three billion tons of topsoil are lost from American farms each year—also the direct result of the use of agricultural chemicals. Chemical farmers and growers add concentrated salts to the soil in order to grow food. Wind and rain are always blowing and washing topsoil away, so these farmers lose massive amounts of their most precious resource each year.

Organic growers, on the other hand, add massive amounts of organic matter to their soil. At the end of the year, they've *added* tons of topsoil to our nation's land.

After a hundred years of exclusively chemical farming, this country would look worse than the most lifeless desert in the most famine-prone portion of the world. Forget even sterile, lifeless soil—you'd be lucky to find patches of sand among the rocks and bleached bones of former chemical salesmen.

After 100 years of organic growing, you'd see Eden. Rich, black soil.

Want another reason why we grow organically? Because we are *gardeners*. People who use chemicals don't "garden." They kill everything that flies, walks, crawls, or slithers into their path and force their plants to grow by shoving the horticultural equivalent of anabolic steroids down their roots. At the end of 20 years, they know nothing more than the day they started. And they probably spread enough poison around in that time to wipe out a small city.

## Gardeners Do No Harm

Organic gardeners *garden*. When an unfamiliar life form appears in their patch, they learn if it is friend or foe. If it is a pest, they learn about its life cycle, its natural enemies, its weaknesses to traps and other nontoxic techniques. They feed their soil with composted kitchen scraps, yard wastes, manure, and other materials that would otherwise clog our overloaded waste stream. At the end of 20 years of gardening, they have acquired much wisdom about the natural world, improved their soil, protected local wildlife, and done no harm.

But the suppliers of agricultural chemicals have a $35 billion to $50 billion a year business to protect. So they find the craven ones, the ones who have rejected every principle of true science, and they pay them to create lies.

One of my biggest concerns when I took this job was whether I would be up to refuting the scientific spokespeople of the purveyors of agricultural chemicals.

Little did I know that they have no science. All they have are gross distortions laced with some outright lies. One "study" we looked at (the one that said everybody's food bill would go up hundreds of dollars a week and we'd all starve anyway) not only disregarded every rule of science, but disregarded the very criteria it had established in its funding proposals.

The economic truth, as reported by the National Research Council—the official scientific body of the United States—in their massive 1989 report (in which my water-pollution and soil-loss statistics are cited), is that production costs and yields are essentially the same for organic and chemical farmers.

So this is no time for a middle ground. The war that Frank Capra

### Briefly Quoted
### February 1954
"As for the farmer who undertakes to take everything from the land without making any restitution, his liberty will eventually be taken from him and he will become the servant of wiser men, either on the farm or elsewhere."

*C. E. Thorne*

helped America win clearly showed us that appeasement is no answer. Yes, the "other side" has untold billions of dollars to spend, while we are merely common people who like to work with soil and help things grow.

But strikingly similar common people fought and won a war of independence two centuries ago to free that soil. And the other side's resources are limited by their twisted mission, by the senseless destruction that is the logical conclusion of their goals. They cannot be allowed to win; this planet is too precious to surrender to those who would imperil her for personal profit.

There will always be people who deny the existence of such evil. During World War II, some said Hitler was getting a bad rap; others said that no matter what was going on, *we* shouldn't be involved; others laughed and cheated and lied to get their unfair share of meat and gasoline.

Then we saw the concentration camps, and we truly understood the plans of our enemies and the outcome if they had won.

Objective? Middle ground? Not here. Not now. Not ever. The problem may not be invading armies this time, but the prize is the same. Which world do *you* choose for your children to inherit? Your children's children?

I hope that someday those children can look back at the choices we make here and now, and see this as yet another time that the forces of life would not be denied. Maybe they will echo the words of a great man who

saw his people rise to such a challenge and say with pride that "this was their finest hour." He said that with half his nation in flames.

He could have tried to be objective; he could have tried to seek a middle ground; he could have tried to figure out which conquerors were less dangerous than others, which occupied nations were less important. He could have stopped the shouting.

Thank God, he didn't.

We do our part—by offering you information, resources, and encouragement. You do yours by growing what you grow without toxins; by adding life back to the soil; and yes, by standing up to those who turn their heads and make excuses while they poison our planet and imperil our future. I realize that last part can be difficult.

No one ever said it would be easy. Only that it would be right.

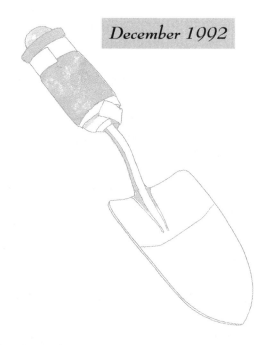

*December 1992*

# Chapter 2

# *Solutions*

Q and A through the Years

 Questions sent in by *Organic Gardening* readers over the years, on subjects ranging from compost to roses to controlling pest problems.

 Answers you can use to make your garden the best it's ever been.

# Q and A
# through the Years

### Compost for the Lawn

 I am interested in maintaining a healthy lawn without resorting to chemical fertilizers. Would you tell me what is the best method in applying compost to an established lawn?

H. D. W.
*Athol, Massachusetts*

 Use slightly acid compost, made without lime. Make the compost fine by grinding, by chopping it with a hoe or otherwise, and passing it through a ¼-inch sieve. The sieved compost should then be spread over the surface of the lawn to the thickness of ½ inch and raked into the soil. Bare spots should be reseeded. This treatment will make the lawn grow so vigorously that weeds, including quack grass, will be crowded out. By fertilizing the lawn in the fall with compost, the grass will get an early start in spring and occupy the ground so completely that quack grass, which spends the winter in the seed stage, will not get started.

*January 1948*

## How to Use Seaweed

 I live only five blocks away from the Pacific Ocean and have access to seaweed that comes in on the high tides. I was wondering if I could put this in my compost pile or rotary till it into my garden. Would the salt content be harmful?

Lloyd Beauregard
*Imperial Beach, California*

 Seaweed contains 400 pounds of organic matter per ton. The chemical analysis of fresh seaweed is rather similar to barnyard manure; it contains somewhat less nitrogen, half as much phosphorus, and twice as much potassium. Dried seaweed is 20 to 50 percent minerals, and it contains many essential trace elements. Without a doubt, seaweed is one of the most valuable organic soil builders.

Fresh seaweed can be spread directly in the garden, buried in little pockets, or used as a mulch around plants for booster feeding. Don't heap up the seaweed to allow it to decay; its nutrients easily leach out. If only limited amounts are available, use it in the compost pile as it decomposes quickly and helps to heat up the pile. You can make a seaweed tea by putting 2 pounds of chopped weed in 1 gallon of hot water and allowing it to soak overnight. Use as you would manure tea.

Some gardeners wash off seaweed with a hose to remove any salt, but this isn't really necessary as the amount of salt that might cling to the outside of the plants is minimal.

## *February 1976*

## Taming Tough Clay

 My soil is gray clay that I sink into up to my ankles in winter, but in summer it gets so dry it develops wide cracks. I tried raised beds filled with topsoil, but yields were poor. How can I rebuild this soil?

Bob L. Hunt
*Santee, California*

Stick with raised beds. There's no point in improving soil in the walkways. Even more important than the topsoil you added is organic matter. You will need to add lots of it annually. We recommend a three-part program: compost, mulch, cover crops.

One of our correspondents in California, John Meeker, has done wonders with heavy clay. To start he applied *three* dump truck loads of compost on 800 feet of raised beds, then tilled it in. Timing is critical, says Meeker, since there is only a brief period between wet and dry when clay soils will crumble easily in your fingers. Meeker used mushroom compost, but he recommends substituting the best locally available materials. For fastest results the material should be fully composted.

Always keep the soil covered, either with mulch or with cover crops. The mulch keeps soil and compost moist so the plants can make the most of it. As the mulch rots, it adds more organic matter. Cover crops trap the nutrients you have added, and they add more organic matter. Their roots break up heavy soil. Plant a cover crop as soon as a patch of ground has finished for the season, then turn it under one week before planting. Meeker uses buckwheat in warm weather and fava beans interplanted with rye when it's cool.

cellent seedlings, you can do just as well by using standard fluorescent tubes, such as cool white alone (which produces short, stocky seedlings) or a combination of cool white and warm white or daylight.

Grow the seedlings as close to the lights as possible without having the leaves touch the tubes, moving the tubes up or the seedlings down about an inch at a time as the plants grow. Since light intensity is highest near the centers of the tubes, rotate plants from the ends to the center if you notice uneven growth.

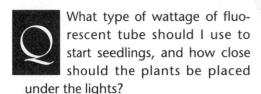

*April 1985*

*April 1988*

## Lights for Seedlings

**Q** What type of wattage of fluorescent tube should I use to start seedlings, and how close should the plants be placed under the lights?

J. C. Haskins
*Hampton, Virginia*

**A** Install a fixture that holds at least four parallel 40-watt (4-foot) tubes. In terms of light output, 40-watt tubes are more economical to buy and operate than some less common sizes. They're long enough to provide plenty of light space for seedlings and transplants, but compact enough to fit easily into the average room. While fluorescent tubes designed for plants produce ex-

## Hardening-Off Seedlings

**Q** I have started my own plants and am not sure how to harden them off before planting them out in my garden.

M. S. Inzone
*Kings Park, New York*

**A** Young plants, especially non-hardy ones, are very vulnerable to sudden temperature changes. To put them outside, after their propagation in the protection of a greenhouse or other warm place, may easily be fatal. Therefore to lessen the shock of temperature, wind, and sun, a hardening off process is used, in which seedlings are gradually exposed to the natural elements. The process usually takes about two weeks and should be timed so that the young seedlings end the two weeks in a period warm enough for them to be planted outside safely.

The best way to harden off seedlings is to move them, flats and all, from their indoor location to the cold frame. The frame should be closed for the first two days of the period. On the third day, the top should be opened just a crack, and over the remainder of the period, the air space should be widened more each day until, on the last day, the top is removed entirely.

If you haven't got a cold frame, you can simulate the same conditions that it provides. On the first day of the period, place flats outside in a sheltered place for only a few minutes during the warmer part of the afternoon, covered with a burlap screen. Gradually expose them more each day until the process is completed.

If plant protectors made of plastic, waxed paper, or glass are used to cover plants when first set out, hardening off is not as important. Tomato and strawberry baskets and the little glass tents known as cloches are effective in shielding tender plants from sun or windburn. You can place them to cover the plants entirely or tilt them to allow air to circulate underneath and, if a late frost is announced after you've removed the protectors, you can save your seedlings by bringing them out again.

*February 1976*

## Should Tomato Plants Be Pruned?

 How shall I prune my tomato plants to keep them healthy and get a good crop? Should they be staked or not? Cultivated or mulched?

B. M. Van Matre
*Flora, Illinois*

 A thick mulch of straw or grass clippings under tomato plants will help to keep the fruit clean if the plants are allowed to sprawl on the ground, and will keep the moisture content of the soil more uniform, thus preventing much blossom end rot. Tomato plants permitted to sprawl without pruning will set and mature more fruit than plants that are pruned, but the fruit will be smaller and much of it may be lost by rotting on damp ground, by damage from slugs and insects, and by becoming overripe while it is hidden under a dense mass of foliage. If allowed to go unpruned, tomatoes will make branches at each leaf node, and sometimes fruit cluster stems will extend to form additional branches. Whether the vines are to be trained or not, these fruit cluster branches should be pinched off just beyond the cluster in order to throw all the nourishment from that stem into the fruit.

When vines are to be trained to one stem, all side branches should be pinched back after they have made one set of leaves. Suckers arising from the root after the main stem has made a good growth should also be removed. If two or three stems will be permitted to grow, the branches on the first leaf nodes are allowed to develop. Each branch is then tied to its own stake and treated in the same way as the parent stem.

Once pruning has begun, it must be repeated every week throughout the growing season. If it is started and then abandoned, tops of the plants will develop heavily and many suckers will take the strength from the plants without providing much fruit.

Six weeks before the first expected frost, nip out all growing tips, including that on the main stem. This will stop vine development and permit the plant's nourishment to concentrate on the maturing fruit. New blossoms may also be pruned out after this date, since fruit set late will not be large enough for use.

### *April 1975*

## Saving Tomato Seeds

**Q** I'm saving tomato seeds from this year's crop to plant next season. How can I separate the seed and pulp?
Darren Harrelson
*Jasper, Tennessee*

**A** The best way to separate tomato seed is to ferment the fruit, since this destroys the tomato-canker bacteria, which

otherwise can cause the plants to wilt and white spots to form on the fruit. Be sure your tomato is fully ripe, or even overripe.

Cut open the fruit, and scoop out the seeds and pulp. Put the mixture into a jar or glass with $\frac{1}{4}$ cup of water and let it ferment at room temperature. Stir at least twice daily. The fermentation turns the pulp into a thin liquid and allows the viable seeds to sink to the bottom of the container. The fermentation will take four days at 60 degrees, three days at 70 degrees, and two days at 80 degrees. It's best to keep the mixture at 70 degrees or less to prolong the fermentation period. At least three days are needed to destroy the bacteria of tomato canker. After the seeds have sunk to the bottom of the container, pour off the liquefied pulp and the seeds that are floating on the top. Spread the remaining seeds on newspaper or paper towels to dry. After drying, rub the seeds off the paper and store in an airtight container.

### *September 1983*

## Confused Cauliflower

**Q** My white cauliflower picks up the color from my purple cauliflower. Should I plant them farther away from each other?
Carolyn C. Respess
*Catonsville, Maryland*

The neighboring purple variety isn't the problem. Sunlight on the cauliflower head (called the "curd") causes it to turn from white to purple, yellow or green, depending on the variety. Blanching will prevent it from coloring. To produce a white curd, start blanching as soon as the developing head begins to push back the inner leaves. Make sure the head is dry, then gather up the longest leaves around the head and hold them in place with a strip of cloth, soft twine or clothespins. You can also rip off a large bottom leaf and place it over the head.

Many of the new varieties are self-blanching. They have longer leaves that protect the curd.

*May 1983*

## Split Garlic

When I dig my elephant garlic bulbs, the skins are split and the cloves inside are green. Why does this happen?

Ivan L. Zatlukal
*Rosebud, Texas*

You may be feeding the garlic too much nitrogen and not enough phosphorus and potassium, says Betty Walker, manager of Nichols Garden Nursery in Albany, Oregon, a source of elephant garlic.

To get strong skins and large cloves, work in bonemeal for phosphorus, and greensand or kelp meal for potassium, before planting. Exposure to sunlight due to shallow planting turns garlic cloves green, says Walker. Green cloves are usually too bitter to eat, but can be used for planting. Set cloves 4 inches deep, harvest as soon as the tops wither, and dry the garlic in a shady place before storing.

*January 1988*

## Transplanting Rhubarb

A friend with a huge rhubarb patch has offered me some plants. How do I transplant them?

Millard Guerry
*Baltimore, Maryland*

Dig rhubarb crowns as early as possible in the spring, before they break dormancy, or in the fall before the ground freezes. Divide the crowns, including as much root as possible. Each piece should have at least two large buds. Four to six pieces can usually be split from each crown. Don't allow the divisions to dry out before planting them. Plant the rhubarb 2 to 3 inches deep in a well-drained location.

*April 1983*

## Window Well Storage

 It seems to me that we could make use of our window wells to store food over the winter. Is this a safe idea?

Edwina Wilson
*Lewisburg, Pennsylvania*

 Actually, it's a great idea. Since window wells are adjacent to the house and below ground level, the temperatures inside them should remain fairly constant throughout the winter.

Cover the wells with screening and wood. When very cold weather hits your area, raise the temperature in the well by opening the basement window to allow some house heat to enter. When the temperature in the window well gets too high, remove the wood from the top of the well to permit the cold outside air to cool the area. If basement windows open inward or are sliding type, access is convenient during the winter months.

*November 1980*

## Transplanting Bulbs

Q I would like to relocate some of the tulips and daffodils now blooming in my yard. When and how is it best to transplant hardy bulbs?

Mrs. M. Flohr
*Monroe, New York*

 Dig them up when the foliage is about half yellowed. By then, the bulbs will have ripened but will still be easy to find, and the dying leaves will give you a convenient handle to lift the clumps out of the ground. Separate the bulbs and replant immediately in well-drained soil enriched with compost and a sprinkling of any complete granular organic fertilizer. Be careful to set each species at the proper depth and spacing.

*April 1988*

## Plants to Brighten Shady Areas

 What sort of plants can I set out along the house foundation wall that's almost always shaded or in some parts of the yard that stay mostly in shade? Nothing that looks cheerful seems to grow in those places.

 Drab, shaded areas can be perked up by several good bedding plants suited to growth in the shade. Among them are balsam, lobelia, pansies, browallia, begonias, calendulas, torenia, nicotiana, coleus, myosotis, impatiens, and wall-flowers. For best results,

set them in well-drained, well-aerated soil. Work some coarse sphagnum peat moss or other material into heavy soils, along with coarse horticultural-grade perlite if drainage is poor. Water bedding plants thoroughly right after planting, saturating soil to a depth of 6 to 8 inches.

## October 1966

### Winter Mulch Protection for Roses

**Q** A few of my roses were killed by cold temperatures last winter and others were injured. Will mulching keep winter freezing from damaging my roses?

**A** Most winter injury to roses comes from alternate freezing and thawing of soil during warm spells in winter. This problem can be minimized by proper application of a good mulch around the plants to prevent the soil from freezing too deep, and also to act as an insulator to keep it that way.

Don't apply it too early, though, since doing that may prevent soil from freezing, thus allowing plants to sprout too soon in the spring—before danger of killing frosts has passed. Wait until the ground has partially frozen, then spread 6 to 8 inches of material. If you already maintain a summer mulch, be sure to replace it completely for winter. In the absence of mulching materials, soil can be mounded around the base of the plants, but this involves considerable work, and the soil must be hauled in rather than being pulled up from the rose bed.

The best mulches are kinds that do not tend to pack down tightly. Coarse ground corncobs make an excellent mulch; others that work well include clean straw, wood chips, and peat moss.

## October 1968

### Aphid Problems

**Q** Last year we had trouble with aphids and ants in our garden. They were over everything, and my tomato plants developed mosaic from them. Do you have any suggestions for what I can do so this won't happen again this year?

Mrs. J. M. Hoppe
*Arlington Heights, Illinois*

**A** Aphids, or plant lice, are small, soft-bodied insects distinguished by their pearlike shape, long antennae, and pair of tubelike appendages that project from the back end. There are dozens of species, many named for their favorite food preference.

Aphids suck plant sap and cause withering of foliage and a loss of plant vigor. Excess sugars and sap are emitted from the insect's anus and are known as honeydew. Ants feed on honeydew and will tend aphids as farmers do cows. The ants distribute the aphids from plant to plant, quickly spreading any plant diseases with the aphids. In fall, ants carry aphid eggs into their nests to be carried back out in spring and set on plants, making control very difficult. During a season, two or three generations of aphids will be produced.

The best-known predator of aphids is the ladybug. Other predators include soldier bugs, damsel bugs, big-eyed bugs, pirate bugs, spiders, assassin bugs, syrphid flies, and lacewings. Both ladybugs and lacewings are commercially available for augmentation to control severe outbreaks.

What you must do is attack the aphids on two fronts. First, develop a very fertile soil to produce healthy plants, which aphids have shown a tendency to dislike; and second, to battle peak populations, use one or more of the many controls available.

The simplest remedy is to gently rub leaves, crushing the aphids. In some cases, aphids can be repelled by growing nasturtiums between vegetable rows. If the aphids are attracted to the nasturtiums, wait until the plants have a good infestation, then pull them from the garden and destroy them, aphids and all. Other companion plants include garlic, chives and other

alliums, coriander, anise, and petunias.

Aphids can be washed from plants with a forceful spray of water. A soapy-water spray is effective, but plants should be rinsed with clear water after applying it.

Since ants are often the major cause of aphid problems, you should also try to control them. Ants can be contained by borders of small amounts of bone meal or powdered charcoal. A band of cotton, made sticky with Tanglefoot or Stick-Em adhesives, can be wrapped around the base of larger plants to catch ants. Good garden sanitation and quick removal and composting of plant debris will also help cut down aphid and ant populations.

*February 1978*

## Cucumber Beetle

**Q** I have found a striped bug on my cucumber leaves. Is there anything I can do to get rid of it? We have composted for only a year as yet.

J. H. J.
*West Virginia*

**A** That is probably the striped cucumber beetle. We have not been bothered with them after using the compost method, but have heard of a successful method: Put a handful of lime and a handful of wood ashes in a 2-gallon sprinkling can, stir well, then apply with the can or with a sprayer, taking care that the underside of the leaves is just as much covered as the top. This will not kill the beetles, but seems to drive them away. By next year, when composting has produced a balance in your soil, you will indubitably get along without this.

## The Great White Worm

Q A fat, white worm, about ½ inch long, gets into the stems and destroys my squash and melon vines. I read that the organic way to kill the worm is to "search and destroy" him with a small knife, but I end up ruining the stem as well. What is this worm and how can I get rid of it?

Lynne Breakstone
*St. Louis, Missouri*

A You're observing the larval form of the squash vine borer, a large brown, reddish orange and black flying insect in the moth family. It lays eggs on the stems of squash vines. The larvae hatch and burrow into the stems where they feed on the plant unnoticed and safe from predators. A gummy sawdustlike substance oozing from holes in stems and leaves near the base of the plant is a sure sign that squash vine borers are at work. Leaves of infested plants will droop severely on sunny days.

Slitting the stems and killing the worms (there may be three or four worms in one tunnel, and two or three tunnels per plant) is the best control. Kill the worm with the knife blade or a piece of wire, then bandage the slit with tape.

Another preventive measure is to pinch off the growing point while the plant is young and before the borers attack. That forces the plant to branch out, becoming multistemmed. Then cover the stems with soil. This encourages the vine to root at the joints from which the leaves grow. Or you might want to try a delayed planting, which may miss the egg-laying moth. Earlier plantings (under cloches) can work, too, because the adult borer doesn't begin laying eggs until July, by which time the plants are larger and much more tolerant of attacks. When a plant dies, don't let it lie. Find all of the larvae and kill them so none overwinter.

Winter squash varieties like HUBBARD and most summer squash varieties are severely damaged by attack. BABY BLUE and BUTTERNUT are somewhat resistant.

## Habitat for Toads

**Q** We have acquired toads along with our new property. We're concerned that as we straighten up our yard, the toads' habitat will be ruined. Can you tell us their requirements for living?

Katherine Hostetter
*Santa Clara, California*

**A** During the day, toads usually will seek moist, sheltered places beneath loose boards, under garden mulch, or in the shade of low-growing shrubbery. At night, with the safety of darkness, they hop about in search of cutworms, potato beetles, ants, slugs, and a number of other small creatures. Although the backyard garden patch is hardly the ideal habitat for this rough-skinned amphibian, special provisions can be made to entice it to stay.

Toads need water, both to breed and to drink through their skin when sitting submerged. Put a shallow pan in the garden with enough water to allow for both these activities. Given enough fresh water, females lay up to 15,000 small black-and-white eggs in paired jelly strings. The eggs hatch in 3 to 12 days into black tadpoles, which gradually transform into small toads in six to nine weeks.

Be sure to wet down the shrubbery on hot days, and perhaps provide a modest shelter for additional shade. Sink a box or inverted flowerpot a few inches into the ground and cut a small entrance hole for the toad's access. If the weather is moderate, toads remain active from March to mid-November, and in that time, a single toad can eat up to 15,000 insects.

*June 1978*

## Quack Grass

**Q** In spite of my careful tending, my lawn and gardens are invaded by quack grass each season. How can I get rid of quack grass?

G. U.
*Milwaukee, Wisconsin*

**A** Quack grass grows as an annual in Wisconsin. This means that it produces seed and spends the winter in the seed stage. It can be controlled by frequent and careful cutting so that it cannot go to seed. Also, this grass cannot stand shade or crowding, so that it can be crowded out if the regular lawn grasses are given a dressing of compost in the spring so that they make an early and luxuriant growth.

*February 1949*

# Chapter 3

# OG 101

# What Is Organic Gardening?

*Ruth Rodale*

Organic Gardening and Farming

en Planning Issue

## What Every Organic Gardener Knows

Human health is more precious than extra-high yields and insect-free crops. Any methods to bolster yields should be adopted only after we are thoroughly convinced that future generations will not be injured. Fertilizers and insecticides now on the market have been tested only briefly, and even then no one becomes excited unless a chemical causes outright death. How long can a civilization exist while embracing this careless philosophy?

The balance of nature must not be overlooked. Each part has its own sphere of activity as well as intermeshing with other related parts. What alters one part may affect half a dozen others—most often to our own disadvantage. Spraying, for example, kills off beneficial insects and birds, contaminates the soil, leaves poisonous residues on crops, and is a financial burden on the farmer.

Soil is a storehouse of living organisms, which must be fed and cared for like other organisms. Bacteria, fungi, insects, and earthworms inhabit the

*You need not look far to find ingredients for your compost pile. Grass clippings and fallen leaves are excellent and readily obtainable additions, as are vegetable trimmings, coffee grounds, and even shredded newspaper.*

phate supply phosphorus, while glauconite marl and granite dust release potash. These fertilizers dissolve slowly, benefiting crops for several years. Rock fertilizers, in addition, do not leach quickly into the drainage waters. Millions of tons of natural rock fertilizers await further discovery by enlightened fertilizer companies.

No concentrated, completely soluble fertilizers (known as "chemical fertilizers") are recommended in the organic method. Relying on harsh chemicals year after year will produce nutritionally poor crops. Flooding plant roots with chemical fertilizers may cause trace element deficiencies. The soil becomes strongly acid, unless lime is constantly applied. Earthworms and beneficial bacteria and fungi are driven away or killed. Toxic residues, like chlorine and sulfur, build up year after year. Last, organic matter is quickly depleted from chemically fertilized soils.

Some natural insect controls may be necessary until and possibly after the gardener has been practicing the organic method for several years. The soil must become rich and fertile: insect parasites and predators must be encouraged. Safe measures for control that we advise are hand-picking of insect pests, encouraging birds, interplanting with crops that repel insects, planting resistant varieties, and setting out traps and attractant lamps. Exterminating all harmful insects is not our goal: good yields, truly safe food, and sensible insect controls is the answer.

Sprays and dusts that decay insects certainly are not free from some toxicity to human beings, remarked a prominent scientist recently. The same can be said about potent weed killers, fungicides, and other chemicals that violently disturb the natural functions of plant and animal life. Keep these facts in mind when tempted to invest in spray equipment.

*August 1952*

soil by the millions, using organic matter as food and in turn preparing it for living plants. Concentrated chemicals, on the other hand, cannot be continually added to the soil to destroy harmful insects and bacteria without doing just the same to the needed microorganisms.

Plants fed with natural fertilizers are well balanced in trace elements and vitamins. Using chemical fertilizers like superphosphate may supply excess phosphorus while crowding out magnesium. Well-nourished plants are more resistant to insect attack than deficient crops, probably because of the latter's vitamin abnormalities and more attractive odor to pests. These two theories were recently supported by experiments at the Bartlett Tree Expert Company and the University of California.

## What the Organic Gardener Practices

All suitable organic matter goes back to the land by mulching or by composting. A mulch is a layer of organic matter (plant or animal wastes) placed on the soil surface that protects the land while fertilizing it. Only those materials ordinarily not applied directly to the soil (garbage, for example) need be composted. Organic matter can be piled in bins or open heaps to decay, or compost. This method often reduces the mineral content of fresh organic matter, so mulching is preferred.

Pulverized rock fertilizers, rich in phosphorus, potash, and trace elements are broadcast on the garden plot or incorporated into the compost pile once every few days. Raw ground phosphate rock and colloidal phos-

**CROSS SECTION OF HEALTHY SOIL**

*The correlation between soil health, plant health, and human health is a cornerstone of organic gardening.*

# Course in Organics

*J. I. Rodale*

## Introduction

In this section, we will discuss the many meanings of the word *organic,* particularly the meaning that interests organic gardeners. You can consider this chapter a minicourse in organics; if you pay attention and pass the test at the end, you are well on your way to understanding the basis of organic gardening. Take the challenge, and see if you can make the grade!

ORGANI-CULTURE

## What Is Organic Matter?

Organic matter is a term applied to both plant and animal matter, alive or dead. But regardless of whether it is dead or alive, organic matter is the life of the soil. Plant and animal matter includes the bodies of bacteria, fungi, yeasts, protozoa, and the like. Organic matter represents material that has been in living tissue or that has come from it. Some examples are manure, plant sap, sawdust, and olive oil. It consists of matter that may have been alive long ago, like peat (which may be thousands of years old), or coal (which may be hundreds of thousands of years old).

Organic matter represents the remains of all kinds of plants, animals, and microorganisms in various stages of decomposition. But actually, the expression *organic matter,* as we sometimes refer to it, is a misnomer, for it includes both organic and inorganic substances. A corncob, for example, is usually referred to as representing organic matter. But if you burn it down to its ash, destroying all the organic matter, in that ash, or residue, there remains a significant amount of minerals. In nature all of what we usually consider organic matter contains some inorganic compounds. So we must be aware of this confusion when we use the term *organic matter.* Perhaps it would be more correct to say that corncobs are a form of substance containing both organic and inorganic materials. We might say that it is an organic type of material.

## Examples of Organic Matter

Typical examples of organic matter, in the common usage of the term, are leaves, weeds, grass clippings, manure, the bodies of cows or pigs, and the human body. A piece of stone would not usually be referred to as organic matter, although in extremely rare cases rock may be found that does contain some. A piece of cotton or woolen cloth might be termed organic matter because it comes from a plant or an animal, respectively, although each cloth usually has some inorganic minerals included in its makeup. Dirt that is swept up from a floor would usually be a combination of organic and inorganic material. Hair is organic. Metallic iron is inorganic, and such substances as calcium and sulphur are inorganic.

Some organic matter is in a raw state; other matter is in an intermediary stage of decomposition. Organic matter in a more advanced state is sometimes referred to as humus, but that is an inaccurate statement. The raw materials usually placed in the compost heap, except the lime, are referred to as organic matter. To review the terms, we might say that *organic matter* is placed in a *compost heap* to form *humus.*

To review the definition of organic matter, then, we find that it is a substance that is alive or that was once living. In the biologic field the dictionary will define the word *organic* as pertaining to or deriving from anything that has life. The only known substances that are alive are in plants and animals. Among the lower forms of plants we find bacteria and molds. Many persons believe that germs are tiny animals. This is not so. They are bacteria and molds and the like, which are lower forms in the plant world. People confuse them with protozoa, which are one-celled animals.

In the upper 7 inches of an acre of soil the weight of bacteria might average 400 to 800 pounds. In the form of animals in the soil (excluding the protozoa), there are nematodes, rotifers, and other minute animals. Between both groups (plant and animal lower forms), their functioning and death furnish considerable amounts of organic matter.

## Green Matter

The term *green matter,* in the sense we use it, differs from organic matter in that it includes only plant materials. It is applied to any plant matter, regardless of whether it is freshly cut or actually green. It might consist of fresh or withered lawn clippings or weeds, dry leaves, cured hay, or sawdust.

## Leaf Mold

The term *mold* is often used in the expression *leaf mold,* and according to the dictionary, it is a soft, rich soil or an earthy material. The word *molder* means to crumble by natural decay, and that is exactly what happens to leaves that fall and are not removed by man. They decompose into a form of compost called *leaf mold.* In other words, leaf mold is compost composed entirely of leaves. It is organic matter in its second stage.

## Organic Residues

The term *organic residues* indicates a vast array of decomposable materials that are in the category of organic matter (organic and inorganic). They include city garbage, leather dust of shoe factories, cannery wastes, apple pomace of cider mills (skins), spoiled milk, and hundreds of other materials. Much of this material today is wasted. By proper handling and quick decomposition processes, organic residues can be turned into valuable organic, humus-containing fertilizers.

## Total Organic Matter

Sometimes we use the term *total organic matter* to refer to organic materials in general, using the term *humus* for the real organic fraction of it that is realized when the processes of decomposition go into action.

## Organic Compounds

The term *organic* has several meanings. One of them is in the sense that it is something living. It is the *organic* part of the expression *organic matter.* The other meaning is entirely different: an *organic* compound is anything containing carbon. Since all organic matter contains carbon, the organic matter that the gardener and farmer use must be considered carbon compounds also. But there is another class of carbon-containing compounds, which we would not consider a type of organic material usable as a fertilizer. One such compound is petroleum. Impregnate your soil with a fair amount of this oil and you will destroy its ability to raise crops for a long time.

There is an entire field of chemistry devoted to the study of this second type of organic substance, or carbon compounds, some of which are known to cause cancer. For a long time, a yellow organic pigment, called *butter yellow,* was used to color butter. It was banned by the government when experiments proved that it caused cancer. In our consideration of organic materials valuable as fertilizer we must completely exclude these types of chemical carbon compounds.

## Compost

Thus far we have discussed various aspects of organic matter. Now we come to a process called *composting,* which we will find interesting to study. *Compost* has two meanings. First, we give the general definition: a *composition, mixture, or compound.* The word *compote,* which means fruit stewed in syrup, has the same origin. The way some people make compost, throwing the ingredients together helter-skelter, you can safely call it a compote, or stew.

The specialized meaning of the word *compost* as it applies to farming and gardening, according to Webster's New International Dictionary, Second Edition, unabridged, is "a mixture for fertilizing or renovating land in which plants are grown; now, especially a fertilizing mixture composed of such substances as peat, leaf mould, manure, lime, etc., thoroughly mingled and decomposed, usually in a heap called a compost heap." This is not a bad definition, but it is not the best. The important thing is that the material must be decomposed in order to be called compost, and it is not to be called compost until it is. There are two basic things about a compost heap. You must have organic materials, and there must be the proper conditions to make them decompose. The degree of decomposition may be referred to in terms such as *finished* or *unfinished compost.* In a more or less finished compost the materials would be greatly reduced in the extent of their fibrous appearance.

In an agricultural textbook, you might find the following type of definition: "A compost is a fertilizing mixture of partially decomposed organic materials of plant or animal origin, or both, and may include substances such as ash, lime, and chemicals."

In the organic method we would exclude the ash, if it is from coal, and would also condemn the addition of the usual fertilizing chemicals.

In review we can see that organic matter is the raw material of the composting process, a process that hastens the formation of humus. Composting, then, is a process of making humus.

---

### Briefly Quoted
### February 1954

"The soil must be considered not merely a dynamic or even a biological system, but a living system."

*Selman A. Waksman*

# Test Your Knowledge

## Instructions

Read each question and refer back to the article for its answer. Then read the questions a second time, attempting to give the answers from your mind. Correct your written answers by comparing them with the text of each lesson and mark your work accordingly.

## Questions

1. Describe the term organic matter.

2. Give 12 examples of popular forms of organic matter.

3. Give examples of some of the higher and lower forms of plant life.

4. Give one example of a lower form of animal life that lives in the soil.

5. Give two examples of organic matter that is thousands of years old.

6. What is wrong about the popular conception of the term organic matter?

7. By what processes can you separate the mineral element from a corncob?

8. Give an example of a substance that rarely contains organic matter.

9. What part of organic matter in an advanced state is formed as a separate substance when organic matter decomposes?

10. What would be the approximate weight of bacteria in the upper 7 inches of an acre of soil?

11. How does green matter differ from organic matter?

12. What is another term used in reference to organic matter to classify it before it begins to decay?

13. What is leaf mold?

14. What does the term mold *itself* mean?

15. Give three examples of organic wastes.

16. What does the term total organic matter mean?

17. What is meant by an organic compound?

18. Give three examples of organic compounds.

19. What are the main raw materials of a compost heap?

20. What are the two basic things about a compost heap?

21. Name the three stages of matter in the production of organic fertilizer.

*February 1953*

# Organic Methods

*Roger W. Smith*

PLANTS    ANIMALS

**ORGANICULTURE**

Often the gardener has to make the best he can of the small piece of ground that goes with his house. "This is your garden," he is told. So he takes a look at his "garden"—a terribly poor piece of ground it is after years of mistreatment. How can he bring to such a spot a touch of life? How can he convert it into a verdant garden?

The city gardener is not the only one who faces this problem; many suburban and rural gardens are unproductive beyond belief.

What we wanted to know was what organic methods could do under the worst of all possible conditions, keeping in mind the gardener's being one person of limited means. Just what could the ordinary gardener do, without great expense, to turn a dead back yard into a fertile garden?

The garden soil of the place we selected was about as hard as concrete. Few weeds were able to survive. The area was not excessively shaded by crowding trees. It was open to full sunshine, and because of this, its surface was hard-baked. After a heavy shower, excess water soaked in easily, although much of it ran off.

Such a garden, we estimated, might be cared for in the usual manner for many years before it became really productive. Under present conditions it would never be worthwhile. We proposed to make it productive quickly. So we began "spot gardening" in its most primitive form.

We dug a hole, placing the "dead" soil on the compost heap. The hole was about 4 feet wide and about 1 foot deep. At that depth, the shovel failed to penetrate the hard subsoil.

What should be used to fill the hole? We could obtain compost humus, but it seemed wasteful to use only mature, rich humus. Finally we decided upon a mixture made up of one-third sifted compost humus and two-thirds clean sand.

A hole filled with such a mixture would have all those qualities the surrounding soil lacked. It would retain moisture and would be as well-drained as the subsoil permitted. The sand would maintain a steady temperature.

We wondered if the garden soil was really as dead as it appeared and whether the effects of traffic and mistreatment might be remedied by organic methods.

Well-watered when the need arose, the hole—we got to calling it "the hill"—produced magnificently. Planted with cucumbers and nasturtiums, the garden stood out like a brave, green island in a sea of deadness.

## An Improved Method

Corn and squash and many flowers grow naturally in hills—what about growing pole beans, melons, and tomatoes by this method?

The following year we improved upon the crude "dig a hole" method. A good recipe for this improved method goes something like this. Dig a hole about 4 feet in diameter and 1 foot deep. In the bottom of this hole dig another hole about 3 feet deep and 1 foot in diameter. Fill the lower hole with good compost humus, pack well. Fill the wide upper hole with clean sand. Rich topsoil or well-rotted manure may be used as a poor substitute for mature humus.

The spot should be soaked with 6 to 12 gallons of water, preferably rainwater. After the spot has settled, it should be filled up with clean sand, but a slight depression should be left to indicate the hill and to collect moisture. The deep, compost-filled hole serves as a reservoir for moisture, laden with natural plant nutrients within easy reach of plant roots.

That year we had excellent results from our spot gardens. We gave some of our flowers to the lady who lives down the street, and she won a prize with them in the flower show at the schoolhouse. We had made a big improvement by using spot gardening and were beginning to understand how to use organic materials and to appreciate the value of clean sand and rich compost humus.

Then somebody told us about the

"sunken barrel" method. In some ways this is an improvement over the dig-a-hole method. It goes something like this: Dig a hole at least a foot deeper and a foot wider than the butter tub or other container to be placed in it. The sides of the container should be perforated with many small holes. Butter tubs are scarce these days; metal drums may be used if these are free from paint and oil and the like. We used many corrugated cartons and found these satisfactory.

In the bottom of the hole, place about a 1-foot-deep layer of sand. Upon this place the container. Fill the container with good, rich compost humus and fill in around it with clean sand. Soak well with 10 gallons of water. Replace the settled material with more of the same kind. The edge of the container should stand about 1 inch above ground after you are through with your work.

In the sandy strip around each sunken barrel we planted seed. One hill was given over to cucumbers, another to mignonettes, another to melons, and so on. During dry weather a bucket or two of water was poured into each hill.

We had a very peculiar garden that year, but everything flourished. The flowers were more fragrant and the melons more flavorsome than our neighbors'. The dead backyard was no more.

From spot gardening and the "sunken barrel" it was an easy step to organic "bed gardening." Today we use spot gardening and the sunken

barrel to take care of unproductive corners. Under such conditions the sunken barrel can work wonders with strawberries, pansies, cucumbers, and the like.

## Building Wide Beds

Instead of making a fertile spot with the use of compost, sand, and water, why not construct a wide bed?

To be practical, we thought of the surface of the dead garden as the subsoil that it really was. Leaching, erosion, and excessive tillage had removed or destroyed the topsoil. Suppose we marked off a small area and replaced as best we could what had been lost?

We looked over what organic materials we had—a couple of years of good compost, many leaves, some hay and stable litter, and so on. Then we marked off a small area some 9 feet by 16 feet. The area took up one corner of the lot, the most promising corner. We worked and planned and wondered and went ahead.

Over the marked area we spread a layer of rough straw and dried weeds with some stable litter. This we watered and rolled and stamped down as much as we could. When it was first applied, the layer was about 4 inches deep.

This was followed by an inch-deep layer of rough compost material. Upon this was spread a 3-inch layer of a mixture of well-rotted straw, partially rotted leaves, spoiled hay, and fresh grass clippings. The children did most of the trampling down of this layer and loved it. They stomped and stomped, and with faces glowing with eagerness, they asked permission to do more stomping.

Then the bed was soaked to make it as compact as possible. The watering was discontinued just as soon as water began to run from the bed. That was enough work for one day. The bed rested overnight. The foundation had been laid; tomorrow we would build upon it.

We felt that a wooden frame would be necessary to hold the rest of the bed in place. So we gathered up a number of old boards and planks about 6 inches wide and made a frame slightly smaller than the bed we had built. This frame was filled with a 5-inch layer of a mixture made up of equal parts of ripe compost humus, clean sand, and rich topsoil.

The bed was again compacted by soaking, and additional compost was used to take care of settling. We found that mature compost had no real substitute, although well-rotted manure might be used in its place if necessity demanded this.

A bit later our bed garden simply bulged with flowers and vegetables. We eventually built four beds with neat straw-covered paths surrounding them. By using organic methods, the dead, can-strewn garden flourished.

We learned from experience the value of a mixture of compost and sand. A shovelful of rich compost humus and some clean sand can work wonders. It is difficult to say just why this should be so. But if we had to take over a badly treated, dead backyard, more than likely we'd spread over it a 3-inch layer of sand and a 1-inch layer of sifted compost humus and dig these in lightly.

This might not work as well as the spot garden or the bed garden, but in it we have approached the problem of making the whole of the garden fertile and that is something.

*November 1948*

# The Meaning of the pH Scale

How to tell if your soil is acid or alkaline—and what it means to your plants.

**A**cidity and alkalinity of soils are the result of the chemical nature of the rock from which the soil is derived and the partial or complete decomposition of vegetation. High alkalinity, as far as the growth of plants is concerned, is confined to the rather limited areas of limestone, the salt marshes, and the alkali deserts found in the West.

The term pH means hydrogen ion activity. This activity is nearly as important as temperature in many biological and industrial processes. It is of such great importance in the vital processes of soil organisms and of higher plants that every gardener and farmer should have a clear understanding of pH.

From a practical gardening and farming standpoint, there is a need to determine with reasonable accuracy the degree of acidity or alkalinity of individual soil sites, and to base the selection of plants and much of the soil treatment indicated accordingly. As a means of expressing such relative degrees, the term pH and the scale devised by chemists is employed.

Briefly, pH is a measurement of the acidity or alkalinity of a substance. Just as an inch is a measurement of a distance and a degree is a measurement of temperature, so a pH unit is a measurement of acidity or alkalinity.

As an example, it is known that lemon juice is sour, or acid. But what does that mean? There is no more definition to this expression than to say, "Water is hot." One person may think of "hot" as boiling—another may think of it simply as uncomfortable to the touch. Now, if the temperature of water is 160 degrees, as established by a thermometer, a definite value for "hotness" is stated, which no one can mistake.

And the same with lemon juice. To state simply that it is acid or sour is too indefinite. But if the acidity is stated to have a pH of 2.6, then a definite exact value for "sourness" or acidity is established.

To understand pH fully, we must first understand the pH scale. There are many acids, ranging from strong sulfuric ($H_2SO_4$), which dissolves iron like sugar, to weak acids like boric ($H_3BO_3$), which is used as an eyewash. Despite the widely diverse properties of individual acids, all owe their acidity to the single property of producing hydrogen ions ($H^+$). Strong acids produce high concentrations of hydrogen ions; weak acids produce low concentrations. So the measure of acidity is the numerical value of the concentration of hydrogen ions.

The numerical values for hydrogen ion concentrations, expressed in chemical terms, are extremely small fractions—$1/10,000,000$, for example. Such expressions are inconvenient. As a result, a scale was introduced, de-fined mathematically as the negative logarithm of the hydrogen ion concentration. Or, the power to which 10 must be raised to equal the hydrogen ion concentration. As a result of this mathematical conversion, acidities are expressed on a convenient numerical scale that runs from 0 for an acid solution of unit strength, to 7 for a neutral solution such as pure water. This scale is called the pH scale.

The range of pH values of general interest lies between 0 and 14; pH 7 being the neutral point, or the value of superpure water. Numbers less than 7 express increasing acidity, and numbers greater than 7 express increasing alkalinity. Also, a unit change in pH represents a tenfold change in acidity or alkalinity. As an example, a soap solution of pH 10 is ten times as alkaline as a soap solution of pH 9, and one hundred times as strong as a soap solution of pH 8. Similarly, an acid solution of pH 3 is ten times more acid than an acid solution of pH 4, and a hundred times more acid than an acid solution of pH 5, and one thousand times more acid than an acid solution of pH 6.

For practical agricultural purposes we may classify soils as follows: pH 4.0 as very acid; pH 5 as acid; pH 6.0 as slightly acid; pH 7.0 as neutral, that is, neither acid nor alkaline; pH 8.0 as alkaline.

***Very Acid Soils (pH 4.0):*** Very acid soils occur in peat bogs covered with sphagnum moss and in the duff under coniferous trees.

***Acid Soils (pH 5.0):*** Acid soils include peaty upland soils, rotted wood, some pine-barren sands, and heavily fertilized but seldom limed fields and gardens. Some plant indicators of acid (pH 5.0) soil are dwarf cornel or bunchberry (*Cornus canadensis*), golden thread (*Coptis groenlandica*), trailing arbutus (*Epigaea repens*), mountain laurel (*Kalmia latifolia*), trillium, and mountain ash.

***Slightly Acid Soils (pH 6.0):*** Slightly acid soils occur in most gardens in non-limestone regions, and in gardens in which manure or other organic matter is never used and seldom limed. Garden plants that prefer this type of soil are potato, watermelon, tobacco, and spinach.

***Neutral Soil (pH 7.0):*** Neutral soils occur in ordinary gardens in which manures, organic matter of other types, and lime are used. Also most composts, rotted manures, and black leaf molds are neutral. In this soil most of our garden plants thrive.

***Alkaline Soils (pH 8.0):*** Alka-line soils occur in salt marshes, limestone soils, and heavily limed soils. Plant indicators of alkaline soils are rough bedstraw (*Galium aparine*), oxeye daisy (*Chrysanthemum leucanthemum*), and *Trifolium medium*.

## Soil pH in Relation to Shrubs and Trees

Few shrubs and trees are acid tolerant. The most common acid-tolerant shrubs and trees are birches, oaks, alders, currants, bunchberry, mountain ash, and sweet bay magnolia

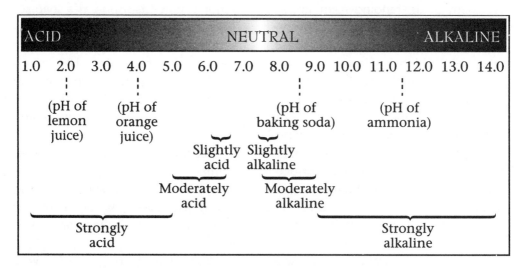

*The pH scale ranges from 1.0 to 14.0, representing values from strong acidity to strong alkalinity. A pH of 7.0 is considered neutral—neither acidic nor alkaline. Although soils are called acid or alkaline, their pH values tend to be much closer to neutral than to either the low or high ends of the pH scale. Most soils are less acidic than orange juice and less alkaline than baking soda. Gardeners often refer to alkaline soils as "sweet" and acid soils as "sour."*

(*Magnolia virginiana*). Some are mesophilous (pH 4.8 to 7.2) and are intolerant of any degree of alkalinity. Rhododendrons, raspberries, azaleas, birches, oaks, hollies, elms, junipers, dogwoods, pines, spruces, and hazelnuts are examples.

Acid-tolerant are apple, cherry, plum, pear, elm, beech, box, species of maple, and the most common ornamental shrubs and trees. While these shrubs and trees can tolerate acids, they should be limed occasionally.

## Soil pH and Lawn Grasses

The best lawn grasses available for putting greens and bowling greens are brown top (*Agrostis tenuis*), Chewing's fescue (*Festuca rubra* var. *fallax*), and *Festuca ovina* var. *tenuifolia*. All three of these grasses form a turf best under definitely acid conditions (pH 5.2 to 5.6), which excludes some undesirable weeds and is attained by adding acid peat or composted oak leaves.

## Plants Requiring a Decidedly Acid Soil

The following plants prefer or demand a soil at least as acid as pH 6.5, and thrive best at pH 4 to 6.

| | |
|---|---|
| Azalea | Marigold |
| Bayberry | Mountain laurel |
| Blackberry | Oak |

| | |
|---|---|
| Blueberry | Peanut |
| Butterfly weed | Pecan |
| Cardinal flower | Pink potato |
| Cranberry | Radish |
| Flax | Raspberry |
| Heath | Rhododendron |
| Heather | Spruce |
| Huckleberry | Sweet potato |
| Lupine | Trailing arbutus |
| Lily | Watermelon |
| Lily-of-the-valley | Yew |

## Plants That Prefer Alkaline Soil

Moderately alkaline soil favors the growth and productiveness of many garden plants. The use of lime, wood ashes, and some of the natural rock powders creates or increases the alkalinity of the soil. Certain alkaline-soil plants like peas, clovers, and alfalfa may become stunted or even sickly in acid soil. The more common alkaline-soil plants in the garden follow.

| | |
|---|---|
| Alyssum | Geum |
| Asparagus | Iris |
| Bean | Lettuce |
| Beet | Nasturtium |
| Cabbage | Onion |
| Carnation | Phlox |
| Cantaloupe | Rhubarb |
| Cauliflower | Squash |
| Cucumber | Sweet pea |

## Compost and the pH of the Soil

Humus functions as a buffer in the soil. Garden and crop plants are far less dependent upon a specific pH in the soil when there is an abundant supply of humus. For instance, potatoes require a distinctly acid soil when the humus content is low. In less acid or neutral soils low in humus, potatoes are highly susceptible to potato scab. In practical potato growing, it often is desirable to follow potatoes by crops not tolerant of soils too acid, such as cabbage, cauliflower, and brussels sprouts. According to Hugh A. Ward (*The Organic Farmer*, August, 1949), with the application of compost and the accompanying low soil acidity (pH 6.0 to 6.8), it becomes possible to follow early potatoes with cauliflower or brussels sprouts, which are transplanted in the fields in late July or early August for harvesting in October and November. If it is not desirable to grow these other vegetable crops after potatoes, the pH of the soil is favorable for such legumes as vetch and cowpeas for increasing the nitrogen content of the soil. Mr. Ward also reported that he can grow potatoes free from potato scab in a soil having a pH as high as 7.2 when he has plenty of humus in the soil. This observation emphasizes the importance of soil pH on the occurrence of plant diseases in general, and also the need for humus in the soil.

## pH and Plant Diseases

The relationship of pH to plant diseases involves both the pH of the soil and the pH of the sap and tissues within the plant. Many bacteria and fungi tend to change the pH of the medium in which they grow. Many disease-producing bacteria may raise the internal pH of a living host, while numerous acid-producing saprophytic bacteria lower the pH of their medium. Disease-producing fungi seem to decrease the internal pH of plants.

Plants with very acidic juices are reported to be immune to crown gall. Fungi are more acid tolerant than bacteria. The metabolic "health" of plants attacked by disease-producing fungi and bacteria seems to depend to some considerable extent upon the relation between the metabolism of the plant and the pH value of the soil solution from which it absorbs its nutrient substances. In soils low in humus, the finger and toe disease of turnips is rare in soils above pH 7.0, corky scab of potato does not develop in soils having a pH below 6.0, potato scab is rare in soils below pH 5.2, violet root rot is uncommon when the soil pH is above 7.0, heart rot of beet is rare below pH 6.7, wilt of tomato is minimal at a pH above 7.4, and the black root rot of tobacco is rare in soils with pH below 5.5.

*January 1954*

# Chapter 4

# Soil Improvement

# How My Garden Soil Grew and Grew

## John J. Meeker

There's a priceless lesson for gardeners everywhere in how this backyard soil-builder turned his cracked, caking California clay into top-grade, top-growing topsoil.

Visitors to our garden accuse us of trucking in high-grade loam to avoid the challenge of tightly caked clay typical around here. And unless they have some experience in the organic treatment of soil, we have a difficult time convincing them that besides vegetables and flowers, we also "grow" our own soil.

The same caked clay of the old orchards all my California neighbors have in their yards is also in mine, but the appearance of mine has been considerably altered, and its usefulness has been improved a hundredfold. No cracks appear

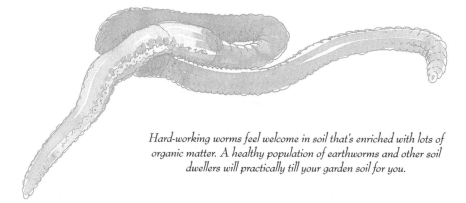

*Hard-working worms feel welcome in soil that's enriched with lots of organic matter. A healthy population of earthworms and other soil dwellers will practically till your garden soil for you.*

in my soil when wind and sun dehydrate the ground. In my garden, no plant's roots suffocate from standing water. And no one suffers back pains from cracking big pieces of earth into little ones.

The visitor may dig down deeply into the soil with his fingers. The earth smells sweet and is filled with tiny rootlets from the plants around. One of my periodic tasks is to cut out my neighbors' hungry roots that invade my soil over the property line. If I scoop up a soil sample in my hand, I can crumble it or pack it like rough brown sugar. Inspecting the texture, one discovers things like partially rotted twigs, half of a prune pit, a bottle cap bent double and oxidized into a lump of rust, bits of wire, bamboo stakes from tomato props three seasons ago, and a petrified tongue depressor.

In the seven years we have lived here our small plot—dug in between the cement of two patios—has risen 10 to 12 inches above the concrete around it. When we first moved in, a rank crabgrass lawn was well-established in a depression where the garden is now. Today we have to terrace the soil above the concrete and retain the earth with boards to keep it from spilling over on the cement.

## Elbow Grease and Organic Material

Our soil grew up because of two main ingredients: elbow grease and organic material. I wouldn't swear that one is more important than the other. Liberal dressings of compost or compost material—such as leaves and manure—will visibly change the condition of any soil, but deep cultivation to get the organic matter thoroughly mixed into the soil is essential.

By spading and hoeing mulches and dressings deeply into the earth, we have accomplished two important operations: addition of the organic matter to feed microscopic animal life, which in turn changes the organic matter into nutrients available to the roots. Physically breaking up the soil by spading and cultivating creates millions of tiny air pockets in the soil, giving the microorganisms air to breathe and making the soil fluffy.

Compacted clay soil that dries out to hardpan in the summer is—to an organic gardener, at least—simply precious garden soil with all the organic matter removed. When we moved here, we saw the problem in organic terms. It was just as important to start growing soil as it was to set out our first tomato plant.

The first year we dug up the 10-by-10-foot crabgrass lawn. We had to treat the earth first with long water soaks before we could slice the sod into 6- to 8-inch strips. Those slices became the start of my first compost pit at this house. Between the slabs of patio concrete, the excavated garden bed-to-be looked like the bottom of a pan from which a burned chocolate cake had been scraped. The clay bed looked unpromising. Further soakings were necessary to dig the ground. Of course, we were careful not to break down the body of the soil even further by digging it when it was sopping wet. We waited until most of the moisture had drained off and the soil was just about dry. Turning the clay, we broke it up with a shovel and by breaking clods between our hands.

The barrelful of sand I tried to include would probably have made things worse if I had not added at the same time a pile of unrotted sycamore leaves saved from the previous autumn, a bale of peat moss, a sack of "compost mix" from a factory experimenting with reconstituted garbage, and about 8 cubic feet of rotted oak leaves we had collected from the mountains while picnicking.

## "Expanding Soil" Starts Proving Itself

By the time all of this organic material was spaded and forked into the ground, the level of soil had reached the concrete of the patio. I noticed that the earth's level would rise with each spading. More than giving credit to additions, I believe that the greatest cause of expansion was the spading itself. With each deep spading (I attempted to work down to 18 inches), more air was worked into the composition of the soil.

The first year, we grew only tomatoes and cucumbers, crops grown commercially on nearby farms. Not a very adventurous garden, I admit, but we assumed that proven crops were best until we grew better soil.

That autumn I dug in rotted leaves that my neighbors had thrown away, and I plowed under the dead vines from the summer's crops. I had not become interested in the possibilities of winter gardening at that time, so I allowed the ground to rest and mulched it with leaves raked up during the fall. By now, the level of the earth, not counting the mulch, was about even with the cement of the patio.

Spring came, and my spade slipped through the mulch into the ground without too much effort. I felt as if I had a garden for the first time since the year we moved here. There was no sign of the vegetative matter of the summer's crop nor of the first organic applications. Under the mulch, at the line where the leaves began to dissolve into earth, a myriad of tiny earthworms wriggled when I disturbed them.

By the time I added the contents of the compost heap—those crabgrass sods we had lifted a year earlier, plus kitchen refuse, lawn clippings, and some leaves rescued from the street cleaners—the soil level had come up about 8 inches above the patio. We had to start making a terrace of earth at the boundaries of the garden to confine the soil and water when we irrigated.

At this time I was given an interesting comparison in my neighbor's garden. He had the same space to work in, but he just scratched and planted without periodically digging deeply and without adding organic materials. We took no pleasure from the fact that he had failures and middling successes. We were getting infected by the organic faith at that time, and like new converts to a religion, we wanted to get others to join. Our neighbor didn't seem convinced, even though the soil in his garden remained a clay-baked crust while ours was visibly changing. There could be no clearer evidence that we were doing the right things, at least most of the time.

## System Adds Humus All Season Long

Since that first year, never once at the beginning or end of a growing season have we failed to add liberal amounts of organic material. And through a system of creating passageways through our densely planted vegetables, we have added organic materials even during the growing season.

My method is to excavate the pathway carefully, throw in the refuse or leaves, and replace the soil over it. Although a few small roots from nearby plants are invariably cut into by this method, I have not found that it noticeably interferes with plant growth. The pathway larded with rotting leaves and

refuse becomes a bed for plants during the following season.

I can see a danger in this technique if one puts green or half-composted vegetable matter too close to growing plants. For soil bacteria to break down organic materials, nitrogen must be available. To do their job these organisms must take available nitrogen from the soil. When they have broken down the organic matter, they release the nitrogen and make it available once again to plants. The result is that plants are robbed of the nitrogen that they need. Green-manuring while plants are reaching maturity will starve the growing plant rather than feed it. I try to avoid this condition by digging in green manures and half-composted matter a distance *away* from the rows of growing things. I couldn't say that this technique is particularly good except for those gardeners who need to utilize every inch of space and who do not have room for all their available compost—and so benefit by using unused space as a pocket for decaying vegetable matter.

## Mixing Mulching and Cultivation

Not only does our ground have at any moment a pocket or two of vegetable refuse composting, but we practice mulching throughout the year. Shortly after spring shoots and seedlings get well-established with adult leaves, we begin to apply a mulch of compost.

The tender young plants require my best finished compost, of which we usually have a great deal by the end of winter.

Mixing mulching with cultivation, we see the first light application of mulch and the topsoil merge together very quickly. When the plants get taller we apply a mulch of straw or leaves and clippings that have not fully composted. Any dampness in this material soon evaporates, and the mulch forms an insulating layer for tomatoes, cucumbers, eggplants, and the root vegetables. The mulch becomes a pad as well as an insulator for melons and squash.

We save a lot of money on water bills with our mulch. However, we don't mulch everything. We do not mulch beans for two reasons: the few insects that find the mulch a nice home seem to become more of a problem on beans, and more important, pole beans appear to need a drying-out period to produce well— so without mulch our soil holds just about the right moisture for beans.

As soon as we harvest a crop, the remains of the plants are fed to the compost pile and the mulch is spaded into the soil. In about 30 days, winter or summer, there is little sign of the mulch. Admittedly, however, our California winters are mild.

## Year-Round Mulching

We mulch winter and autumn crops as well. During the winter months, however, we use only finished compost—whether it be leaves, garden refuse, or kitchen garbage. Snails, slugs, and earwigs seem to love the partially composted materials, but if we use finished, sweet-smelling compost as a mulch, pests do not seem to be attracted to it.

All the garden is raked and put in trim in the fall, and with the resulting refuse along with autumn leaves, we start a new compost pile for the winter. The summer refuse, now fully composted and clean, serves to mulch the prewinter turnips, potatoes, carrots, beets, leeks, shallots, and lettuces. We find autumn mulching particularly valuable because the winter rains often do not come when one expects them, and those fall droughts can fool the unwary gardener. A mulch helps conserve the water then as it does in summer.

For many years, during midwinter we stopped gardening. Now, though, we're never without a winter garden anymore because we've found that a lot of vegetables do well despite our light California frosts. But whether we have plants in the ground or not, we find a winter mulch a particularly nice way to get tilth into the soil. Clean straw, spoiled by water for consumption by animals, makes an especially good winter mulch. By spring the action of water and soil bacteria have it reduced almost to invisible plant nutrients in the soil.

We discovered what nice things clean hay does for the soil one winter when a neighbor moved away, leaving his son's archery target, a bale of good hay. As a farewell gesture he let us have it, and I mulched about half the garden in which we had planted a single crop of garlic. That occasion marked our third winter in this garden, and the following spring the soil turned up more workable than ever before. The hay had "melted" to about 3 inches, and in some places you could see the earth. We turned the ground in March, and by April there was hardly any sign of hay. By the time the spring sowing came up, one could find nary a straw. I thought I could almost hear the earth belch.

Of course, every organic gardener is a witness to the expansion of his soil to some extent. What has made the growth of ours so dramatic is the unchanging level of the concrete patio by which we can measure how the soil expands.

Now if you compare our soil to that of our neighbors around us, it does appear that we have trucked in some rich loam. Our care and feeding of the soil make it fat, and fat soil makes rich produce. Fortunately, rich vegetable produce alone doesn't make fat people. Our waists haven't increased in proportion to our soil—and happily we still weigh what we did when we first lifted the sod seven years ago!

*February 1971*

# Building the Soil Naturally

*Mark Kane*

You can't put too much organic matter on your garden, but you certainly can overwork yourself.

I've done some arithmetic for weary gardeners and concluded that a 30-by-40-foot garden like my own needs about 400 pounds of organic matter a year to match what the plot would grow if nature had her way. That's about ten bales of hay.

When I started gardening, my clay soil was fit for pottery—heavy and sticky in the spring, and hard as adobe in the summer. The first season, I spread 45 bales of straw and hay and tilled them in. According to my arithmetic, the clay should have turned into good soil, but by midsummer it turned to brick instead.

After two years I had turned under 80 bales of hay and straw and four wagonloads of manure—enough manure to fill a dump truck—and they had disappeared. The only sign of change was that walking through the garden, I no longer picked up 10 pounds of clay on each boot. Since I never had any trouble getting hay, straw, and manure, it took me some time to realize that I was squandering organic matter—and my own labor.

In those first years I spread and tilled in organic matter in spring, and planted by the instructions on the seed packet, laying out rows 2 and 3 feet apart. Then I tilled and hoed and weeded until the soil around my plants was bare. All that cultivation and bare ground burned up my organic matter. What I gave with one hand, I took away with the other. I put organic matter where no plant grew and then helped it vanish. Instead, I could have concentrated it on half the ground, grown just as much food, and done more good for the soil.

All this time, there was a good example of natural soil-building right under my garden fence. Falling down from age, the fence was overgrown with weeds, grass, and tree sprouts that had raised a ridge of soil and roots 3 inches higher than the surrounding ground. The bottom wire of the fence was engulfed, and in some places pinned down by roots that took an ax to sever. The soil was light and crumbly, nothing like the heavy clay in my garden and the adjacent pasture.

Where did that ridge of good soil come from? The fencerow plants were responsible for making it. Plants are the only producers of organic matter, and they know how to use it. They mulch themselves with their own leaves and toppled stems, sheltering the soil from the elements and providing a small, steady supply of organic matter to feed soil life.

## Soil Dwellers Do the Work

On the average, half of all fresh organic matter is transformed to humus in just two months by the bacteria, fungi, insects, and other animals that teem in the top 6 inches of soil. Their numbers are as dizzying as a night full of stars—a gram of soil may hold a hundred million bacteria, and in an acre of topsoil the bacteria may weigh 3 tons. There are thousands of species of soil life, each with its specialty. Earthworms, for example, feed on litter, dragging it into their burrows. Worms are the main reason mulch disappears. I mulch my asparagus patch each fall with 6 inches of hay, and the old mulch is so thin that when I kneel under the plumes of foliage to spread the hay, I can see the ground and the worm holes.

Mulch is not the only soil builder. Roots contribute astonishing quantities of organic matter and put it directly in the soil, some of it far deeper than I would care to dig. Roots are also the main agents in making the soil lighter and more open because their probing—and some cement drawn from humus—bonds soil particles together into long-lived aggregates, the "crumbs" that are the mark of rich soil.

At the end of the second season, I planted winter rye for a cover crop. When I tilled it near the end of March, the rye was 12 inches high and the roots were so thick they looked like small mops. (One admirable researcher tape-measured a rye plant and found 387 miles of roots and over 6,000 miles of root hairs.) Instead of the cold clods I expected to turn up, the soil shattered into crumbs. Wherever the garden had gone bare all winter, the soil clung to my boots, but where the rye had grown, I had a seedbed ready for planting.

Between the winter rye and the overgrown fencerow, I finally learned my lesson. A garden can't produce as much organic matter as the same patch of ground would if nature did the gardening. And we gardeners shouldn't expect it to. But we can see to it that our gardens produce as much of their own organic matter as possible and do as much of their own soil building as possible. That way, the organic matter we supply to make up the deficit will go further.

The main problem with my early soil-building efforts was too much bare ground and not enough plants. I was squeezing nature out of a job and overworking myself, fetching organic matter and turning it in when plants could have done more to build the soil. Humus was burning up. Nutrients

*Growing your plants in wide rows lets you make the most of garden space, moisture, and organic matter. By reducing the number of paths in your garden, wide rows keep more of the soil surface covered. This helps to keep out weeds and reduce moisture loss and allows you to apply organic matter where it's needed most.*

were leaching down without roots to catch and bring them up. Aggregates were being destroyed faster than plants could build them.

We should adopt methods that conserve organic matter and humus instead of burning them up. Here are the rules I've learned to follow:

**Keep the soil planted.** Bare soil should make you shudder. Wherever the soil is neither mulched nor growing plants, you can be sure organic matter is being consumed and nothing is replacing it. Plan for mature plants being close enough to shade the ground. Where you're not growing food, grow a cover crop. Remember that you can't build soil without plants.

Plant in wide rows or beds. Both let you cover more ground with plants than narrow rows, and concentrate organic matter where the plants will grow. With beds 3½ feet wide and paths 18 inches wide, less than 30 percent of your garden goes bare, while with narrow rows and wide paths, as much as two-thirds of your garden is bare (and you do all that cultivating or haul enough mulch to cover it all).

**Cultivate sparingly.** Cultivation exposes the soil to drying, which breaks apart aggregates and releases the humus that cements them. At the next rain, the plants get a boost from the released humus, but beware of gardeners who boast that this is a benefit of cultivation. You pay for the benefit with your soil's organic matter.

Cultivation also speeds up the oxidation of organic matter and humus, burning up your supply faster than plants can capture and use it.

From what I have read, there's nothing to the idea that cultivation during dry spells makes a "dust mulch" that keeps water in the soil. Once the soil surface has dried out, there's no difference in the rate of evaporation whether the soil is cultivated, undisturbed, or mulched.

**Keep the soil mulched.** Soil life needs constant feeding. It's better to put organic matter or compost in the soil in small, regular amounts than to turn under your whole supply at the beginning of the season. If you give the soil one big feeding, you'll get a microbial population explosion and then a collapse. Nothing feeds the soil better, with less work from the gardener, than mulch.

When I put my garden in wide beds, I didn't want even the paths to go bare, so I dug them out to a depth of 8 inches, spreading the soil on the beds, and filled them with sawdust. Watching the sawdust drop year by year—it's down about 3 inches in four years—gives me the smug feeling that nature's making topsoil out of the clay underneath.

**Put your organic matter in the topsoil.** There's no point in burying organic matter deeply. Nature keeps humus in the top 6 inches of soil and so should you. That's where the soil life is.

About 85 percent of all roots are in the first 6 inches of soil. The ones that go deeper are mainly in search of water. They leave a modest amount of organic matter in the subsoil, but it turns to humus only slowly, since there is very little oxygen to support soil life. Most of the subsoil nutrients leach down from the topsoil or are released by acids.

Once I began to cooperate with nature, my soil improved quickly. I saw the usual signs: lots of earthworms, dark, crumbly soil replacing clay, and so on. But the most dramatic sign was the appearance of new and thriving weeds, like dock, with its long lancelike leaves and yellow root, which never gives up sprouting no matter how many times it's cut. Dock annoys me, but it makes me proud, too.

A final point about organic matter: There's a limit to how much your soil can use efficiently, and it's not set by how many pickup loads of manure you can haul in a season. In the North, where cool summers slow down the loss of humus, you can pat yourself on the back if you build up the organic matter in your soil to 4 percent. In the South, where hot, humid summers burn up humus, you'll have to work hard to reach 2 percent. You can put on as much organic matter as you like, or have energy for, and surpass the natural limits. I don't go out of my way to try, however. I'd rather be gardening.

*May 1981*

# How to Use Compost

Y our compost's finished. After carefully following the recommended steps for turning the year's bounty of organic materials into rich, mellow humus, you want to be certain that it's used right—that it benefits your soil most and helps to insure a natural abundance and health in your coming crops.

Let's examine some of the better methods of garden compost applications. By doing so, perhaps

Here's the way to get the most from the best of fertilizers.

*A wheelbarrow of finished compost is a treasure trove of nourishment for your soil and your plants.*

many people who have recently begun gardening the organic way will find a number of very practical and worthwhile suggestions on making the optimum use of nature's valuable fertilizer. Even those who are "old hands" at tilling the land and following the recommendations of the organic method may discover some downright helpful ideas and hints.

## When to Apply

The principal factor in determining when to apply compost is its condition. If it is half-finished, or noticeably fibrous, it could well be applied in October or November. By spring it will have completed its decomposition in the soil itself and be ready to supply growth nutrients to the earliest plantings made. Otherwise, for general soil enrichment, the ideal time of application is a month or so before planting. The closer to planting time it is incorporated, the more it should be ground up or worked over thoroughly with a hoe to shred it fine. A number of garden cultivating tools and machine equipment offer an excellent time- and labor-saving hand in accomplishing this. Several will help spread compost evenly and mix it thoroughly with the soil.

If your compost is ready in the fall and is not intended to be used till the spring, it should be kept covered and stored in a protected place. If it is kept for a long period during the summer,

the finished compost should be watered from time to time.

## How to Apply

For general application, the soil should be stirred or turned thoroughly. Then the compost is added to the top 4 inches of soil. For flower and vegetable gardening, it is best to pan the compost through a half-inch sieve. Coarse material remaining may then be put into another compost heap.

Where compost is desired to aid a growing crop, there are cautions necessary to avoid injuring plant roots growing near the surface. In order not to disturb these roots of established plants, the compost may be mixed with topsoil and together applied as a mulch. This is the best means of adding what is often termed a top dressing. It serves a double purpose in that at the same time it is providing plant food which will gradually work itself down to the growing crop, it also affords an effective mulch to the soil, giving protection from extremes of temperature, hard rains, and so forth.

## How Much to Apply

For best results in gardening, compost should be applied liberally, let us say, from 1 to 3 inches in thickness per year. Within a few years your garden will become the wonder and envy of your neighborhood. Of course, you can get by with as little as $1/2$ inch of compost, but in gardening with small plots, put it on heavy. There is no danger of burning due to overuse, such as is always the case with the chemically concocted fertilizers.

You can apply compost either once or twice a year. The amount would depend, of course, on the fertility of your soil originally and on what and how much has been grown in it. Incidentally, an average figure of weight for 1 cubic yard of compost (27 cubic feet) is 1,000 pounds. There would be variations depending on the materials used and the length of time composted.

## For Orcharding and Trees

Compost should be applied under each tree. Start about 2 to 3 feet away from the trunk, and go to about 1 foot beyond the drip line at the end of the branches. How thick should it be applied? If you are going to apply it every year, 1/2 to 1 inch will do. First cultivate under the tree to work the grass mat into the soil; then work in the compost, keeping it in the upper 2 inches. It is a good practice then to apply a mulch of old hay or other green matter. A layer of compost about 3 or 4 inches thick would be sufficient for three or four years.

Where there are poisons in the soil from many years of spraying, a 3- or 4-inch layer of compost worked into the soil will tend to counteract somewhat their harmful effects.

## The Ring Method

To save time, the compost can be made right under the tree. Thus it acts as a mulch also. It is called the ring method because you place the raw materials 3 feet away from the trunk, like a ring. Apply the materials as if you were making compost, but instead of making the heap 5 feet high, make it only about 2 feet high. To hasten the formation of compost, add lots of earthworms to the material.

## For Flowers

All flowers, like any other growing plants, respond well to the organic method and, of course, to applications of compost. Compost may be safely applied even to acid-loving flowers such as the rhododendron. If a gardener has a considerable number of acid soil plantings, which include several of the berries as well as many flowers, it would be advisable that he prepare an acid compost. This is done by making the compost without lime or wood ashes, just as it is done for those soils that are quite alkaline.

For potted flowers, compost should not be used alone, but should be mixed with soil. Try screening and applying friction to it before using in a flower pot. Then mix about one-third compost and two-thirds rich soil.

*October 1954*

# Finished Compost in 14 Days

## Robert Rodale

Modern methods return a useful, better-quality compost in just two weeks.

The big news in composting today is speed. Why wait for three months or even a whole year for compost to break down when by using modern methods you can be assured of usable compost in as short a time as two weeks? And there are other advantages. Speed-compost is richer because it is subjected to rain and sun for a shorter time. It saves space in your garden, because you can make and use 1 to 5 tons of compost during a two-week vacation.

Shredding of all material before it goes into the compost heap is the key to fast com-

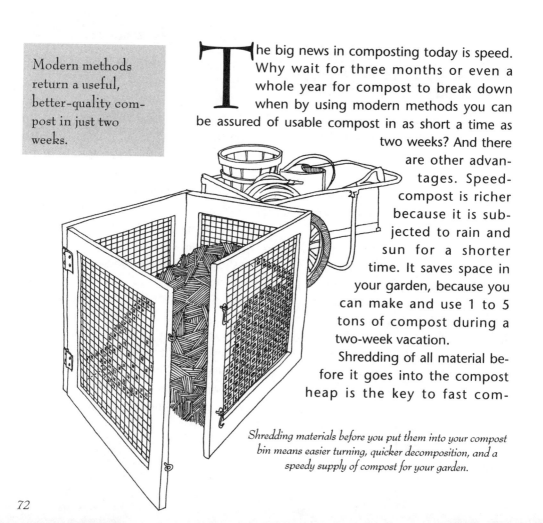

*Shredding materials before you put them into your compost bin means easier turning, quicker decomposition, and a speedy supply of compost for your garden.*

posting. We proved that with our own experiments at the Organic Experimental Farm and in our own home gardens. Frequent turning—as often as every three days—is also important. Shredded compost is very easy to turn. It offers little resistance to your shovel, and a 1-ton heap can be turned in five to ten minutes.

We are now convinced that the small amount of time it takes to shred weeds, leaves, straw, spoiled hay, manure, and other raw materials before composting is easily repaid by reduced labor later.

In order to present to readers an accurate picture of fast composting methods, we got together the three garden-size compost shredders that are now being marketed. They were the Kemp Model 6, the Keston Shredder, and the W-W model 2-XB. The Kemp and the W-W shredders were equipped with 2-horsepower gasoline engines, and the Keston with an electric motor.

For purposes of comparison, we first made an ordinary compost heap, using spoiled hay and chicken litter as the two basic ingredients. The heap was made in layers, following the original Sir Albert Howard method. It occupied an area 5 by 10 feet, and was 5 feet high. It was well-watered after being made. After a week the heap was turned, but little heating had occurred. After three weeks this ordinary heap was still in a fresh and undecayed condition.

The heap would certainly have decayed in time, but it was not suc-cessful by any means. Our main difficulty was keeping the heap moist during hot weather. The spoiled hay was so tough and kinky that it did not create a favorable environment for bacteria to work. Turning the heap was extremely difficult, because the hay formed itself into tough mats.

The first shredder to arrive was the Kemp Model 6. We took it to our own backyard, along with two more bales of the spoiled hay, two drums of dry corncobs, and a drum of horse manure. I also used a few shovels of finished compost for a starter.

## Finished Compost ASAP

We were determined to produce finished compost in as short a time as possible. I wanted to show the neighbors that composting did not have to drag on over two seasons. First, we began putting through the machine several bushels of iris that a friend had contributed. They were mashed up admirably, but the stringy stalks could stall the engine if they were fed too fast. We found that feeding a corncob with each large handful of iris cleared the machine nicely.

The cobs themselves were shredded all right, but they made a lot of noise inside the machine. That started us feeding some hay with the cobs, in order to cushion them. Finally we ran through the hay and manure. Both were shredded into quite small particles.

All in all, we were quite impressed, because the Kemp (and the W-W) is primarily intended as a grinder of finished compost and soil. It worked well for our purpose, however.

After watering our compost mound, we retired to the bathroom to soak off what had clung to our own bodies. I expected fast developments, but was quite surprised next morning to see the temperature up to 130 degrees. Even more interesting was the color, which had changed from a light yellow to a light brown overnight.

## Quick-Cooking Compost

By afternoon, the temperature was up to 140 degrees. I was using my wife's meat thermometer, and the red line was up to "beef rare." So you can see that the compost was really cooking. Monday evening I turned it for the first time, noting that the color was even darker and the heat greater. A ring of white, air-loving fungus had begun to grow around the edges of the heap. According to scientists, the area around the edges of a compost heap breaks down first, because of the action of these fungi. The strongest decay-causing organisms need plenty of air. That is why the heap should be turned often.

The following Saturday—one week after the heap was made—it was turned for the second time. The ring

mold was very noticeable. From a distance of a few feet, the heap looked finished already. But close up you could see that it needed some time to simmer down.

Ten days after the heap was made, it was inspected by Phillip Wells, well-known compost authority. He was surprised to hear that it was just recently made, for by that time it was quite dark brown and soft to the touch. Together, we transferred the heap to a Keston-Lehigh compost bin, in order to get some photos of the bin in use.

Three days later—two weeks after it was made—I judged the heap finished and ready for use. It had not stopped heating entirely, but it certainly looked like finished compost, and its nutrients were in a readily available state. We had succeeded in making compost in two weeks, using commonly available materials. There is no reason why you cannot do the same thing.

*February 1982*

# Compost Piles That Work

### Jeff Cox

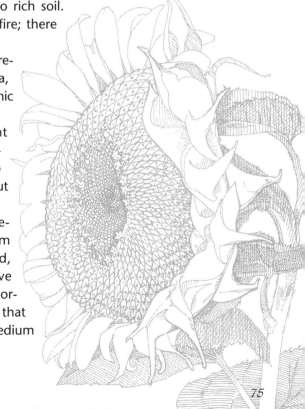

With the right ingredients in the right proportions, you can't miss. It's the heat in the compost pile that's always been most fascinating; the biological fire steaming refuse into rich soil. There's no magic to summoning this fire; there are only requirements.

For a pile to heat up properly, it requires air, moisture, nitrogen, bacteria, heat, sufficient size, and plenty of organic matter to digest.

Special ingredients like succulent green matter, the methods of shredding, and equipment like tumblers help raise the pile's temperature quickly, but are not essentials.

Let's examine those essential requirements. A lack of any one of them can limit the heap's temperature and, therefore, the reactions that conserve nutrients, kill weed seeds and disease organisms, and produce the substances that make compost the superb growing medium that it is.

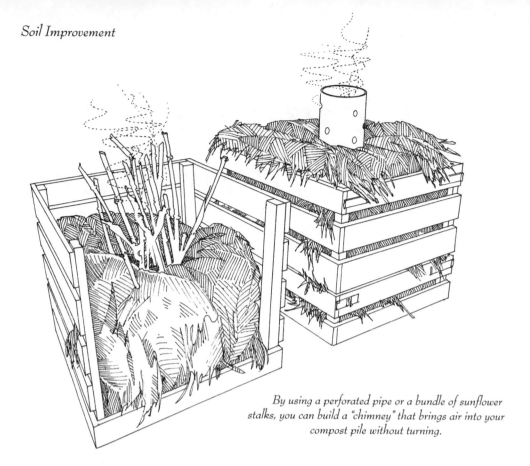

*By using a perforated pipe or a bundle of sunflower stalks, you can build a "chimney" that brings air into your compost pile without turning.*

## Air

Sunflower stalks build air channels into Warren Pierce's compost at the Community Environmental Council's Mesa Project, an urban gardening experiment in Santa Barbara, California. Air is essential for the aerobic bacteria whose furious proliferation and action within the pile cause the intense heat.

"Sunflowers have stalks with soft centers which rot out quickly," Warren says. The stalks themselves rot through and bring air right to the middle of the pile.

"Place numerous stalks of this type as the bottom 2- to 4-inch layer of your pile. Then put the first 12-inch layer of moistened compostable materials on top of the stalks followed by ¼ inch of soil. Now place a few stalks on top of the soil layer, followed by another 12-inch layer of moistened compostables and ¼ inch of soil on top. This layering process goes on until the pile is 4 feet high. The last layer should be 2 inches of soil," he says.

Cornstalks, by the way, do not rot easily, and neither do their centers, so cornstalks shouldn't be used for air channels.

In my new garden, Jerusalem artichokes are the peskiest weed, and Warren's advice led me to inspect the dried stalks of last year's growth. The stalks are papery, and the centers are soft—perfect for air channeling. When I put my pile together last week, I used artichoke stems in every layer. Check the dried stalks of other weeds available to you—if the centers are hollow, you're in business.

Turning the pile every week or so aerates it and speeds up the process. Another time-honored trick for good aeration involves layering poles into the heap and withdrawing a few every day or so during the major heat buildup. You can also stick the pile with the tines of a pitchfork to open air channels.

One of the main benefits of a compost tumbler is the aeration that tumbling provides.

A commercially produced model of the tumbler-style composter stands on a tube-steel base and holds 14 bushels of material. A crank on the end turns the tumbler, and screened vents allow air into the composting mass. You only have to rotate the drum for five complete turns to achieve finished compost in 14 days. Because of the amount of air it lets in, you'll have to water the pile almost daily. A similar tumbler could be constructed at home using a 55-gallon drum with holes punched in it, mounted on an axle.

Another method for aeration involves building the pile on chicken wire or hardware cloth about a foot off the ground, allowing air to enter from the bottom. Stretch the wire tight so it holds the weight of the pile, which can reach several tons in a large heap. You can lay plastic sheets under the mass to catch any liquids that drain out, returning them to the top of the pile for double action.

*Tumbling takes the place of turning when compost is made in a tumbler instead of a pile. By rotating the barrel on its axle, you add air to the ingredients without lifting a fork.*

## Moisture

"You want it to be like a moist sponge," says Professor James R. Love, a soil scientist at the University of Wisconsin in Madison. "Grab a handful and squeeze it. No drops of moisture should come out." Too little moisture slows down decomposition and prevents the pile from heating up. The microorganisms need a steamy environment. Too much moisture drives out air, drowns the pile, and washes away nutrients.

Country folks know how a haystack sheds water—a well-made haystack keeps the bulk of the hay dry through winter rains. This effect can be a problem in a compost you wish to keep moist when you're using hay as an ingredient. Counter this by keeping the hay layers to 6 or 8 inches and wetting each layer thoroughly as you build the pile. To control the moisture in an exposed heap, cover it with a few inches of hay, which should help shed rain. Some cover their compost with black plastic and remove it during selected rains.

For watering while the pile is working, dig out a little hole in the top and pour your buckets in or stick the hose in it. Since my garden hose doesn't reach the composting site, I carried buckets as I built my pile. The finished pile stands 4 feet high, has a 3-foot-square plateau on top, and tapers out to a 5-by-5-foot base. It took 24 buckets of water.

Check the moisture content when turning the pile, especially.

## Nitrogen

Lack of enough nitrogen is probably the main reason why composts fail to heat up. Scientists talk of the carbon-to-nitrogen ratio, but the home composter doesn't need numbers.

Manure is the basic nitrogen-rich compost ingredient, and it should comprise about a quarter to a fifth of the pile, the rest being plant wastes. Chicken droppings, being the highest in nitrogen of any commonly available manure, just about guarantee that the pile will get hot. I used two 20-gallon garbage cans full in constructing my pile this spring, paying a dollar a can at a local egg ranch, but you may be able to get it free. It really does the job, but it's difficult to work with. While you want it to form a nice, even layer (it works best if you spread it on top of the hay or main layer of green matter), it wants to clod up into lumps. I take thin slices with the shovel and lay them over the hay, then wash them into the hay with water.

Fresh horse manure, kitchen garbage, and special materials like blood meal, guano, and cottonseed meal are also rich in nitrogen. Fresh cow or pig manure is good, but not so good as those described previously, so just use a little more of these manures.

Hay that's been used for animal bedding is an added nitrogen source, although you'll still need manure to get the pile cooking. We have two goats on our small homestead, and compost-making was preceded by forking the winter's layers of bedding out of the goat house. The bottom layers were soaked with urine and peppered with goat manure, which is perfect for boosting the pile's nitrogen content. Bedding used for horses or sheep, or litter used for poultry, would also be excellent. Just make sure that it hasn't been exposed to rains that would wash the soluble nitrogen in the urine out of it.

Additionally, some hays or grasses contain more nitrogen than others. Alfalfa is high in this element;

timothy hay is low. Grass clippings are high (stick your hand into a pile of fresh grass clippings—they begin to heat up alone very quickly); leaves are low in nitrogen.

## Bacteria

Bacteria are the agents of the transformation of wastes into gardening gold in a compost heap. They exist in the raw ingredients, but they might not be the right mix of the right types. Most composters seed their piles by finishing each layer with a thin covering of good garden soil, which contains just the right kinds of microorganisms—bacteria, fungi, and the free agents called actinomycetes.

There are commercial bacterial compost "starters" on the market, but garden soil that's been enriched with actively decaying plant matter works fine.

## Heat

It will be next to impossible to get a pile working during the cold months. The warmer temperatures of spring through fall provide enough ambient heat to allow the pile to work. A fall-built pile can be insulated to work into the winter, but it's trouble, and who needs lots of finished compost in January? Better to compost while it's still warm enough, cover the pile from winter rains, and use the finished product in the spring.

## Size Your Pile for Surefire Heating

The larger the pile, the easier it is to get it to heat up to its optimum 140 degrees. Below a minimum size, which is a cube of material 3 feet on each dimension, the pile may get warm, but it's unlikely to get hot enough to kill weed seeds or pathogens. Try for a heap 4 or 5 feet square on the bottom, rising to 4 feet high, for surefire heating. Composting expert Dr. Clarence Golueke says that in a pile this size, less than half the material—that part right in the middle—is exposed to the highest temperatures. The temperature goes down as you approach the outside of the pile. When turning, shovel the undigested materials from the outside portions of the pile into the middle. This often causes a second heating as this material gets a chance to decompose in the heart of the heap.

Dr. Eberhard Spohn, a consultant in waste recycling and soil health in Heidelberg, Germany, uses what he calls a "wandering compost pile." Fresh ingredients, such as kitchen refuse (minus meat or animal fat), are tossed on the sloping front face of the heap, which is 3 feet wide and high and at least 3 feet long—the minimum size. Finished compost is sliced from the back, which means the pile creeps forward about 6 inches a week. Dr. Spohn screens the finished compost and uses the large particles left in the screen to cover additions to the front face, thus seeding them with bacteria. This method continuously composts household, yard, and garden waste in a pile the right size for suburban and small-scale composters.

## Organic Matter

Any plant material will compost, but some materials have drawbacks. Leaves, for instance, unless they are finely shredded, tend to mat into tough layers that thwart the intense heating we're after. All tough, stalky matter, wood chips, and other refuse high in lignin resist rapid breakdown.

The folks who follow bio-dynamic principles are fond of using stinging nettles for the compost, and with good reason—the nettles, before flowering, are soft and succulent and are easily colonized by decay organisms. This kind of "explosive green matter" helps the pile heat up quickly. I used an inch or two of fresh nettles between layers of my pile, since they grow rampant in one corner of my property. May is a good month for finding this kind of soft and juicy material. Later on in the year, the plant tissue tends to toughen up. A shredder then proves to be a very useful tool.

Besides its richness in nitrogen and green matter, alfalfa may have an added benefit. A recent *New York Times* article by Boyce Rensberger reported on the work of Dr. Stanley K. Ries of Michigan State, which shows that a substance (triacontanol), found in minute amounts in alfalfa, seems to boost yields of many crops from 10 to 40 percent when applied in just the right amounts to a garden or field. The right amount is 104 pounds of alfalfa per acre, Dr. Ries says. That is equivalent to about a pound of dry, ground-up alfalfa per 640 square feet of garden space.

A pound or two of alfalfa meal in the compost may or may not have an effect (the active substance could be changed in the composting process), but it can't hurt.

When the pile has stayed at 140 degrees for the better part of a week and cools down to 100 degrees, it is finished. It's very beneficial to have the final phases of digestion completed in the soil. Top yields are the result when you follow this method. A recent study by F. P. Eggert of the Plant and Soil Sciences Depart-ment of the University of Maine at Orono showed that compost alone with rock phosphate out-performed four other fertilizing systems in total yields, including the French Intensive method, commercial fertilizer, commercial plus seaweed extract, and compost plus seaweed mulch.

*August 1977*

# Chapter 5

# Fertilizers

# That Cover Crop...

## IS MORE IMPORTANT THAN YOU THINK

### Thomas Powell

*Sometimes called green manures, cover crops add nutrients and organic matter to the soil. By keeping your garden's soil covered during times when you're not growing vegetables, cover crops also prevent erosion and help keep out weeds.*

The gardener who neglects to sow a cover crop is letting his garden—and himself—down hard. Cover crops serve a variety of purposes. They decay and add humus to the soil and act as a binder to prevent soil erosion and cracking by frost. They store up precious plant foods and prevent them from being drained down out of reach of the plants' roots.

Some cover crops, such as vetch, peas, and clover, manufacture nitrogenous compounds from nitrogen in the air and make it unnecessary to buy nitrogenous fertilizers. Cover crops hold leaves, which will form humus, and snow, which will add moisture to the soil when it melts. For the gardener who likes to have a neat garden all year, a cover crop presents a fresh, green appearance through late fall, winter, and early spring.

Some cover crops live through the winter, while others are killed by frost. Both have their advantages and disadvantages. If you sow a delicate crop, there'll be no worry of its growing in the spring. If you sow one that will survive the winter, you must take care to work it into the surface layers of the soil before it grows more than 8 or 9 inches high. If allowed to grow too high, not only is it harder to dig under, but it also becomes woody, decaying more slowly and even interfering with the development of your vegetable crops.

Sow a cover crop when the vegetables are nearing maturity and before they are harvested; this may be as early as July or as late as October. Apply some composted manure or an organic fertilizer like bonemeal shortly before sowing. Its nourishment will be used by the cover crop and returned to the soil when the plant residues decay.

Sow the seed for the cover crop either by drilling it between the rows of vegetables or by broadcasting it around them. If you intend to sow a cover crop of legumes that you have never planted in your soil before, inoculate the soil or seed just before sowing. This supplies the symbiotic rhizobial bacteria the crop needs to capture nitrogen. Various kinds of in-

*In the mid-1980s, gardeners at the Rodale Research Center tested the soil-building effectiveness of more than 20 different nitrogen-fixing legumes. In a 1987 Organic Gardening article, they cited hairy vetch, Austrian winter pea, alsike clover, crimson clover, Hubam sweet clover, and yellow blossom sweet clover as the top performers for home garden use.*

oculants are procurable from seed suppliers. Tell the supplier exactly what crop you intend to sow in order to get the most efficient inoculant for that crop. If you know of some gardener who has recently grown the same crop, get a wheelbarrow full of his soil and spread that on your plot instead of buying the inoculant. If you grow the same legume each year, there is no need to inoculate the ground before each sowing—the bacteria last many years.

Now let's take a look at some of the cover crops you may decide to plant in your garden. *Soybeans,* tender annuals that grow from late spring to midsummer, are among the best. Being erect plants, they hold many wind-blown leaves and snow and are fine sown with low cover crops like cowpeas or Canada field peas.

*Cowpeas,* which will not survive frost, are also good grown on a bare piece of ground from June through August. They form large numbers of rapid-growing vines that cover the ground thickly. Plow them under in September and plant a winter cover crop like vetch or rye on the same plot. *Canada field peas* also produce a large quantity of vines and roots and are best sown with oats, rye, or barley to help support their tops.

*Crimson clover* and *hairy vetch* will both survive not-too-severe winters on well-drained ground. Vetch, a trailing vine, will make the best growth if sown with cow peas, buckwheat, or soy beans in July or with rye in September or October.

*Buckwheat* may be planted from late spring to midsummer. It is a non-legume, which is generally killed by the first frost, but it should not be plowed under until it has had the opportunity to catch a good supply of wind-blown leaves and snow. It forms large amounts of foliage that decays quickly when plowed under. For best results, sow buckwheat with vetch or crimson clover in midsummer.

*Turnips, cowhorn turnips, mustard,* and DWARF ESSEX *rape,* all non-legumes, should be sown in September or October. In the cool autumn weather, they make a profusion of roots and foliage that are usually killed by heavy frost. Plow these under early in spring to avoid their offensive decaying odor.

*Rye* is a hardy winter grain that will grow all through the fall and winter whenever the ground is not frozen. It should be sown in early fall and dug under early in spring, before it is more than 7 or 8 inches tall. If it grows any higher, cut it with a scythe and use it for compost, with only the stubble being plowed under.

Your garden will benefit more by your sowing a cover crop, which is inexpensive and takes comparatively little time and energy, than by constant applications of commercial fertilizers. So take the time to sow a cover crop this year; you'll have a good-looking garden all winter and better vegetables next year.

*May 1948*

# Wood Ashes Are Worth Money!

*Doc and Katy Abraham*

The energy crunch has done one good thing. It's made dollar-minded people use their fireplace for something besides a decoration. There's no question that more people are using fireplaces this year than ever before. Our neighbor figures he cut his fuel bill in half last year by putting his fireplace to work.

Any wood will burn and give off heat, of course, but if you have a choice, select ash, oak, maple, or beech for slow-burning qualities as well as heat.

> Anyone with a fireplace or woodstove has a by-product that's valuable in the garden, lawn, or compost heap.

Then, *save your wood ashes.* They're an important by-product of your fireplace. Did you know that wood ashes are twice as high in acid-neutralizing power as ground limestone? That doesn't mean you can put them on your garden year after year. Naturally, you can overdo anything. We don't advocate applying wood ashes onto soils without checking every other year to see how acid your soil is. Most plants will thrive in a *slightly* acid soil. It's just the highly acid soils that should get plenty of wood ashes.

You *can* over-alkalinize, so be sure by taking a soil test first. Avoid using wood ashes on acid-loving crops such as radishes, potatoes, watermelons, blueberries, rhododendrons, hollies, and azaleas, to name a few.

A simple "acid" test can be made by taking a soil sample, moistening it with a small amount of distilled water or deionized water. Then dip a piece of pH testing paper (litmus) into the soil mixture. You'll get a quick reading by a color change, which can be compared with a color chart that comes with the kit. Garden supply stores now handle these simple but effective pH testing papers.

## "Pot Ashes" Contain Needed Potassium

For many years wood ashes have been valued and used by gardeners because of their potash content and high percentage of lime. The word *potash* is derived from "pot ashes," which were obtained by leaching wood ashes and evaporating the solution. The residue consisted of potassium carbonate plus other salts.

Unleached wood ashes contain all the mineral elements that were in the original wood. They are a good source of potash, the plant nutrient that encourages stiff stems and prevents "lodging" or falling over. Potash imparts increased vigor and disease resistance to plants and gives winter hardiness to others. At one time, wood ashes were the chief source of potash.

Various woods you burn in the fireplace differ greatly in potash, but if you burn a ton of elm (a common fireplace wood today), you get about 9 pounds. Twigs are richer than mature wood. Besides potash, wood contains about 2 percent phosphorus, the plant nutrient that stimulates growth and root formation. Wood ashes also contain oxides or carbonates, which give them an alkaline (sweet) reaction.

Another bonus from using wood ashes is that the potassium in them has a tendency to slow down growth that may have been caused by excessive amounts of nitrogen, and also acts to prevent early maturity resulting from too much phosphoric acid. Within the plant, potassium plays its role in food manufacture (photosynthesis) and the translocation of foods made in the plant (starches). Wood ashes are helpful in supplying potassium, which is essential for making chlorophyll (green pigment) in the leaves and stems.

You can tell if your plants need potash by looking at the leaves. Since potassium is mobile within the plant it moves upward out of lower leaves to the upper ones. When there's a lack of potash in the soil, the lower leaves will show a marginal yellowing; they later turn brown and appear scorched. In addition, mottling and yellow spotting of lower leaves may appear.

Hardwood ashes contain more potash than softwood, but there's no truth to the notion that they are caustic or harmful. Both are okay to use in the flower garden or vegetable garden. Do not use wood ashes year after year on potato land as it may cause scab, a disease favored by sweet soils. On the other hand, wood ashes have been used for years to force a stubborn peony bed to bloom.

Elements in wood ashes are soluble, so don't make the mistake of piling them outdoors—until you're ready to add them to your compost heap or garden soil. Store them in a dry place in the garage. If your soil tests quite acid, use wood ashes in spring, fall, or winter at a rate of about 5 pounds per 100 square feet.

## Wood Ashes in the Compost

Wood ashes are excellent for the compost pile. Many acids are present in organic residues cast onto the pile. If the material is too acid, it can slow down decomposition. That's why it's a good idea to add wood ashes to the pile to neutralize acidic conditions, except, of course, where the soils are quite alkaline.

If not neutralized, too much ammonia released in the pile might kill or impair earthworms and other important soil organisms at work in the compost. We scatter a layer of ash on each layer of soil, garbage, and lawn trimmings. This is repeated until the pile is 3 feet or so high.

With a proper amount of wood ashes and organic matter, your compost will be naturally inoculated with a variety of helpful decomposer organisms. Nature was generous to those who make compost piles. Spores, eggs, and other dormant stages of organisms that help break down wastes are present in soil, on surfaces of organic debris, and even on household garbage. Wood ash helps these naturally occurring decomposers work better. Use about 1 peck per yard of compost.

On soils receiving wood ashes (or lime), dead plant materials are broken down into plant nutrients by microbes. These same microbes tend to be inactive when the acidity increases. This means that the supply of phosphorus, nitrogen, calcium, and magnesium is not built up in the soil and is therefore not available as plant nutrients. The wood ashes can act as a key to unlock plant foods. In humid areas where rainfall exceeds 25 inches per year, garden soils and lawns tend to become gradually acid, all the more reason why wood ashes can be valuable in your compost pile.

## Other Uses for Ashes

If your lawn or garden soil is heavy clay, wood ashes are helpful in making them "breathe easier." Clay is composed of tiny particles that have a large surface to soak up water. High water content causes clay to be sticky. If you add wood ashes—about 10 to 15 pounds per 100 square feet—you can do a lot to loosen it up.

As for shrubs, we scatter wood ashes in our perennial bed and around rose plants, applied in fall or spring. Roses like them at the rate of ½ to 1 pound around each plant. Other shrubs can have wood ashes applied at the same rate. Rains carry the nutrients down to the root zone.

If snails are a problem to tomatoes, peppers, lettuce, or other vegetables, fight them with wood ashes. Scatter several handfuls around the base of each plant. Snails don't like crawling over dry ashes. The calcium in the ash helps plants build cellulose walls, and when you eat the produce from the garden, that same calcium is healthful in building up bones and teeth.

Certain disease organisms that live in the soil may also be checked with the addition of wood ashes. These include root rot of corn and clubroot of crucifers (cabbage, cauliflower, broccoli, turnips, etc.).

Lawns can benefit, too. Hardwood ashes of good quality contain lime equivalent to that of high-grade, finely ground limestone used for lawns. They contain about 4 per-cent, or 80 pounds of, potash in 1 ton plus about 1.5 to 2 percent phosphoric acid, or from 30 to 40 pounds per ton. Most lawn grasses will do best when the soil reaction is around a pH of 6 or 7 (meaning almost neutral); at that level, plant foods are easily available to be taken up by grass roots. Also, the soil microbes—the tiny organisms that decompose thatch and other organic matter—are highest at that level.

Grasses on a well-limed soil (or those that get more wood ashes) are more aggressive than those on an acid soil and are better able to hold their own against weeds. Even acid-tolerant grasses, such as fescues and bent grasses, grow much better on close-to-neutral soils than on strongly acid soils.

However, if a lawn has weeds in it, it's not necessarily an indication that the soil is "sour" and needs wood ashes. Liming is not a cure-all. It can be beneficial in controlling weeds only if the soil is so acid that plant nutrients cannot be absorbed. Do not use fresh ashes on newly germinating seeds or let them come in contact with roots.

Your fireplace can give your home extra heat, at little or no expense. It can also give you a by-product no other fuel does—wood ashes. That bonus can help you grow better plants. For that reason alone, ashes are well worth saving.

*January 1976*

# Choosing and Using Manure

## James Jankowiak

Not so very long ago, some livestock owners would practically pay you to haul away their accumulated manure. Not so today. Manure may not be worth its weight in gold, but its price is on the rise, and the more we learn about it, the more valuable it seems.

Manure and compost are the very best all-around fertilizers available to organic gardeners, adding humus to the soil—something *no* chemical fertilizer does. Manure releases its nutrients into the soil on both an immediate and an extended basis, helping crops grow steadily throughout the season.

In fact, manure, like compost and other decayed organic matter, *is the basis of continued soil fertility.* It supplies nitrogen, phosphorus, potassium, and trace

> Manure is the basis of natural soil fertility and top production.

elements. It furnishes carbon as a source of energy for the soil life system.

## Hot and Cold Manures

Animal manures are divided into two basic groups—hot, or those that contain a relatively high proportion of nitrogen, and cold, or those that contain a relatively low nitrogen proportion. The former includes duck, goose, hen, sheep, turkey, and rabbit manure. The latter group includes cow and hog manure on the low end and horse manure on the high end. Naturally, any manure will vary in nutrient content depending on what the animal has been eating, whether it is pregnant, nursing, or growing (in which cases the nutrients in the manure are less), and how the manure has been treated in terms of being mixed with bedding or exposed to improper handling or leaching. In addition, there will be varying amounts of trace elements needed for proper plant growth, plus all that wonderful humus. Remember that as commonly sold by the bag or by the truckload from farm or feedlot, manure is not straight dung, but a mixture of dung and other materials. Not only that, manure unlocks nutrients already present in the soil, and its fertilizing value is much higher than chemical analysis shows.

For instance, poultry litter sometimes comes as a mixture of wood shavings or sawdust and droppings. Some people say that if a bedding contains a high percentage of fresh sawdust, it is not fit for the garden because it locks up nitrogen, gives off harmful acids, and encourages harmful fungus growth. I've used sawdust and shavings by the ton as poultry litter, animal bedding, and directly on the soil as an amendment or mulch, and have never noticed any harmful effects. The part about locking up nitrogen is true, but in a fertile garden this won't make any significant difference. Besides that, the nitrogen is not lost—it's released later from the decaying sawdust, which in the end is humus. So don't hesitate to use sawdust, or manure that is made with straw. Straw tends to be a good absorber of liquid manures and has the advantage that it breaks down quickly and cleanly.

## Manure Three Ways

There are three basic ways manure is sold: fresh, rotted, and air-dried. Fresh is cheapest, and dried most expensive. The dried costs more because the percentage of water is less and the percentage of nutrients and humus is correspondingly higher. For example, hen manure that renders 20 pounds nitrogen, 16 pounds phosphorus, and 10 pounds of potash to the ton will come out about 40-30-19 dried. Chicken, sheep, and steer manures

usually can be found dried and bagged at nurseries and even at supermarkets. But because of their cost, I recommend their use only when unprocessed manure is not easily available, or for special uses like potting, or where handling it fresh is difficult, such as for people physically unable to load and spread tons of manure.

If you do have to buy your manure, and you're getting it unprocessed, make sure you know something about the way it was handled, or you might be getting less than you paid for. For example, if it's sold by the ton you might be buying a whole lot of water the seller sprinkled on the night before. Also, you might be getting "burned" or "fire fang" manure. This is manure that has been piled up in a relatively dry state. The process of composting starts after a fashion, but then the manure heats up so hot that it actually uses up much of its nitrogen as well as ruins some of the humus value.

The other major problem is leached manure. The nitrogen, potash, and phosphorus found in manure are for the most part water soluble, and that means that if the manure heap is exposed to rain, the nutrients leach out with the runoff. The resulting matter still has humus value but should not be considered a complete fertilizer.

With all these possibilities of spoiling the manure, how should we handle it? My sentiment leans in two ways. First is compost. Every time we cleaned out the henhouse we had stacks of weeds, eelgrass, and garden trash ready near the compost bins. I started the compost heap using the chicken manure in 1-inch layers over 6-inch layers of green matter, and under caps of 1 inch of dirt. (In case you have to use other fresh manures, cow bedding should go on in 2- or 3-inch layers, depending on the quantity of the mixed-in straw or shavings.) The resulting compost heats up fast, turns easily, and makes a rich product for general garden use.

The second use is broadcast spreading, but this presupposes that you have a lot of manure and ground to work at the same time. If you do, just haul out the manure, spread it over the ground, and turn it in. Sometimes this is not the most pleasant-smelling work, but it is the best way—next to composting—to conserve all available nutrients.

## Handling Fresh Manure

If you're buying fresh manure and are not going to use it right away, or if you have a steady supply, the thing to do is to cover the day's yield or each incoming load with a layer of soil or some organic matter like peat moss or sawdust (both of which will help absorb odors). If the manure is wet, like chicken droppings or cow dung, use absorbent material like peat. If it is relatively dry, like horse manure, use soil.

Keep the pile moist, but not so moist that water is running out the bottom, and not so dry that the pile can heat up uncontrolled. The last step is to turn the pile every few weeks to ensure even decomposition. The resulting material can be used at any time. However, if your object is to have rotted manure ready to apply directly to the garden, you'll have to stop adding new material at some

## Manures and Their Uses

*Horse:* Good for general fertilization. Put up in 4-foot stacks, it decomposes quickly if kept moist and turned over three or four times in a six-month period. Intensive turning can speed up the process to mere weeks. Horse manure is recommended for hot-frame operating.

*Cow:* More liquid and less strawy than horse manure. I like it for liquid measure and "tea." Bagged and dried, it's convenient to use as a seedbed or potting ingredient.

*Hog:* Decomposes slowly and makes a good amendment for heavy clay soils, especially when used with peat moss.

*Poultry:* Good for compost making. When it is well-rotted, I use it to side-dress leafy green vegetables that like lots of nitrogen.

*Rabbit:* Use it like poultry manure or add to worm beds and use with the castings for potting mixes and seed flats.

*James Jankowiak*
*October 1980*

point, and start a second heap. Allow the composting process to go its full course with the first pile, and you'll have a rich, earthy-smelling product after a few months that is fit for immediate application to vegetables and flower gardens.

If you haven't followed these steps and your manure is green, you must take some precautions to protect your plants if you want to apply the manure right away. Green manure, because of the active decaying process, the heat, and the high percentage of available nitrogen, can harm plants if directly applied. Furthermore, some vegetables, like carrots, respond to fresh manure with undesirable altered growth, such as forming forked roots. Some experts suggest that well-rotted manure be incorporated into the soil no later than two weeks before planting. The recommendation for the fresh manure is two to three months before planting, or in the fall for an early spring crop. In all cases, the manure should be plowed under. When using fresh manure in the summer, I've turned it under a month to three weeks before planting and have had good results. When it is well-mixed with a high-humus-content soil, the microorganisms, beetles, and worms seem to get right to work so that, except for carrots and other root crops, you should discern no bad effects.

A minimum manure application is about 10 tons per acre, and a generous one about 20 tons. The latter works out to about 1 pound per square foot of soil. To get things down to garden size, a 2- or 3-inch layer spread over the area to be fertilized will average out to around 10 to 15 pounds per square yard.

## Mix It In

If you're short on manure, don't spread it broadcast, but down the rows. I usually dig a trench about 5 inches deep, toss in the manure, and cover with soil. Then I make my furrows and plant. This puts the nutrients right where developing root systems will make the most use of them. Whenever I use this method, I plan on supplemental feeding later in the season. The object is not to get the manure down deep, but to mix it well into the first 5 or 6 inches of soil when you're broadcasting. If it is all in a solid layer, 6 inches down, it will take some time for the plant roots to get there. Meanwhile, the nutrients will be leaching downward. If you can evenly spread the manure throughout the surface soil, there's a better field for root growth.

A rotary tiller is the best piece of equipment I've found for incorporating manure in this way, but a lot of elbow grease and a shovel will achieve the same results. And you can expect such an application to benefit your garden for three years—one year for the highest nutrient advantage and three years for the humus value.

## A Low-Work Method

There is another, less-work method than turning under your manure, and that's to simply broadcast it and let the rain take the nutrients under. If you're fertilizing an already established stand of something—say a pasture or herb bed—or just starting such a crop, you might do well to apply composted manure to the surface and hope that a well-timed rain or overhead irrigation will take the nutrients under. However, you will still lose some plant food to the air. This can be offset when you consider that the nutrients will be right at the top of the topsoil, where the seedlings or the roots of shallow-rooted crops can quickly make use of them. Another plus is that topdressing doesn't disturb existing growth.

While it can be said that you can't apply too much manure in terms of its wonderful humus value, there is a law of diminishing returns. For example, an application of 16 tons to the acre will often produce 80 percent of what 32 tons will produce. Similarly, a manure application around woody perennials toward the end of the season could result in lush, sappy growth that could be very susceptible to winterkill. The idea is not maximum manure usage, but optimum usage, or getting the best possible results without an excessive outlay of work, manure, and cash.

*October 1980*

# Give Your Crops a Midsummer Feeding

*M. C. Goldman*

The difference between a bumper yield and one that's only fair may be just a little boost in soil and plant nutrients at midseason.

Eggshells for tomatoes? That's what John Shealy gives his plants when the summer hits its peak. First he mixes a dozen eggshells with a quart of water, and then runs the combination in a kitchen blender for about a minute. The result? An ideal mixture for his tomatoes and other garden plants. The blend helps to control blossom-end rot in tomatoes, says the Johnston, South Carolina, gardener, and produces better, healthier plants in general.

Shealy's experience underscores a basic point: Vegetables and fruits continue to need nutrients as they approach maturity. Most plant growth as well as the onset of edible crops shift into rapid high gear at midsummer. That's when a boost for the slower-acting organic materials in your soil is a logical step. Adding just a little at this critical time can act as a catalyst, a literal fuse to ignite and release more of the nutrients waiting to feed plants. And it can mean a better yield of tastier, more nutritious foods for you, as vegetables or fruits have essential trace elements made available.

Broccoli, squash, corn, snow peas, cabbage, pole beans—nearly every garden vegetable—benefits from

*A ring of crushed eggshells does double duty around young plants like tomato seedlings. The sharp, crushed shells repel hungry slugs while adding calcium to the soil.*

a summer booster feeding. Late-planted fall crops, usually set out where earlier crops have been harvested, need added fertilizer to balance nutrients already used. Berries, especially those that fruit at the season's end, do well with more food now.

Tree fruits, most of which produce their delectable harvests as the summer wanes, respond appreciably to a modest feeding.

## Water with a Wallop

Two of the best techniques comprise irrigating with an easily enriched water—employing either manure or compost "tea" or fish emulsion. The first, a booster solution prized by many gardeners, is prepared simply by suspending a cloth bag (burlap or cheesecloth will do) of any animal or poultry manure or compost in a water-filled bucket, barrel, trash can, or similar container. Stir the sediment thoroughly in the solution, keeping the finished product to a "pale-tea" consistency. For small outdoor areas, the greenhouse, or houseplants, make some compost water by filling a sprinkling can half with finished compost, then half with water, and stirring a dozen times. Reuse several times, since soluble nutrients won't wash out in a single watering.

Fish emulsion, one of the most concentrated boosters, is valuable anywhere the garden needs a mid-season perking up. While the N-P-K reading on the label may not be high, the liquefied fish wastes deliver a rich trace-mineral bonus and stimulate soil microorganisms into making more of the waiting food available to plant roots. Directions advise how much to

*Steeping a burlap or cheesecloth bag of manure or compost in a bucket of water yields a nutrient-rich "tea" that you can water your plants with or spray on as a foliar feeding.*

dilute the emulsion—usually a table-spoon or so to a gallon. Added to liquid compost or manure tea, it makes an even more potent "irrigation feed" of your solution.

Make sure the liquid nutrients soak down into the soil close to plant roots when you apply them. For late-season growth, succession plantings, or crops set out in midsummer, the extra feeding can help speed up fruit-set and maturing, often preventing loss because of unripened vegetables by the time frost arrives.

California garden-writer Warner Tilsher, who uses a furrow system to stymie the heavy rains or hot sun he gets, notes: "On some crops, such as beans, corn, potatoes and cabbages, we pull over the opposite edge of the furrow and build up the soil around

Spraying your plants with a dilute solution of fish emulsion or liquid seaweed gives them a needed nutrient boost during the growing season.

the base of the plants. This buries the roots a bit deeper and insulates them from the sun's heat. Just before we do this we side-dress the crop with fish emulsion or sewage sludge. We then fill the furrow with mulch. Another big point for the furrow system is that it gets the water down below the root zone and the plant goes after it. Evaporation losses are reduced and this will show up in your water bills."

Foliar feeding (applying liquid fertilizer directly to plant leaves) has also come into its own. It is now regarded as a valuable supplement to soil feeding in many circumstances, such as correcting iron deficiencies and compensating for lower nutrient up-take in very wet or dry summer spells. Trace elements in foliar fertilizers like liquefied seaweed and fish emulsions are especially effective. During the 1976 drought, Iowa farmers who sprayed their corn with seaweed and fish solutions reported harvesting three times as many bushels per acre as they had expected. There is evidence, too, that liquid seaweed sprays confer increased resistance to diseases and insects, notably fungi, aphids, and mites.

If you're also growing roses, a note in the *American Rose* magazine (March 1978) will be of interest. Powdered brewer's yeast, fed at 1 or 2 tablespoons to a gallon of water, helped Richard French overcome the midseason blahs his roses were suffering, and produced greener foliage, sturdier growth, and improved bloom.

## Side-Dressings and Mulch

Dry fertilizers effective in midsummer booster applications include compost, well-aged manure, dried blood, cottonseed meal, leaf mold, seaweed, and kelp. Ground rock and bonemeal fertilizers also help supply minerals that may have been used up by earlier crops. Granite dust or greensand can be sprinkled by the handful for potassium simply as a topdressing.

Wood ashes are good when used as a side-dressing a few inches from the plant base. (Remember, they're alkaline and raise soil pH when applied in quantity.) Phosphate rock is a good source of phosphorus with the added benefit of containing trace elements such as boron, zinc, and nickel needed for plant vitality. Phosphate rock can be surface-dressed around or even dusted on plants as an insect repellent with no concern about overdosage.

Veteran gardener Ruth Tirrell recommends that beginners start by growing tomatoes, beans (green or wax), cucumbers, and both summer and winter squash. They're all prolific, she explains, and reasonably easy to grow, and most of them also provide food for winter. And, she points out, all must be planted rather late—after danger of frost—so they include good choices to follow "catch crops," faster-growing early vegetables like radishes,

onions, lettuce, and the like, which use a temporarily open patch of garden until it's needed. These later arrivals also require midseason feeding, notes Miss Tirrell, and for this she uses her own version of "spot fertilizing."

Once her plants are up, she explains, she mulches heavily with whatever is at hand: leaves, hay, weeds, grass clippings, and so on. "Or use some of the contents of a compost pile (which need not be broken down if applied on the surface). This organic material, as it decays, adds more nutriment. Besides, I dose the plants once a week up to harvesttime with manure tea, applied to the base of each plant under the mulch. Each tomato is thus growing in its own oasis of fertility, no matter what the condition of the overall area."

Mulching, of course, goes right along with the midsummer program, helping to preserve moisture that roots draw upon. Side-dressings of a nitrogen-rich material such as cottonseed meal or blood meal will add to the feeding value of the decaying mulch. Or, try mixing a handful of these and perhaps some ground rock directly into the mulching materials.

## Apples Take a Shine to Fish Emulsion

Asked what feeding program he recommends for top yield of apples, longtime orchardist A. P. Thomson replies: "Use the fish fertilizer annually as insurance for enough trace minerals in the soil. Start with 1 teaspoonful to 5 gallons of water concentration at planting time, and increase 1 teaspoonful each year, up to a quart for full-size trees, half that much for dwarfs. Apply in three stages: a third in early spring when trees are dormant and before buds emerge, another third after blooms fall, and the last third in early summer to boost fruiting. The mixture suggested provides the equivalent of 50 pounds of fish per tree in fertilizing value."

For fruit and other trees in general, nurseryman Lewis Hill advises that slow-acting organic fertilizers and mulches can usually be applied safely at any time of year, although he prefers spreading them in early spring and late fall. Rain works the fertilizer down toward the tree's roots, he explains, ready for it to use for growth and setting its fruit. "Since most soils are worn out or badly eroded, fertilizer is something they always seem to need."

One important point about feeding trees is understanding the root zone, Hill notes. "The tree root zone covers just about the same area as that of the branches, and it looks much the same. As with the branches, the large roots are near the trunk and the small, fibrous hair roots that actually pull in the nutrients are farther away. The roots that feed the

### Bones

We have always kept our dog bones, and when we are ready to plant a fruit tree or even berry vines, we bury a couple of bones 1 foot below where the roots will be. The result is very profitable. My husband was an agricultural chemist and banked a great deal on organic gardening and compost treatment.

*Mrs. S. H. Hartung*
*Burlingame, California*
*May 1947*

tree are therefore in a circle beginning about a foot or two from the trunk and continuing to the outside spread of the branches. The fertilizer you put too close to the trunk or spread much outside the branch area is likely to be wasted."

### Feed 'Em and Reap

It's the returns from the care you give your garden that count—that get to the family table or into the larder. This season, when food costs and quality are critical factors, make the most of your growing opportunities. A midsummer feeding keeps crops on the grow—and the gardener's storage bins and freezer full!

*August 1978*

# Hunger Signs in the Garden

## Charles H. Coleman

Plants are like humans. If they don't eat the right things, they get sick from malnutrition. And of course, sick plants are not the most healthful to eat. They are deficient in some of the nutritional elements needed by humans for the best health and vigor.

Sick plants are also more susceptible to attack from insects and plant disease. The produce from sick plants sometimes brings lower prices on the market, since something is obviously wrong with it.

Like sick humans, sick plants exhibit certain symptoms that are characteristic of specific nutritional deficiencies.

With a little keen-eyed observation you can diagnose many hunger symptoms in the plants in your garden. Once you have done this, treatment of the condition is easy with proper organic fertilizer.

> Are the leaves of your carrots curled and turning brown? Do you find small, brown spots on any leaves? These are only two of the many "hunger signs" that plants exhibit. It's their way of telling you they need nutrients. Learn to spot hunger signs, so you can correct them in your own garden.

## Nitrogen Deficiency

Nitrogen is especially important for vegetables of good quality since it is essential for the synthesis of natural proteins. Plenty of nitrogen gives a good, normal deep-green color to foliage and stems. In general, a nitrogen deficiency is characterized by slow growth; slender, fibrous stems; and foliage and stems that fade to yellow.

**Corn:** The most prominent symptom for corn that is deficient in nitrogen is the yellowish green of the plants rather than the normal deep green color.

**Cucumbers:** When deficient in nitrogen, cucumbers exhibit stunted growth. The green of the plant turns yellow. Roots turn brown and die. Nitrogen deficiency is also what causes cucumbers to point at the blossom end. These market as low-grade produce.

**Radishes:** Radishes deficient in nitrogen are retarded in growth. The leaves are small, narrow, thin, and yellow. The stems are slender and weak. And the edible roots are small

*Cucumbers suffering from nitrogen deficiency show stunted growth. Fruits may develop a pointed shape at the blossom end.*

and imperfectly developed, with a faded reddish color.

**Tomatoes:** Tomatoes deficient in nitrogen exhibit very slow growth at first. This is followed by the green of the leaves becoming lighter, starting at the top of the plant. The leaves remain small and thin, and the veins may become purple. The stems are stunted, turn brown, and eventually die. Flower buds turn yellow and are shed, and the yield is reduced.

### Treatment for Nitrogen Deficiency

Use compost or any organic fertilizer high in nitrogen. Some of the best products available commercially are blood meal (15% nitrogen), hoof meal and horn dust (12.5% nitrogen), and cottonseed meal (7% nitrogen). These products could be mixed with compost in ample quantities and applied to the soil in fall, or in very early spring. Always allow at least six weeks for complete decomposition of organic materials in the soil.

## Phosphorus Deficiency

In general, plants deficient in phosphorus are slowed in growth. The underside of leaves assumes a reddish purple color, and the plants are slow to set fruit and mature.

**Celery:** Celery deficient in phosphorus exhibits poor root development and slender stalks.

**Corn:** Corn deficient in phosphorus

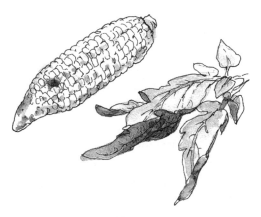

*Phosphorus deficiency causes corn to produce ears with missing kernels, especially at the tip. Tomato leaves turn reddish purple underneath, and the whole plant may take on a purplish tinge.*

has a yellowing of leaves similar to nitrogen starvation. After the ears set with kernels, check to see if the rows are filled, and if the kernels fill out to the end of the ear. If they don't, this is a sure sign of phosphorus starvation.

*Radishes:* The leaves of radishes deficient in phosphorus may be reddish purple on the underside.

*Tomatoes:* A phosphorus deficiency causes a reddish purple color to develop on the underside of leaves, and the whole foliage eventually assumes a purplish tinge. The leaves are small, and the stems are slender and fibrous. The plants are late in setting fruit.

## Treatment for Phosphorus Deficiency

Use either phosphate rock (30% phosphorus) or bonemeal (21% phosphorus) either applied directly to the soil or mixed with your compost. The amount you apply depends on how much your soil needs. A soil test would be very helpful in determining the correct amount of any fertilizer to apply.

## Potassium Deficiency

General symptoms of potassium deficiency in plants include reduced vigor, poor growth, poor yield, and greater susceptibility. Ashen-gray leaves are observed instead of the good, normal deep green color. The leaves develop brown edges and crinkle or curl. Later they become bronzed.

*Beets:* Beets deficient in potassium develop long, tapered roots rather than the preferred bulbous type.

*Cabbages and Brussels Sprouts:* The leaves become bronzed on the border, and the color spreads inward. The leaf rim parches, and brown spots appear in the interior of the leaf.

*When they're not getting enough potassium, cabbages develop bronzed leaves that become parched looking with pale brown spots at the margins.*

**Carrots:** Carrots exhibit the first symptoms of potassium deficiency in curled leaves. The rim of the leaf becomes brown, the inner portion becomes grayish green and finally bronzed.

**Cucumbers:** Leaves of cucumbers deficient in potassium exhibit a bronzing and dying of the leaf margin. The fruit has an enlarged tip. This is just the opposite symptom of nitrogen starvation, where the fruit has a pointed tip.

**Radishes:** Radishes deficient in potassium have leaves that are dark green in the center while the edges curl and become pale yellow to brown. Extreme deficiency is indicated by a deep yellow color of leaves and stems. The leaves may become thick and leathery. The roots are more bulbous than normal.

**Tomatoes:** Tomatoes deficient in potassium grow slowly, are stunted, and have a low yield. The young leaves become crinkled. The older leaves turn ashen-grayish green at first, developing a yellowish green along the margins. This progresses further into bronze-colored spots between the longer veins. These may become bright orange and brittle. Leaves turn brown and die. The stems become hard and woody and fail to increase in diameter. Roots are brown and not well-developed. Fruit may ripen unevenly; that is, a tomato sliced across may show traces of green on one side while being red-ripe on the other. The fruit may lack solidity.

## Treatment for Potassium Deficiency

By placing 6 inches of green matter to every 2 inches of stable manure in your compost heap, you supply adequate amounts of potassium for gardening purposes. Once the moisture of green plants is eliminated and the material is broken down, a great percentage of the solids consists of potassium. If your soil is particularly low in potassium, add potash rock, granite dust, wood ash, or some other potassium-rich organic material to the compost—or apply these materials directly to the soil.

Heavy mulching also seems to help maintain the potassium supply. At Purdue University, Clarence E. Baker found that mulching with manure, straw, and soybean hay eliminated symptoms of potassium deficiency in a peach orchard. The check trees, which received no mulch, did not recover.

## Calcium Deficiency

In general, plants exhibiting calcium deficiency are retarded in growth and develop thick, woody stems.

**Corn:** Corn deficient in calcium exhibits the most startling symptom of all plants. The tip ends of the leaves are stuck together as if they had been glued.

**Peas:** Red patches appear on the leaves near the center and spread out. The healthy green of the leaves changes to a pale green, then white. Growth is slow and the plants are dwarfed.

*Calcium deficiency causes the upper leaves of tomatoes to curl and turn pale yellow.*

**Tomatoes:** The upper leaves appear yellow. This distinguishes the deficiency from that of nitrogen, phosphorus, or potassium, where the lower portion of the plant has discolored leaves while the upper leaves and stem remain more or less normal. The plants are weak and flabby and lacking in firmness. The terminal buds die and the nearby stem becomes spotted with dead areas. The roots are short and brown.

### Treatment for Calcium Deficiency

Use any good grade of ground natural limestone. About 60-mesh is a good grind.

## Magnesium Deficiency

Magnesium deficiency is widespread. Plants deficient in magnesium are, in general, late to mature and do not mature uniformly. They have poor market quality. Magnesium-deficient plants exhibit a characteristic lack of green color, with the lower leaves being affected first. The areas between the leaf veins turn yellow, then brown, while the veins remain green.

**Cabbages:** Mottled light-colored spots appear on the leaves of cabbages deficient in magnesium. The lower leaves pucker. The edge of the leaves may turn white or very pale yellow. These may turn brown and die. If only magnesium is deficient, the entire leaf becomes mottled with dead areas. If nitrogen is also deficient the entire leaf turns a light green color, then yellow, and finally develops a mottling of dead areas. Potassium deficiency, which is sometimes confused with lack of magnesium, can be distinguished by the bronzing that occurs before the dead areas appear.

**Carrots, Cucumbers, Squash, and Lima Beans:** These show the typical characteristics of mottling and then browning of foliage.

**Corn:** Magnesium deficiency is very easy to tell in corn plants since they develop a yellow striping or white streaks only on the older leaves.

**Tomatoes:** Tomatoes deficient in magnesium have brittle leaves that curl up. A yellow color develops in the leaves. This is deepest farther from the vein. The older leaves of mature plants are the ones that most commonly show the symptoms. There is little effect on stems or fruit.

**Turnips:** The leaves of turnips deficient in magnesium develop brown areas around the rim. These dry up and drop out. The inner areas are mottled with light-colored spots.

## Treatment for Magnesium Deficiency

If obtainable, add 1 quart of sea water to each 100 pounds of compost. Or use dolomitic limestone since this contains quite a bit of magnesium.

## Boron Deficiency

A deficiency of boron in plants causes plants to grow more slowly. Severe deficiency causes crop failures, since plants die. Unlike the other nutrient elements, which produce general changes in most truck crops, boron deficiency produces more specific changes in different vegetables. Beets and turnips develop corklike areas in the edible root, and a hollow stem develops in cauliflower, while celery cracks. The leaves may be stunted and twisted with dark spots on the tips of young leaves, which grow larger as the leaves mature.

*Beets, Turnips, and Other Root Crops:* These, when affected by boron deficiency, develop what is commonly known as brown-heart disease. Dark brown water-soaked areas appear in the center of the roots. Sometimes a hollow, discolored center results. The roots do not grow to full size and may have a rough, unhealthy, grayish appearance. The surface may be wrinkled or cracked. The plants are stunted, and the leaves smaller, twisted, and less numerous than normal. Leaves sometimes develop yellow and purplish red blotches, and the stalks may show splitting.

*Cauliflower:* Deficiencies of boron cause discolored, water-soaked areas in the stem of cauliflower. These areas may spread beyond the stem. The leaves around the curd may be stunted and deformed.

*Celery:* Celery deficient in boron develops a brownish mottling of the leaf. The stems become brittle and have brown stripes. Crosswise cracks appear in the steam, and the tissue curls back and turns brown. Roots turn brown and die.

*Lettuce:* Lettuce deficient in boron exhibits malformation of the more rapidly growing leaves and spotting and burning of leaves.

*Tomatoes:* Deficiencient plants have blackened areas at the growing point of the stem, and stems are stunted. Terminal shoots curl, then turn yellow and die. The plants have a bushy appearance, and the fruit may have darkened or dried areas.

## Treatment for Boron Deficiency

Use plenty of manure.

## Iron Deficiency

Iron deficiency in plants is characterized by spotted, colorless areas developing on young leaves. Yellow leaves appear on the upper parts of plants. The growth of new shoots is affected, and plant tissues may die if the deficiency is severe. Too much lime causes iron deficiency to develop.

## Treatment for Iron Deficiency

Plenty of manure, crop residues, dried blood, and tankage are the best methods for correcting iron deficiencies.

## Copper Deficiency

Copper deficiency is usually confined to peat or muck soils. Plants deficient in copper exhibit slow growth or complete cessation of growth. Leaves become bleached looking, and leaves and stems are flabby.

*Lettuce:* Leaves become bleached looking. The stems and the rim of the leaf are affected first.

*Onions:* Onions deficient in copper have an abnormally thin scale, which is pale yellow rather than the usual brilliant brown. Growth may be stunted or fail entirely.

*Tomatoes:* Tomatoes deficient in copper have stunted shoot growth, and very poor root development. The foliage may be a bluish green, and the leaves curled. There is an absence of flower formation, and leaves and stems are flabby.

## Treatment for Copper Deficiency

Use plenty of manure.

## Zinc Deficiency

Zinc deficiency occurs in peat soils. In plants, it is particularly characterized by leaves that are abnormally long and narrow. The leaves may also turn yellow and be mottled with many dead areas.

*Corn:* Corn deficient in zinc exhibits older leaves that are dead, while yellow striping appears between the veins on the newer leaves.

*Squash, Mustard, Tomatoes, and Beans:* These plants usually are the first in the garden to exhibit the typical symptoms of zinc deficiency as described previously.

## Treatment for Zinc Deficiency

Use plenty of manure.

## Manganese Deficiency

Plants deficient in manganese are slow to grow and mature late and unevenly. The areas between the veins of leaves become yellow, then brown, while the veins remain green.

*Beets:* The leaf takes on a deep red to purple color, which gradually becomes yellow. Dead areas finally appear between the veins. The growth of roots and tips is stunted.

*Cucumbers, Cabbages, and Peppers:* These plants, when deficient in manganese, have small, slender, weak stems. The leaves turn yellowish white while the veins and midribs remain green. The blossom bud may turn yellow.

**Snap Beans:** Whole leaves turn a golden yellow, and small brown spots appear between the veins.

**Spinach:** Spinach deficient in manganese exhibits a loss of color at the growing tips. This spreads in toward the center of the plant. The normal green color gradually changes to a golden yellow. White, dead areas eventually appear.

**Tomatoes:** Leaves have a typical lightening of green color, which gradually turns to yellow farthest from the major veins. Dead areas appear in the center of the yellow areas and spread. Growth is stunted, and there are few blossoms and no fruit.

### Treatment for Manganese Deficiency

Use plenty of manure.

### Become an "Organic Plant Doctor"

Although at first glance it may appear somewhat difficult to diagnose the problem in a garden where the plants are sick, it is easy if you pick out one vegetable and concentrate on that. For example, if cucumbers are pointed at the end, then the soil is deficient in nitrogen. If cucumbers are narrow at the stem and bulging at the flower end, then the soil is deficient in potassium. In just a few minutes of careful observation, you can tell what your garden's soil is deficient in.

In general, plenty of manure or good-quality compost made with kitchen scraps and a wide variety of plant materials such as weeds and grass clippings will correct all soil deficiencies. At the same time, manure and compost will tend to neutralize an unfavorable soil pH and will also reduce the harmful effects of previous applications of toxic chemicals. Whenever there is doubt concerning the cause of sick-looking plants, it is recommended that heavy applications of manure or compost, or both, be used.

After becoming well-versed in applying the powers of observation, you can state rather definitely what is causing your plants to be sick. Then, once you are able to prescribe organic methods for their recovery, there's no reason why you can't become the first "organic plant doctor" in your neighborhood. You can help out your friends' and neighbors' gardens as well as your own.

*March 1957*

# Raised Beds and Friends

# Easing into Raised Beds

*Anthony DeCrosta*

Here are three sensible options that are a lot less work than double-digging.

There is more than one way to raise a bed. So don't make the mistake of attempting too much too fast. After all, gardening intensively means gardening intelligently. Sure, experienced gardeners like John Jeavons of Palo Alto, California, can double-dig an entire 100-square-foot garden bed in two hours, but there's no reason you have to match his breakneck pace. A

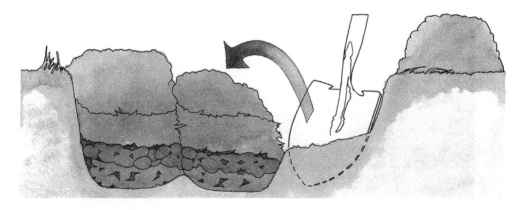

*To double-dig your garden, dig a 1-foot-wide, 1-foot-deep trench across one end of the bed. Put the soil from the trench aside. Use a spading fork to loosen the soil in the bottom of the trench, then top it with a shovelful of compost or other organic matter. Dig your next trench beside the first one, shoveling its soil into the original trench. Repeat this process down the bed; use the soil from the first trench to fill the last one.*

modest 3-by-3-foot area double-dug in less than an hour your first season makes an excellent growing bed for root crops, for example.

But no matter how much of a double bite you take, everyone agrees—the first year is definitely the toughest. Here's some practical advice from Jeavons to make the digging easier:

- *Set realistic goals.* The "ideal" is to loosen the soil to a depth of 24 inches. If you can go down only 15 inches the first year, be satisfied. Don't strain. Each year, digging will get easier and the soil depth will increase inch by inch. If you hit bedrock or wet muck at 12 inches deep, erect boards around the sides of the bed and shovel soil from the paths to the top of it. You'll create a deep bed of loose, friable soil.

- *Thoroughly moisten the soil two days before you prepare the bed.* Digging a hard, dry soil pulverizes its structure. Wet soil is heavy and compacts easily. At the right moisture level, soil digs four times easier. Your soil is too dry for digging when it is loose and will not hold its shape after being squeezed in the palm of your hand. Soil is too wet to work when it sticks to the spade.

- *Get a digging board.* Use a ⅝-inch-thick plywood board, 2 to 3 feet long by 3 to 5 feet wide, to stand

on. Whatever you do, don't stand on a just-dug trench—that will only recompact the soil.

- *Pace yourself.* It's a lot easier to dig for two, three, or four hours straight—perhaps resting at one-hour intervals—than to stop every few minutes to catch your breath because you're working too fast. Attitude's important, too. *Believe you can do it!*

- *Take as much time as you feel you need.* You're doing something good for your body, you're getting fresh air and sunshine, and you're converting compacted earth into cultivated soil that will support a bountiful harvest. What's the rush, anyway?

## Tilling and Hilling

Quicker and more convenient than a spade and a fork, a rotary tiller can be used to prepare raised beds. You have two choices if you use a tiller. You can either till the whole garden and then mark off the beds, or mark off the beds and then till them separately. For economy and thoroughness, tilling and fertilizing only the growing beds is the better approach. Use a rear-tine tiller, if possible, since you can walk in the path while running the tiller in the bed. With front-tine tillers, you have to walk where you've just tilled, thus compacting the soil again.

Allow your tiller to determine the

width of each bed. Since a large tiller will churn an area about 3 feet across, one pass will make a good, but narrow, bed. Two passes—one in each direction with plenty of overlap—tills up a fine bed, almost twice the width of your tiller. As always with garden beds, the idea is to have a bed just wide enough for you to reach the middle from either side.

Tilling produces a soft, level cushion of soil 6 to 11 inches deep. Although this level of cultivation is deep enough for some shallow-rooted crops like peas and beans, it is not ideal for deep-rooted ones like beets, parsnips, and carrots. Also, keep in mind that just beneath the level at which the tiller tines work, a crust of hard-packed soil—called a hardpan—gradually evolves as fine soil particles are ground against each other. Plant roots can't easily penetrate a hardpan, and some actually turn outward instead of down, making the plants susceptible to drought, nutrient deficiencies, and wind damage.

If you opt for tilling the entire garden area and then marking off the growing beds, remember to take the topsoil from the paths and place it on the growing beds.

Intensive gardener Steve Coker in Evergreen, Alabama, uses a bed preparation program to loosen his garden soil to the 2-foot mark while effectively suppressing this subsoil barrier. Called "tilling and hilling," the method starts with tilling the planting area to a depth of 11 inches, then replacing the standard tiller tines with a shovel-like blade attachment called a hiller. That attachment pulverizes the soil some more and also allows Coker to direct the cultivated soil exactly where he wants it, giving him an almost perfectly shaped growing bed. He can also adjust the depth of the cut—creating loose and friable soil 24 inches deep.

"After planting, hilling should be done at least twice," says Coker. "These later hillings keep fresh soil turned to the plants, adding support while feeding shallow roots. If the soil becomes packed or hard, tiller tines should be used before the hiller attachment to loosen the soil so it will easily roll to the plants. Don't till or hill when plants show signs of maturity. Root damage during flower or fruit set will diminish the harvest."

## Planting in Sod

When you lack the time to work the soil of the entire garden, use the mulch technique. This works even on sod. Planting vegetables directly into a mulched lawn is as close to problem-free gardening as I've ever tried. Not only was double-digging, rotary tilling, or merely turning over the top layer of soil with a shovel in the springtime unnecessary, I hardly had to lift a finger between planting and harvesttime. For the past few years I have watched with interest the vegetable-sod trials taking place at the Organic Gardening and Farming Research Center under the supervision of Steve Ganser. All anyone needs to try it on an established lawn is enough hay, alfalfa, or grass clippings with which to mulch it 6 inches deep.

I live in a center city row house with a well-trodden backyard that measures 12 feet wide and 30 feet long. A narrow sidewalk runs down the middle of the yard. I decided to convert one side into a vegetable-sod garden bed and maintain the other side for picnics. I worried that the soil under the grass might be so compacted from years of pedestrian traffic that it would strangle any root growth. Happily, I was wrong.

## A Mulch-Made Bed

Here's all I did. After watering the lawn for a few hours to build up its moisture reserve, I spread a 6-inch-thick layer of hay over the sod, which killed the grass within a week. (One bale was enough to cover the 5-by-20-foot area.) I know gardeners who spread a few layers of newspapers over the grass and then cover them with mulch, but I think that makes for a lot of extra work. A thick organic mulch works just fine for me.

I planted a little of everything, making sure I chose compact or bush-type cultivars of tomatoes, squash, lettuce, beans, broccoli, and eggplant. Seeds and seedlings were planted at conventional spacings. To plant, I had only to push back the hay, pull out a 4-inch-square plug of turf, plant the seeds or transplants, and then cover each hole with the soil clinging to the tuft of sod.

Although I kept no yield records, the crops flourished under far-from-ideal conditions. Like much of the United States during the summer of 1980, the Northeast suffered from heat and drought. In backyards all around my own, tomatoes wilted and beans shriveled. Eggplants dried out and rotted on the vine, as did squash. In my yard, on the other hand, the crops thrived—even the lettuce and broccoli, which were planted later than normal. The thick mulch helped maintain adequate soil moisture, as did twice-weekly waterings. The mulch also checked the growth of weeds, particularly late in the season.

Vegetable-sod planting can be done in any type of lawn grass, although rank quack grass, whose rhizomes quickly spread into cultivated soil, could pose a problem to vegetables planted in it.

I'm delighted with the results from last summer's vegetables-in-sod bed. This year I plan to double-dig the previously sod-planted area and build a raised bed. But on the other half of the lawn, I'll do it the lazy man's way. I'll just spread a few inches of hay and plant my seeds and seedlings through the sod. I'm sure my family will get used to summer outings in the park.

*February 1981*

# Remaking My Garden in Raised Beds

*Walter Chandoha*

With fewer walkways, there are fewer weeds and more rows of vegetables in the raised-bed garden.

Without adding an inch of space to my garden, I almost doubled its output by planting vegetables in raised beds. I used to grow onions in long, skinny rows a foot apart. But in a 3-foot-wide raised bed, I can space onion rows 6 inches apart because I don't need a footpath. I can fit five rows of onions where before I grew two rows. Growing crops in long, single-file rows wastes valuable garden space, and wasted space means wasted money. With food costs—it makes sense to go for maximum yields from the garden.

Twenty single-file rows of vegetables in a conventional garden require 20 single-file walkways between the rows. When you can eliminate 2 out of every 3 walkways, you can generally double your productive space and use it to grow more crops. I've found other advantages, too. Because beds are raised, the plants get better air circulation and drainage than flat rows. The ground thaws out and warms up faster in early spring. In my soil, crops can be planted at least two weeks sooner in raised beds.

I wish I'd made the change to raised beds years ago. But I had gotten the idea that such beds ought to be boxed or enclosed somehow. I made a few surrounded with large timbers. But the cost and the time it took me were prohibitive. The carrots and onions were outstanding, but I discarded the raised-bed idea as impractical for a large vegetable garden.

Then on a trip, I saw beautiful vegetables in raised beds with the sides simply mounded or banked, not enclosed. The following spring I converted my entire garden to them.

The conversion was simple. As soon as the soil could be worked, I rotary tilled the entire garden. Then using a pair of lines, I marked out a 3-foot-wide section running the full 30-foot width of the garden. I shoveled the loose soil outside the lines (from what would later be walkways) into the area between the lines. In about 15 or 20 minutes of easy shoveling, the area between the lines was a foot or so higher than the walkways.

As the soil settled, the beds wound up being 6 to 8 inches high. I raked the soil smooth so the top of the bed was flat and the sides were a long, curved slope. When the first bed was finished, I staked out the next 3-foot strip, allowing 12 to 18 inches for paths between each of the raised beds.

The length of the beds is not as important as the width. Plants in the center should be easily accessible from either side. That dictates a maximum width of 4 feet. In a 5- or 6-foot-wide bed, the center would be hard to reach without stepping on the bed. My beds vary between 2 and 4 feet wide. Mostly my beds are 5 to 10 feet long. But I grow a couple of zucchini hills on a 6-foot bed, beans and peas on beds 20 feet long. I also have some 30-footers planted with different vegetables, each divided by a planting of herbs or flowers.

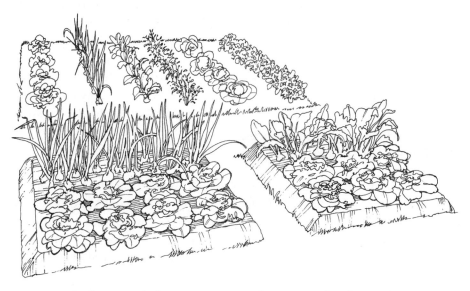

*By eliminating the between-row spacing of a conventional garden, raised beds make better use of space, mulch, compost, and water.*

Rather than making all the beds 30-footers to match the width of my garden, I make small beds to keep plantings small. By staggering planting dates, picking early and often, and replanting harvested beds immediately, we have a steady supply of a full variety of vegetables throughout the growing season. With small beds and frequent plantings, I've eliminated the glut and famine I had when all vegetables were planted in widely spaced 30-foot rows.

There was no rush to make the changeover in a weekend. As I needed ground for planting, I'd prepare just enough space and plant. Then I'd begin another. When the time for putting in melons arrived two months after I planted my spring crops, my changeover to raised beds was complete.

The yearly ritual of rotary tilling has been eliminated in my garden. Since the beds are never walked on, the soil stays loose and is always ready for planting. When it's necessary to add compost or fertilizers, I stand in the path and work them into the beds with a shovel, hoe, and rake.

## Customized Conditions

Raised beds are self-contained units whose soil structure and fertility can be adjusted for each vegetable. For example, cabbage and lettuce grow best in a high-nitrogen soil full of humus. So I grow them together, and before planting, fortify their bed with lots of strawy horse manure. Carrots, on the other hand, should not be grown on a recently manured plot, but they grow straight and long in a sandy soil. By adding a wheelbarrow of sand to a bed that was manured the previous year, I get a perfect carrot environment. Beets like a sweet soil, so I put lime in their bed.

Set or sow vegetables so that each plant has just enough space to spread to its mature size (imagine the space as a circle) before touching the leaves of its neighbors. This arrangement is very space efficient *and* effectively smothers weeds. As the vegetables leaf out, the ground underneath is shaded, discouraging weed growth. Thickly planted beds need weeding only when the vegetables are seedlings. If an errant weed pushes up above the mature vegetables, it's easy to pull it out of the loose soil. Any weeds on the slanted side banks are easily uprooted with a rake. Five minutes of hoeing takes care of any weeds that pop up in a walkway.

Before converting to raised beds, I spread fertilizer over the entire garden. The paths between the vegetables, which took 60 to 70 percent of my garden space, also took 60 to 70 percent of the fertilizer. The fertilized paths encouraged weeds to grow faster and taller. Now fertilizer goes only on the beds and not on the walkways. The same is true of water and mulch. Everything is used more efficiently in the raised-bed layout.

*February 1982*

# How to Plan a Raised-Bed Garden

## Ray Wolf

To plan a raised-bed garden you have to re-think some of your past techniques. Traditionally, designing the coming year's garden involves distance between plants *in* the row and distance *between* rows. With a raised bed, you don't think linearly, but three-dimensionally.

When planning your raised-bed garden, you have three options:

1. *Planting an entire bed all to one crop.* This will give you more production than row gardening and enables you to establish a yearly rotation system. A bed that grew legumes one year would be used for brassicas the next, followed by root crops and then leafy green crops. You may get in two rotations a year if the weather cooperates, one usually being a legume. A monocropped raised bed can be planted on a staggered row plan like the one on the page 116 (top).

2. *Planting close rows without paths.* This type of bed is easy to plant and care for, has many of the advantages of intercropping, but still doesn't make maximum use of the soil. It does, however,

Combining inter-cropping with raised beds will give you a garden more produc-tive than your wildest midwinter dreams.

allow you to group different plants together to take advantage of the polyculture benefits of different feeding characteristics, moisture requirements, sun/shade cycles, and time to maturity. Such a bed would look something like the one shown here (center).

3. *Planting intercropped and succession-planted varieties in one bed.* This method blends the nutrient, space, height, moisture, and seasonal differences of many varieties to give a true polyculture. Problems with such a bed can show up in the planning, making sure that the right varieties are together. Also, when you begin to put seeds in you may quickly forget where you are or where you're going. It is complicated enough to warrant some practice with option 2. If you start with this approach, intercrop only three or four varieties, so your bed will look something like the one shown here (bottom).

For the newcomer to raised-bed gardening, probably the best approach for the first year is planting in rows in a bed. This gives you the insect protection and yield increases of intercropping, plus the space-saving benefits of raised-bed gardening, yet maintains the orderly aspects of row cropping.

To see just how this will work, let's take a look at peppers grown under this type of plan.

Traditionally, you would plan your garden with pepper plants 18 inches

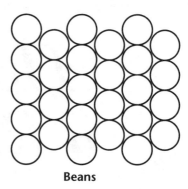

**Beans**

**MONOCROPPED RAISED BED**

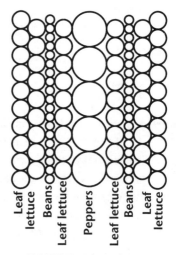

Leaf lettuce  Beans  Leaf lettuce  Peppers  Leaf lettuce  Beans  Leaf lettuce

**ROWS IN RAISED BEDS**

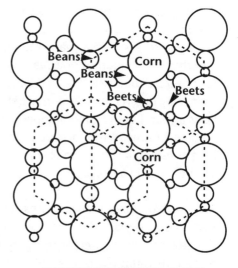

Beans  Corn  Beans  Beets  Beets  Corn

**SUCCESSION/INTERPLANTED**

apart, and 2 to 3 feet between rows. But in a raised-bed garden, what we care about is that a mature pepper plant needs only a circular area of about 12 to 14 inches for its growth. You also need to know that some type of fast, low-growing plant, like leaf lettuce, radishes, spinach, or beets, could be planted close to the pepper plants during the early season, as long as they were out of the garden by the time the pepper plants started their grand growth. If you select a cool-season crop like lettuce, the shading effect of the growing peppers during midsummer may actually extend the harvest period of the lettuce by shading it and preventing it from bolting to seed.

Thus, a standard garden plan for peppers would look like the left side of the profile plan below, and a raised-bed plan would look like the right side of the profile plan.

The bed has peppers down the middle at 12-inch spacings, a row of leaf lettuce 4 inches to the left, and a row of onions 4 inches to the right. These two crops could then be flanked with rows of carrots, spinach, and beets, with bush beans on the outer edge. Try to alternate root crops with leafy crops within the bed to give the roots plenty of room to develop, leaving tops enough space to grow.

Run rows the length of the bed. In the case of a garden designed mainly for salads, you may want rows running across the garden to allow you to replant short rows every few days to ensure a constant supply of fresh, young vegetables.

The width of beds should be kept to a maximum of no more than 5 feet, so you may reach into them from either side to work the middle. If possible, beds should run from north to south to prevent shading of low-growing plants by taller ones. If you

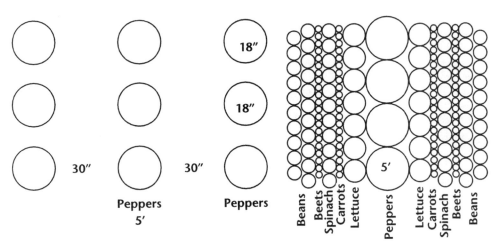

**STANDARD SPACING FOR PEPPERS COMPARED TO RAISED-BED SPACING**

## Raised-Bed Spacing Guide

| Vegetable | Inches required | Raised bed production |
|---|---|---|
| Beans, bush | 4 | Excellent |
| Beans, pole | 10 | Good |
| Beets | 2 | Excellent |
| Broccoli | 14 | Good |
| Brussels sprouts | 18 | Fair |
| Cabbage | 12 | Fair |
| Carrots | 2 | Excellent |
| Cauliflower | 18 | Fair |
| Corn | 12 | Fair |
| Cucumbers, vertical | 12 | Good |
| Eggplant | 18 | Fair |
| Kale | 15 | Good |
| Lettuce, head | 12 | Good |
| Lettuce, leaf | 6 | Excellent |
| Melons, vertical | 24 | Fair |
| Mustard greens | 6 | Good |
| Okra | 12 | Fair |
| Onions | 2 | Excellent |
| Peas | 4 | Good |
| Peppers | 12 | Excellent |
| Radishes | 1 | Excellent |
| Rhubarb | 24 | Fair |
| Rutabaga | 6 | Fair |
| Spinach | 4 | Good |
| Squash, summer | 18 | Good |
| Squash, winter | 24 | Fair |
| Swiss chard | 8 | Good |
| Tomatoes | 18 | Excellent |
| Turnips | 4 | Good |
| Watermelon | 24 | Fair |

must run your beds east to west, keep the taller vegetables to the northern edge of the bed instead of the middle, and your low-growing crops will still get plenty of sunlight.

Certain vegetables team up for a raised bed much better than others. For example, the salad vegetables all go ideally together in one bed. Those vegetables that take up a lot of ground space (potatoes, winter squash, pumpkins, watermelon, and melons) and those that take up a lot of vertical space (corn, sunflowers, and pole beans) do not capitalize on the raised-bed's advantages and are best planted in traditional ways.

### Something Fishy

My family loves to fish, but since we live in town, disposing of the smelly fish heads is a real problem. Last year my husband suggested burying them beside our tomato plants. We knew the rotting fish heads would be an excellent fertilizer for the plants, but were afraid neighborhood dogs and cats would follow the smell and ruin our tomato plants digging them up. Much to our surprise, there wasn't a fishy smell in the garden, and *no* cats or dogs were attracted to the buried fish. And our tomato crop was the best ever!

*Beverly McMasters*
*Stockton, Missouri*
*July 1981*

Consult the "Raised-Bed Spacing Guide" for required spacings for different vegetables and for an appraisal of how well they do in a raised bed. Some do not grow as well in a mixed bed, but in monoculture beds, they greatly out-yield conventional rows. One example is cucumbers trained onto vertical supports. Almost all members of the brassica family (cabbage, cauliflower, Brussels sprouts, and broccoli) do best when grouped into their own bed.

Perhaps the biggest work-saving technique of raised-bed gardening is to establish permanent paths between your beds. That way, you never cultivate, water, fertilize, or apply compost to areas where you walk. All your soil-building and maintenance efforts go into the growing surface. After a few years of such care, the beds will be in very good condition and the paths in such poor condition that not even weeds will grow well.

It takes a lot more than just planting vegetables close together to have a successful raised-bed garden. Having plants so closely grouped puts a higher nutrient demand on your soil than traditional spacings. Thus, you must prepare it for this extra demand. This is where organic gardeners shine.

Working lots of actively decaying organic matter in the form of compost into your soil, plus manures and rock powders, makes sure the increased number of plants will have enough food available throughout the growing season. If you were to try ap- plying that much quick-releasing chemical fertilizer, the young seedlings could be killed, and those that survived would need several more side-dressings during the year.

## Make Room for Roots

To make room for the root systems of the increased plant population, raised-bed gardening requires deep soil preparation before planting. The goal normally is to loosen up the ground to a depth of about 24 inches before planting, without burying the topsoil. That allows root systems to develop vertically instead of horizontally, which reduces the need for watering and heavy fertilization during the growing season.

When you have plants growing close together, you don't need to mulch, as the growing plants shade the soil, forming what is called a living mulch. When you water such a garden, remember that you are watering more plants than you would in the same space in a traditional garden, so water deeply. Toward the heart of the growing season, some plants may begin to show stress from lack of nutrients if the soil isn't rich enough. If this happens, give the heavy feeders a boost with a manure tea, fish emulsion, or foliar feeding of liquid seaweed. Doing that should prove especially beneficial to heavy croppers like tomatoes and peppers.

*February 1977*

# Elbow Room in an Intensive Planting

Make sure that the spacings you plan are based on the real needs of your plants.

The most powerful reason for choosing a bed layout instead of traditional garden rows is the dramatic space savings that result. If you are using 2-foot spaces between rows and switch to 4-foot-wide beds (with 2-foot walkways between them), you will gain one-third more planting space. If you use 5-foot-wide beds, you gain a little more ground.

Another way to look at these gains, or savings, is that you could reduce your garden's size and get the same yields. Some crops will probably give you an even larger advantage when planted in beds because they are well-suited to dense planting. You can plant *ten* rows of carrots down a 4-foot-wide bed. If you were keeping your rows 2 feet apart, you'd get just two plantings of carrots in the same space. Furthermore, you will need to spread less manure, compost, and rock powders. You'll use less water when you irrigate and have less ground to work up for planting.

## Plan for Plants, Not Equipment

But when you begin to plan your garden and flip over the seed packets for the spacing recommendations, you'll read that you should leave 2 or 3 feet between each row of vegetables. Most gardening books will have similar advice. Why? The spacing recommendations for garden vegetables are based on the need to get equipment down the rows, not on the true requirements of the plants. Only a few wide-ranging kinds like squash, pumpkins, and melons really need to be 3 feet from their neighbors (and even they will yield well closer).

Think of a plant's most basic needs: water, minerals, and organic matter in the earth, carbon dioxide and sunlight in the air. The roots of the plant can range deeper and farther than the leaves and branches can spread into the air. And the roots can intermingle freely as they snake through the soil. The

minute root hairs have an astounding number of soil pores to penetrate and particles to cover in their search for nutrients and water. The leaves, by comparison, are much more limited in their spread and freedom to overlap without competition. If a leaf thoroughly shades a neighbor's, it usurps the vital sunlight.

So, as you decide on plant spacings for your bed garden, think of each plant's place in the plan as a circle, described by the spread of its leaves near maturity. If adjacent plants begin shading each other early in the season, neither will develop fully or fruit heavily. Large, vigorous plants can totally dominate small neighbors. If, on the other hand, the plants are spaced so widely that the leaves *never* overlap, the space won't be used to full potential. Where the sun can strike bare ground, water will evaporate rapidly and needlessly. Weeds will sprout. The leaves of neighboring plants should start touching each other right around the onset of harvest, shading the soil with a living mulch. Working with

*A grid of squares based on your plants' mature size is a simple way to space your garden crops efficiently.*

*Equidistant spacing minimizes competition between plants and makes room for more of them in a bed than does lining up plants in rows.*

these relationships is the first step toward successful companion planting.

Intensive gardening does not mean that plants can be crammed into a bed simply because the ground has been worked deeply and well-enriched. No matter what resources are available to the roots, when the tops crowd each other, the stems will become spindly and yields will drop. Garden soils should be so rich and well-watered that competition for sunlight is what determines optimum spacings.

In every garden, plants with vastly different characteristics must be mixed. When each type of vegetable gets its own row, you still have different plants side by side in adjacent rows. In a bed-style garden, the mix can get more complex. Rarely can an entire bed be devoted to one vegetable. With bed gardening, the safest plan is to keep the mixing simple. Here are a few principles to keep in mind.

1. The best spacing is an equal distance in all directions between plants of one kind. The accompanying chart lists distances for many vegetables.

   But remember that some cultivars may be extra large or very compact. Check the catalog or seed packet descriptions and alter the spacings accordingly. Many times the recommended spacing *within a row* is a good number to use for equidistant spacing.

   For small-seeded crops, narrowly spaced rows will yield as well as perfectly equidistant points. That

is, carrots planted 1 inch apart in furrows 4 inches apart will produce the same yields as carrots spaced 2 inches apart in all directions.

2. Your planting plan should get the entire surface of the ground shaded by leaves as early in the season as possible. Again, that means small-seeded vegetables should be spaced closely. I find I need to weed carrots only twice with this method. After the first six weeks, only a few weeds need be pulled. In beds of fast-growing plants, weed control is even easier.

   In beds of widely spaced plants like tomatoes or broccoli, the large patches of ground will be bare for a month or more before the main crop starts to spread. That space can be used by planting very fast-maturing vegetables, like lettuce, radishes, looseleaf Chinese cabbage, and turnips. Treat them as individual plants. Even better, use transplants and gain two weeks of interplanting time. The fast plants should be harvested when the main crop begins to shade them.

3. When possible, restrict each bed to one vegetable. For example, plant corn in one bed, and allow winter squash to spread in another. When you don't need a full bed of a crop, reserve the full width to one crop. Keeping like plants together is the simplest way to prevent overcrowding. Subdivisions of a bed should be more square than rectangular.

## How Far Apart to Plant

| Vegetables | Space between plants | |
|---|---|---|
| Beans | 2" to 4" in rows 12" apart | Gives high yields and efficient use of seed. |
| Beets | 5" equidistant | Beets respond very poorly to overcrowding. Use slightly wider spacing for an extra-early harvest. |
| Broccoli and cabbage | 12" to 18" equidistant | |
| Brussels sprouts | 30" equidistant | The spacing for a equidistant long, cool harvest season. If you need to pick your sprouts all in a few weeks, space plants 20" apart and cut out the top of the plant when the largest sprouts are $1/2$" across. They'll mature more uniformly. |
| Carrots | $1\frac{1}{2}$" in rows 5" apart | Yields are fairly constant over a wide range of spacings. Plant farther apart for fewer, bigger roots and closer for many small roots. |
| Cauliflower | 21" equidistant | For the larger long-season cultivars, space plants farther apart, about 30". |
| Eggplant and peppers | 18" equidistant | |
| Lettuce | 6" to 12" equidistant | Spacing depends on the ideal mature size of each cultivar. Leaf lettuce can be spaced closest. The 12" distance is for crisphead lettuces. |
| Onions | 3" equidistant | For extra-large bulbs, try 4". |
| Peas | 2" in rows 6" apart | |
| Sweet corn | 12" to 18" equidistant | The closer spacing is for equidistant small cultivars, and the wider is for large ones. |
| Tomatoes | 18" equidistant | This is for staked equidistant plants. Close spacing requires more plants, but a larger crop of the earliest fruit results. |

4. Avoid pairing plants with big differences in their times to maturity. For example, a bed partially devoted to early broccoli should be filled out only with other early vegetables, like onions, cauliflower, peas, lettuce, or spinach. Later, the whole bed can be replanted to fall crops. The long-season summer crops should get their own separate beds. This approach makes it easier to plan successions and prepare the soil for planting.

5. When you must mix vegetables, mix plants of similar growth habit and growing season. Carrots and beets can work well next to each other in a bed (not alternating plant by plant). Larger plants can freely alternate if you wish—pepper, eggplant, pepper, eggplant, and so on. Brussels sprouts and late broccoli can be mixed in the same way because they are similar in height and breadth.

6. If you must mix unlike plants (and sometimes you'll have to), always put the taller, more vigorous ones where their shade won't inhibit smaller plants. If your beds run east to west, plant things like staked tomatoes or pole beans in a single row on the north side. Most of the shade will fall on the walkway. If the beds run north and south, locate the tall plants on the west side because most plants can benefit from some shade in the hot afternoon sun. For fall plantings, however, afternoon shade is no advantage.

Or you can spot lone, tall plants around the garden. If they are very far apart, their shadows will be narrow and rotate 180 degrees through the day. No short plants will have to suffer shade for long. There are a few mixes of unlike plants that will work very well. I've had good luck with a slightly delayed planting of cucumbers among a very early patch of EARLY SUNGLOW CORN, a bantam type. Dwarf corn casts very light shade. When the ears were gone and the corn leaves shriveled in midsummer, the cucumber vines rambled on through the stalks. Another year, the cucumbers were a disaster with SILVER QUEEN, a much more heavily leafed and later-maturing corn. Always favor your main crop in an interplant combination.

As you start, stick to the basics and make your initial experiments small. Good combinations will occur to you later as you work among the plants. Most important, observe each plant type so that you learn well what its ideal mature size is. When you get a feel for that, you can give them the room they need to thrive.

*Time brussels sprouts plantings so harvesting will begin after frosts have improved the flavor of the sprouts.*

February 1981

# Chapter 7

# Mulch

# Mulching Comes First

*Virginia Brundage*

For more on mulching, see Chapter 15, where Ruth Stout holds forth on her favorite mulching techniques.

Mulching has become such a common gardening practice that it might be a good idea to review the whole subject, discuss the pros and cons, present some new facts, and sum up everything.

At one time a mulch was merely something you spread around a young plant to keep it from drying out. But times have changed, and mulch is accepted more widely now. A great deal of serious study and experimentation has been devoted to it.

## Benefits of Mulching

1. A mulched plant is not subjected to the extremes of temperatures of an exposed plant. Roots are damaged by the heaving of soil brought on by sudden thaws and sudden frosts. The mulch acts as an insulating blanket, keeping the soil warmer in winter and cooler in summer.

2. Certain materials used for a mulch contain rich minerals, and gradually, through the action of rain and time, these work into the soil to feed the

roots of the plants. Some of the minerals soak into the ground during the first heavy rain. It isn't true, then, that the mulch fertilizes the soil only after it decays.

3. For the busy gardener mulching is a boon indeed. Many backbreaking hours of weeding and hoeing are practically eliminated. Weeds do not have a chance to get a foothold, and the few that might manage to come up through the mulch can be hoed out in a jiffy. And since the mulch keeps the soil loose, there is no need to cultivate.

4. The mulch prevents the hot, drying sun and wind from penetrating to the soil, so its moisture does not evaporate quickly. A few good soakings during the growing season will tide plants over a long dry spell. Have you ever lifted a bit of mulch and

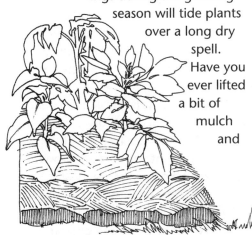

*Mulch benefits your garden in many ways. It reduces moisture loss, protects plant roots from fluctuating temperatures, promotes earthworm activity, prevents weed seeds from germinating, keeps disease organisms from splashing onto leaves, and gradually adds organic matter and nutrients to the soil.*

felt the earth underneath? It is damp and cool to the touch. Compare this with the bare, sun-baked soil of a neighbor and you will see why he must spend his evenings with the hose! We have published in the pages of our magazine innumerable instances of plants enduring a long dry season with practically no watering at all.

5. At harvesttime, vegetables that sprawl on the ground, such as cucumbers, squash, strawberries, and unstaked tomatoes, often become mildewed or moldy or even develop rot. A mulch prevents this damage by keeping the vegetables clean and dry. This is the season when most gardens begin to look unkempt. Everything's over now except for the harvest, so why bother about improving appearances? But the mulched garden always looks neat and trim, no matter what the season.

## When to Hold the Mulch

Now what are the disadvantages of mulching? Are there circumstances when it is best to leave soil uncovered?

1. Seedlings planted in very moist soil should not be mulched immediately. The addition of any organic matter that keeps the soil at a high humidity encourages damping-off of young plants. Damping-off is a disease caused by a fungus inhab-

iting moist, poorly ventilated soil, and can be 90 percent fatal. Allow seedlings to become established, then, before mulching.

2. It is wise, too, to consider the danger of crown-rot in perennials. This disease is also caused by a fungus. If there have been especially heavy rains, postpone mulching until the soil is no longer water-logged. Do not allow mulches composed of peat moss, manure, compost, or ground corncobs to touch the base of these plants. Leave a circle of several inches in diameter. The idea here is to permit the soil to remain dry and open to the air around the immediate area of the plant.

3. Do not mulch a wet, low-lying soil, or at most, use only a dry, light type of material, such as salt hay or buckwheat hulls. Leaves are definitely to be avoided as they may mat down and add to the sogginess. Maple leaves are the worst example.

4. There are a few plants like corn and tomatoes that need a warm soil and a long growing season. These should be mulched only after the soil has warmed in spring.

## How to Mulch

With the instructions given above, it is simple enough to know when and where not to mulch. Except for these instances, the gardener really can't do

without mulching as a wonderful, labor-saving helpmate.

Now to the actual practice of mulching.

In the first place, if you are at a loss as to what materials are best suited to your soil, or you do not know where to acquire them, consult your county agent. He will be glad to advise you.

The average mulch should be 3 to 4 inches deep for the best results. If the soil is dry, wet it down before applying the mulch. By doing this you will maintain moisture from the very beginning. After the mulch has been spread, wet again to prevent it from scattering in the wind. Or you can lay branches over the mulch for the same purpose. Prunings from shrubs and fruit trees are useful here.

It is a good idea when laying sod to spread a mulch on the ground first. This will kill any competing weeds and grass, and will also provide a layer of nutrients for the new roots to feed on.

Use a very light mulch on seed flats, and one with a low nitrogen content. Too much nitrogen will force the seedlings into too rapid growth. Finely ground corncobs are ideal.

Some of the materials for mulching can be found on the home property—leaves, grass clippings, weeds (that have not gone to seed). A little ingenuity will bring other sources to light. Is there a lumber mill in your vicinity? Then you'll find sawdust and wood shavings. Breweries, canneries, and groceries all have waste materials to dispose of. For more leaves, contact your street-cleaning department in the fall.

## Best Mulching Materials

*Grass clippings.* Grass clippings are always available and can be easily applied. They provide a light mulch that dries up quickly, so successive applications will have to be made. The mulch should not be more than a few inches deep, as grass heats up readily in decomposition.

*Weeds.* Weeds should be allowed to dry before applying to prevent rooting. They may be shredded to make a neat appearance and can be mixed with the grass clippings.

*Shredded leaves.* Leaves make an excellent year-round mulch. Shredded leaves do not mat down, and they enrich the soil more quickly than whole leaves.

*Unshredded leaves.* These should be mixed with straw or some other light material so that they do not become a soggy mass. As a mixture the mulch can be spread 8 to 12 inches deep for winter.

Maple and horse chestnut leaves are excellent to use around shrubbery. Oak leaves are acid and are good to spread as a permanent mulch around blueberries, azaleas, and rhododendrons.

*Peat moss.* Peat moss is an old standby. As a bale is greatly compressed and very dry, you'll have to give it a good soaking after it is ap-

plied. Sometimes it will form a crust over the beds, but it can be easily broken up with a rake.

*Salt hay.* According to the Wisconsin Experimental Station, salt hay makes the best mulch for strawberries. Use a 1½- to 2-inch layer here, 3 inches for other uses. This straw is usually cheap and easily obtained. It does not mat down, and remains stiff and firm throughout the season. If used as a winter mulch, it can be taken off in spring and stacked in the corner of the plot to be used again the following winter. However, it is recommended as a year-round mulch, too.

*Alfalfa hay.* Coarse and ragged in appearance, alfalfa hay is most easily handled when green and freshly cut. It has a high nitrogen content and will supply the requirements of fruit trees. Rain-spoiled hay can always be used as a mulch material, so there need be no waste here.

*Oat straw.* Oat straw is considered to be the best of the straw mulches. It is somewhat unkempt and coarse for shrubbery and flowers, but perfectly all right for the vegetable plot. For any of the straws, you can figure that 1 ton will give a 1-inch mulch on 1 acre of land.

*Corn stalks.* Corn stalks to the depth of 3 or 4 inches provide a well-aerated winter mulch, but do not use stalks from a field heavily infested with borers. Lay the stalks crisscross with tops and butts alternating.

*Corncobs.* When ground into 1-inch pieces, corncobs have many uses.

The sugar content will help to increase the microorganisms in the soil, and these will give a better soil granulation. Do not spread this type of mulch on lawns, however, as the lawn mower will jam.

Finely ground corncobs are highly recommended for seed flats. Use lightly. Interestingly, florists using this material claim 100 percent more production and 30 percent savings on operating costs as germination takes place more rapidly and there is no need for frequent watering.

In the opinion of L. C. Chadwick, professor of horticulture, Ohio State University, a ground corncob mulch helps to prevent black spot on roses. This should be good news to rose fanciers! Try it.

*Sawdust.* Sawdust from softwoods provides a good mulch for blueberries. There will be less packing down and better aeration.

A 6-inch layer will smother weeds effectively. If there is quack grass in the soil, its roots will soon lie at the surface just under the mulch. It is easy to run your fingers under the roots and pull them out.

Oak sawdust, used alone, compacts too much and also will produce a gas that will inhibit the growth of the plants.

To counteract the nitrogen deficiency in sawdust, add soybean meal, cottonseed meal, or compost. In fact, it is a good idea to spread a layer of compost under sawdust on all occasions.

*Oak tow.* Oak tow is like sawdust but contains coarser wood strings. It is made by tearing the wood lengthwise in sawing stave bolts. If you can get this material from a sawmill, you'll find it does not compact or blow as readily as sawdust.

*Pine needles.* Pine needles are good for strawberries year-round. Keep in mind that they can be a fire hazard when dry. Use a 2- to 4-inch mulch and renew every year.

We have listed the most common mulches, but there are plenty of other materials that can be used. *Coffee grounds* are excellent. Some people make a deal with restaurants to collect these periodically. *Buckwheat hulls* can be spread 1 or 2 inches deep in summer and a little deeper in winter. They make a clean, inconspicuous mulch, but being very light may blow badly. Some chocolate companies will sell their *cocoa bean hulls or shells,* and these are very good as a mulch. They absorb two and a half times their weight in water. Cocoa bean hulls or shells have been used to advantage over well-rotted grass.

*May, June 1952*

# 11 Ways to Make Hay Mulch Work

## Richard V. Clemence

The method of mulching heavily with hay has enjoyed widespread if unpublicized use for many years. But today, thanks to Miss Ruth Stout and her determined advocacy, there is scarcely an organic gardener in this country who has not heard about mulching with hay.

*Ruth Stout's coauthor offers a wealth of practical ideas—from his own successful experience—on how to obtain top results with mulch.*

It is only fair, therefore, to refer to this sound method hereafter as the Stout system. At the same time, it should be noted once again that many gardeners have, over the years, worked out this method for themselves in much the same way as Miss Stout.

With this in mind, the writer makes the following mulching suggestions, expressing the hope that other organic gardeners will soon make many more. This is to be expected because variations in mulching technique will be dictated by different soils, climates, and growing conditions in different parts of the country.

1. *Planting.* Sweet corn, I have found, can readily be grown by merely pushing the seed kernels into the ground through the hay mulch. A string to mark the rows makes this kind of planting very quick and easy, and the yield is usually well above average.

2. *Plant residues.* After trying many ways of disposing of corn stalks, ranging from composting to chopping and spreading, I have arrived at a nearly ideal scheme. As soon as the corn is harvested, I flatten the stalks to the ground by bending them over and stamping on them. Then I cover the flattened mess with hay. In the spring, any kind of plants can be set with a trowel through this cover. By spreading a little compost, loam, or peat moss on top, even small seeds can be started, and the roots will penetrate into the decaying mass below. The results are astonishing to anyone who has not

*Mulching over crop residues or cover crops can save you the effort of turning them under. Top them with a layer of wet newspaper anchored with shredded leaves or other organic matter. By spring, the bed will be ready for planting. Just dig through the mulch to set transplants, or sow seeds directly into it and cover them lightly with compost.*

tried this method, and the work is reduced to almost nothing. I should add that I am not troubled with corn borers at all and, of course, use no sprays or dusts of any kind.

3. *Fall cleanup.* My annual fall "cleanup" consists of leaving everything in the garden exactly where it is, and covering all crop residues with hay. I prefer to keep this cover fairly thin. If it is only 4 or 5 inches deep, it will be reduced close to ground level by spring, and seeds can be planted on and through it without moving it around. This not only saves work, but also makes it possible to put rows very close together and get far more into the same space.

Row spacing is mainly a question of the gardener's convenience. For most crops, I place the rows the same distance apart as the plants are to stand in the rows. Sweet corn spaced 6 inches each way will do just as well as it will with the rows 3 feet apart, and you get six times as much corn from the same area. Three rows of onion plants occupy a space only a foot wide, and so on, with all the rest. Narrow paths separating crops of different sorts give you ready access.

4. *Weeding.* Hay is a marvelous substitute for thinning and weeding. Instead of pulling unwanted plants out of the ground and disturbing the roots of others, I bend the weeds flat and put hay over them.

5. *Tilling.* On most new ground, a few inches of hay in the fall will make it possible to plant any kind of crop the following year without disturbing the sod. With the Stout system, spading, plowing, and cultivating are all unnecessary and do more harm than good. If a heavy hay cover is laid on even the toughest sod in the summer, plantings can be made through it the following spring. No other preparation of the soil is required.

6. *Transplanting.* Strawberries, tomatoes, and other plants are incredibly easy to set through a thin hay mulch. With a string to mark the row, and a box or basket for the plants, you can move easily along, stabbing a trowel into the ground to make a deep slit. Shove the plant into this slit, step on the raised surface, and move on to the next. I can set a hundred strawberry plants in a half hour without hurrying much. And they grow admirably, too.

7. *Growing potatoes.* Large crops of the highest-quality potatoes can be grown by laying the seed (preferably small, whole potatoes) on top of the remains of last year's mulch. I make double rows, 14 inches apart, with the seed the same distance apart in the rows. The idea of this is not only to get a heavy yield but also to make it easy to inspect the vines from both sides occasionally and to take care of a rare potato bug or a bunch of eggs that the ladybugs have missed.

Having laid the seed in straight rows with the aid of a string, I cover the rows with 6 or 8 inches of hay and do nothing more until several weeks later. After the blossoms fall, I begin moving the hay carefully to see how things are progressing. Small potatoes an inch or two in diameter can be separated from their stems without disturbing the parent plants, and the hay can then be replaced. What these small potatoes taste like is something that no reader of this journal should need to be told. The yield in pounds is reduced, of course, but the returns in satisfaction are maximized. IRISH COBBLERS are the best to eat this way, I think, but any cultivar with plenty of butter and home-grown parsley is a treat that few people have ever had.

8. *Acidity/alkalinity.* If you use hay mulch continuously for a number of years, you can practically forget all

about acid or alkaline soil problems—along with dusting and
spraying and the use of chemical fertilizers and "soil conditioners." I grow
everything from beets to blueberries
under the Stout system, and pay no
attention to acidity or alkalinity anymore. My experience has been that
ample organic matter acts as an effective buffer and helps to neutralize
extremes of pH in any soil.

9. *Soil temperature.* I have noted some
discussion of the Stout system in
journals other than this. Apparently,
some have difficulty obtaining satisfactory results with it. I believe that
the trouble has been due to a mis-
understanding of the method. Piling
a heavy hay mulch onto cold, wet
ground early in the spring is *not a*
good way to begin using the
system. Unless the soil is very sandy,
or unless it is well supplied with
humus, hay will give poor immediate results. Hay applied for the
first time does little more than insu-
late the soil for several months, and
if a beginning is being made in the
spring, seeds should usually be well
started before the mulch is spread.
To improve germination and prevent washing, there is nothing
better than a very thin sprinkling of
peat moss over each row of seed.
This light cover also serves to mark
the rows, so hay can be spread in
just the right places. If peat moss is
thus used, the mulch can be applied
between the rows at any time after
planting.

10. *Garden boundary.* I like to keep
several extra bales of hay along the
side of the garden. In the course of
a year or two they break down into
moist, black humus, filled with
earthworms that enter from below.
Meanwhile, the hay smothers grass
that would otherwise continually
be creeping into the edge of the
garden.

11. *Rotation.* In a recent issue of
*Organic Gardening and Farming,* I
was much interested to learn of
Mrs. Hebble's method of growing
potatoes. Perhaps my application
of the Stout system to a rotation of
strawberries, corn, and potatoes
would be of interest to other
readers. These three crops all present special problems, because they
ordinarily require so much space.
For the backyard gardener to
manage all of them is usually out of
the question, and I have experimented for many years in an effort
to solve the problem. The answer I
have arrived at works very well, but
it may be subject to further improvement, and I hope that anyone
with a better system will let me
know about it.

Since this method is a rotation, we may begin at any stage of
it, so let us start with the strawberries. I will try to show how some of
the ideas I have already mentioned
apply in this scheme. Let me say at
this point that I have eaten strawberries prepared in every way I
could think of, and that my notion

of perfection is to pick the berries dead ripe after the sun has evaporated excess moisture, and eat them immediately when they are still warm, but swimming in heavy chilled cream. If you have not tried organically grown strawberries this way, you may still be wondering if they are worth the time and trouble they require.

## Sweet Corn, Strawberries, and Potatoes

Now for the rotation. I set a new bed every year, buying 100 virus-free plants and spacing them in four rows 1 foot apart, with the plants also 1 foot apart in the rows. The plants are set through a thin mulch left from the previous season, and more hay is added as growth occurs and as weeds need to be smothered. Since I want results, not only on the strawberries, but on the corn to follow, I spread 100 pounds of Bovung and 50 pounds of bonemeal over the bed as soon as the plants are well-started. I remove all runners the first year, which sounds like a lot of work. Actually, however, it takes about ten minutes a week. A walk down each side of the bed, with a pair of grass shears in hand, will take care of the runners about as quickly as you would ordinarily inspect the plants, anyway.

As early as possible the following spring, before the strawberry plants are getting into full leaf, I seed sweet corn between the rows and along each side of the bed. A string keeps the corn rows straight, and I push the kernels into the ground with my fingers, spacing them closely and taking account of the way the strawberry plants are developing. When the berries are ready to be picked in June, the corn should be 4 or 5 inches high and easy to avoid in the harvesting. The corn should be an early and strong-growing selection. I have had the best luck with north star and GOLDEN BEAUTY, but others may be equally good. I count on the five 25-plant rows of corn to yield at least 15 dozen fine ears, and have not been disappointed yet. While the corn is growing it needs no attention at all. The strawberry plants continue to live and to shade the corn roots, and the corn thrives on the extra Bovung and bonemeal applied earlier.

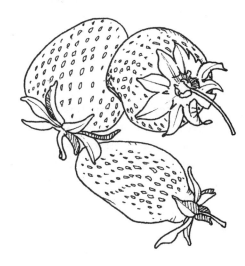

*Strawberries grow better in mulch, since it cuts down on weed competition. A layer of mulch keeps the berries cleaner, too.*

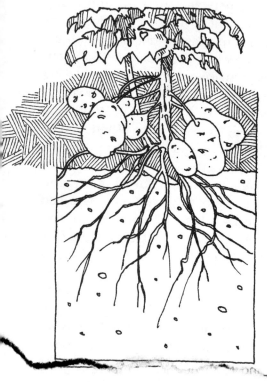

*It's easy to mulch-plant potatoes instead of mounding up soil around them. In the fall, make a hill by mounding up 3 to 4 feet of leaves. The following spring, plant your seed potatoes on top of the partially decomposed mound and cover them with 1 foot of straw or hay, adding more as the vines mature.*

After the corn has all been harvested, the stalks are simply flattened to the ground over the surviving strawberry plants and covered with several inches of hay. The following spring, potatoes are laid on top of whatever remains of all this and mulched with a heavy hay blanket. Again, nothing remains to be done but to gather potatoes as they are wanted. According to the chemical school, everything should be riddled by insects and diseases, but I have barely enough evidence of these to realize what is supposed to be destroying my crops. I harvest all my potatoes with my bare hands, because it is so satisfying to handle the living soil and to discover one handsome tuber after another growing in it. The potato harvest thus leaves the whole space in perfect condition for the next crop. I merely cover the ground with hay and wait for my strawberry plants to arrive.

I am convinced that the Stout system has great potentialities for the home gardener, at least, and that it can be readily adapted and modified to meet all sorts of special situations. I very much hope that these notes will encourage others to try variations on the Stout system, and to report their findings through *Organic Gardening and Farming.*

**January 1959**

# Stone Mulches Protect Winter Plants

## Kathleen and Al Kaule

The ability of stones to hold solar heat for longer periods than most other mulching material (in addition to maintaining an ideal soil condition) got us involved in the ancient gardening practice of stone mulching. By utilizing stones in conjunction with other excellent mulch substances, such as shredded oak leaves, pine needles, straw, and sawdust, we have been able to achieve healthier plants, greater productivity, and a longer crop life span.

When soil begins to cool off rapidly in autumn, the soil of stone-mulched plants will continue to remain warm, extending the plants' growing season for approximately another four weeks. Leaves, straw, and similar materials warm up quickly in the sun, but because of their limited capacity to retain heat, they cool off rapidly at night or on cloudy days, when utilized without stones. On the other hand, stones have the ability to store the sun's heat during the daytime, then release it gradually during the night, warming the lower air temperature surrounding the plants.

Stones are capable of protecting the lower

A stone mulch can give you a jump on the gardening season by providing warmth for heat-loving crops like peppers and tomatoes. The stones collect heat during the day and release it at night, giving tender plants a few degrees of protection against late spring frosts.

## A Heat Bank

Here in Sumpter, in northeastern Oregon, summer frosts are common and the growing season is short. Most summer nights are quite cool. Tomatoes are reluctant to blossom and set fruit, and fruits are slow to ripen.

Since stone is a good material for absorbing and holding heat, I built mortarless south-facing rock walls that would receive full sunlight and store some of the day's heat. I built beds at the bases of the walls and in the walls.

Tomatoes, peppers, and beans survived several 28-degree nights in the summer, and although a 22-degree night in the early fall killed the top leaves of the tomatoes, the plants survived and gave us ripe tomatoes a month later. It took an 18-degree night to kill the plants. Their only protection was the concentration of heat-holding rocks.

All the rock walls are built low enough or at enough of an angle so that the plant areas will not lose early morning or late afternoon sun and will not lose direct sun as the sun moves to its most northern position during the summer season.

*Jon Remmerde*
*Sumpter, Oregon*
*November 1979*

leaves of many low-growing plants against a few degrees of freezing. With a stone-mulched bed, we have been able to keep late-planted fall crops such as beets, lettuce, and broccoli growing weeks after other soil has turned cold and unproductive. Hardy herb seed, like parsley, will germinate earlier and produce healthier plants when sown in such a bed during the fall. Where only a few plants are desired, we have had excellent results by sowing seed in the openings between stones, after filling them with good organic soil.

In spring, soil thaws slowly. Stone-mulched areas, however, heat the soil more rapidly, allowing us to set out tomato and other plants two to three weeks earlier. Using a stone-straw-leaf mulch around tomato plants also has produced a reduction in both cracking and blossom-end rot.

Beds are first cultivated deeply, and good compost worked into the soil, in stone mulching. We also add wood ash, dried blood, and similar ingredients, depending upon specific plant needs. After the bed is prepared and the planting rows marked, we apply a heavy layer of shredded oak leaves, pine needles, and straw (individually or a combination) on both sides of each planting row, extending approximately 1½ to 2 feet in width.

Stones, preferably medium-size rocks, are then set down firmly and close together on the underlying mulch material. The stone's flattest side should be on top. The open areas between the stones are next filled

*Large, flat stones make a useful permanent mulch that conserves moisture, controls weeds, and extends the season by radiating stored heat back to your plants during cool spring and fall nights.*

with gravel, sawdust, or soil. Quick to settle and weather in, this permanent stone mulch may be left undisturbed for years. The only change made is in summer, when a thick layer of straw or leaves is placed on top of the stones to keep them from reflecting too much heat against the plants. In early autumn, this material is raked aside to expose the rocks and soil once more to solar heat.

## Not Just for Vegetables

The practice of stone mulching is not confined solely to vegetables. Fruit trees and rose bushes will also benefit from a combined mulch of stone and other material. A ground corncob-stone mulch around roses will stabilize the soil temperature, preserve its moisture, and greatly reduce the problem of black spot. During a drought, fruit trees will have substantially larger and better-quality fruit when stones are set between two thick layers of straw. Again, the moisture content and soil temperature remain more uniform, which favors better root growth and soil bacterial activity.

In our area there is a saying that "stones hatch out overnight." Instead of just creating a huge rock pile we began using them ornamentally. Later, noticing how plants growing closest to the stones thrived, matured earlier, continued growing later in the season than many others, and stood up better under adverse weather conditions, we began to incorporate stone mulching into our organic gardening practice.

*November 1978*

139

# Chapter 8

# Pest Control

# Getting Garden Pests to Bug Off

*M. C. Goldman*

I t might shock some people to learn that nearly half the food produced in the world today is lost to insects—despite the fact that pesticide use will hit a record 4.1 *billion* pounds this year. One man who's *not* surprised is Dr. David Pimentel of Cornell University. He told the annual meeting of the American Association for the Advancement of Science that chemical use has increased 20 percent in the last five years and now adds up to over a pound of pesticide a year for every person on earth.

Yet progress is not being made against the world's harmful insects, said Dr. Pimentel and University of California's Dr. Ray F. Smith, because the pests are developing immunity to pesticides, and because so much insecticide is being used that it is destroying predators and parasites that are their natural enemies. "Fully 90 percent of all the eggs and larvae of crop pests would be destroyed by their own natural enemies," said Smith, "if we made better use of pesticides."

Another way that poison sprays backfire is by causing what's known as *resurgence*. "You see some bugs on your plants," explains University of California Berkeley entomologist Dr. William

Old-time remedies and new techniques now combine to give home gardeners an edge in battling insects.

Olkowski. "You treat them with a pesticide, and in anywhere from a few days to a number of weeks later, the same kind of bug is back again, only this time in higher numbers than before. What happened?

"Well, you accidentally killed off the pests' natural enemies along with the pest. It is rarely possible to kill off all the pests, and without any predators or parasites to hold them in check, those that didn't die, or those that flew in, were able to multiply without restriction."

Natural enemies do not "resurge" as quickly as the pest, adds Dr. Olkowski, and some insecticides are selectively more toxic to predators and parasites than to pests. At the same time, pests develop resistance, a second major effect of relying on chemicals. "Each time you spray an insect population, you change the balance between susceptible and resistant individuals, because resistant insects survive to reproduce, while most of the susceptible insects are killed," Dr. Olkowski says. "Therefore, the more you use a pesticide to control insects, the faster you produce a population of resistant pests."

## Give Your Favorite Tomato a Pinch

What's the alternative? Using methods that keep pests under control without killing almost everything else—helpful insects, plants that protect other plants, bug diseases, assorted traps, plus some kitchen concoctions that drive bugs up and over the garden wall.

You might start with a pinch—of your tomato leaves, that is. It's an incredible way to ward off tomato pests, discovered by Dr. Clarence Ryan at Washington State University. He found that simply bruising or wounding the tomato plant leaf activates a hormone that causes insects attacking the plant to die of severe indigestion. "Some of the beetles laid eggs on the plants before dying," reported Dr. Ryan. "When the eggs hatched, the young beetles also died after attacking the plants." Dr. Ryan received an $80,000 USDA grant to determine if other vegetables and fruits have a similar hormone, and to look into the possibility of transplanting the hormone of one plant into another to see if it offers a better defense against pests.

Basic gardening practices have a lot to do with discouraging (or inviting) insect troubles. Pay attention to these first:

*Give plants good soil.* Naturally well-fed vegetables and fruits have less appeal to bugs and more resistance to damage or disease. Imbalanced feeding, especially of nitrogen, can increase populations of aphids and other troublemakers. Rich soil also ensures healthy roots, which resist nematode infestation, along with adequate trace-element supplies and moisture—both factors in making plants unattractive to many pests.

*Choose good seed and plants.* Buy varieties with built-in resistance to bacterial or virus diseases, since insects

*Late fall cultivation, after most of your crops are harvested, destroys pests' winter hideouts and exposes their eggs and pupae to the elements.*

have been harvested and before hard frosts set in. That's fatal to many pests that winter in the soil.

*Handpick insects whenever possible.* Don't pass up the chance to debug a few plants as you tend the garden, cultivate or mulch a row, or pick some produce. Simply brush beetles or caterpillars or any other villains into a jar of kerosene or detergent. (Don't just tread them into the ground, though—many are surprisingly tough and may survive.)

## Barriers, Beneficial Bugs, and Bacteria

Three prime pest-control measures revolve around physical barriers and/or traps, carnivorous predators or parasites, and insect diseases that cut pest populations in both the current season and successive generations. One good early-spring barrier idea is the cutworm collar. Use a ring of tar paper, cardboard, or a tin can with both ends removed, shoved an inch or two down into the soil around seedlings just coming up or transplanted.

are drawn to weaker plant growth. Some vegetables and grains also have been bred to mature ahead of the cycle of certain pests, while others ripen after their seasonal visit. Also pick varieties and crops that grow well in your climate and soil.

*Rotate crops.* Many insect pests that tend to attack specific crops live and breed in the ground from season to season. They can be starved to a considerable extent by never repeatedly planting the same or similar crops in the same location. It requires just a little planning, which is simplified if you can group together related plants, such as cabbage, cauliflower, broccoli, and brussels sprouts; cucumbers and squash; and tomatoes and potatoes.

*Plow in the fall.* Turn your vegetable garden thoroughly in late fall or early winter after the majority of crops

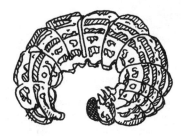

*Cutworms feed at night, severing the stems of seedlings and transplants.*

It's effective against other marauders like slugs, as well as cutworms. Once plants outgrow the protective collars, they're past the critical stage of susceptibility.

Another old remedy is Tanglefoot adhesive, a sticky compound applied to tree trunks either in wallpaperlike strips or by pressurized spray-on containers, which helps keep pests that are overwintering on the ground from crawling up into the trees when they hatch in spring. More recently, diatomaceous earth has been cited as a sharp deterrent to tree pests, in particular, codling moths and leaf hoppers. Dust the ground around the tree's perimeter and paint the trunk with a

*A simple trap, baited with molasses and water, will let you know when codling moths arrive at your apple trees and will catch quite a few of these pests, too.*

solution of diatomaceous earth and flax soap for a sticky spreader. The mixture remains effective for over a month. Seed companies add diatomaceous earth to seed packets to curtail the egg or larval stages of pests like the cabbage looper and bean and cucumber beetle.

One old Pennsylvania orchardist suspends a paper cup containing a molasses-and-water mixture in his fruit and nut trees to trap codling moths. Using a piece of wire fashioned into a loop to hold the cup and a hook to put over a limb, he hangs each so it is about 8 inches below the branch. In it goes a mix of 1 part blackstrap molasses and 9 parts water, filled to the halfway mark. For the average-size tree he uses three or four, and reports he finds them crammed with codling moths.

More trapping notions: Cages made of aluminum fly screen will keep

*A sticky band around a tree's trunk deters leaf-eating caterpillars, such as gypsy moths, that climb up the trunk to feed. Circling the tree with duct tape and then coating the tape with Tanglefoot creates a barrier that's sticky on both sides to keep pests from crawling over or under.*

out the cabbage maggot and other root-burrowing larvae of flies, says Olkowski, who adds, "We turned over clay flowerpots set among the plants to collect snails that wander in during the warm, sunny day and emerge to feed at night. Rolled up newspapers give earwigs places to hide." Lettuce, spinach or cabbage leaves, or slices of raw potato spread along the vegetable rows overnight will collect slugs, snails, cutworms, and grubs—easily gathered and disposed of the next day. Lengths of board can be employed the same way. Aluminum mulch in strips along plant rows confuses aphids, who see the sky reflected and fly off.

Of course, Ruth Stout's beer-baiting idea for catching slugs and snails has become famous. All that's needed is a shallow pan with about 2 inches of stale beer in it, set out where these pests are causing plant damage. Unable to resist the evils of drink (actually the scent of brewer's yeast), the slugs either drown or get so tipsy they can't escape.

Already well-known among the benevolent bugs that help keep pest

*Both adult ladybird beetles and their spiny, alligator-like larvae help gardeners by dining on small, soft-bodied pests such as aphids, scales, mealybugs, and spider mites.*

*The larvae of these delicate-looking insects are voracious consumers of aphids, scale insects, small caterpillars, and thrips.*

populations at a minimum is the ladybug, or ladybird beetle. One ladybug will eat 40 to 50 aphids a day, and a cup or two of ladybugs would be enough for the average garden. These beetles vary their diet, too, becoming gluttons on scale insects, alfalfa weevils, Colorado potato beetles, and other soft-bodied pests.

Let's not forget some other beneficial insects that have been around a long time. A lacewing larva—one of the "eatingest" creatures in the world despite its dainty name—can consume hundreds of plant lice in a few hours and shows no signs of a dulled appetite. The praying mantis, an odd-looking relative of the grasshopper, is another hearty eater, favoring caterpillars and mites among many insects.

Trichogramma wasps, tiny parasites of codling moth larvae (that's the worm in the apple!) come on cards for introduction into fruit tree sections. The tricho wasp lays its eggs on the eggs or larvae of other insects. Thus it breaks the life cycle of the pest insect before it has a chance to develop into an adult and lay more eggs. It does a good job on corn earworm, corn borer, looper, fruit moth (codling), pecan nut case borer, leaf tier, cabbage worm, tomato worm—and will remain in an area as long as there are eggs and larvae on which to lay its eggs.

There are bigger helpers, too. Toads and frogs eat insects constantly and are worth their weight in emeralds to the gardener. So are insect-eating birds, shrews, bats, snakes, and fish in ponds or pools. Bantams, ducks, and geese all have reputations for keeping gardens and orchards pest-free.

Two specific insect diseases have also come along to aid in biological debugging. When caterpillars are the problem (cabbage worms, etc.) you can use *Bacillus thuringiensis* (BT), a bacterial infection that's over 90 percent effective. The most recent tests by Agricultural Research Service ento-

mologists also show BT kills Japanese beetle larvae, although it had been considered useful only against moth species.

For Japanese beetles, too, the milky disease spore—which keeps them from being a major pest in the Far East—can easily be introduced like a "talc treatment" on the soil. The disease, caused by *Bacillus popillae,* infects the beetle in the grub stage, turning it milky white and eventually killing it. The disease is further spread by the diseased grubs or carcasses of the dead ones infecting other individuals.

## Take a Bug to Tea

Teas that turn off bugs are another valuable idea from yesteryear. One of the best "brews" for chasing unwanted pests consists of a blended mixture of garlic, chives, or hot peppers—or a combination of them—in an equal amount of water, with a teaspoonful of plain detergent to help the protective mixture cling to plants. Teas made of wormwood or horseradish are very effective. Slugs, crickets, houseflies, and many tender-bodied insects don't like wormwood. To prepare a tea, gather early-summer leaves in the morning, dry them in shade (or get some dried leaves), then cover with water and bring to a boil. Remove and dilute with 4 parts water, stirring ten minutes to mix thoroughly. For horseradish tea, pour boiling water over the leaves, then dilute with 4 parts water.

*A broken clay flowerpot makes a cool, moist haven that invites insect-eating toads to make their home in your garden.*

Garden columnist George "Doc" Abraham adds some "kitchen arsenal" suggestions: "Take a cup each of fresh spearmint leaves and green onion tops, about ½ cup horseradish root and leaves, and red hot peppers; then run these through the blender, adding a little water. Pour into a gallon of water and add ½ cup of liquid detergent. Dilute by adding ½ cup to 1 quart of water. Makes a good all-purpose organic spray.

"Chop up about 3 ounces of garlic bulbs and soak them for 24 hours in about 2 teaspoons of mineral oil. Then add 1 pint of water and ¼ ounce of liquid soap. Mix well and filter through a fine-mesh screen. Try this against wireworms, cutworms, slugs, and whitefly."

(Be sure to test any homemade spray on just one plant before you spray your entire crop!)

## Use a Good-Neighbor Policy

One of the most interesting weapons against insects is companion planting. Beans and potatoes, for example, make good garden mates; the beans are said to dispell Colorado potato beetles, while the potatoes repel Mexican bean beetles. Other combinations include soybeans planted near corn against chinch bugs and Japanese beetles; tomatoes near asparagus against the asparagus beetle; horseradish or flax in rows between potatoes against the potato bug.

At the same time don't plant crops together that are attacked by the same enemies. Keep tomatoes, for instance, away from corn, since both are victims of the European corn borer. Potatoes troubled by the flea beetle shouldn't have tomatoes planted near them or in the same bed after them.

Herbs head the list of plants that repel insects. Pests simply don't swarm or nibble on their strong-smelling, strong-tasting leaves. Spotting various herbs throughout the garden as a "pest patrol" can keep many troublemakers feeling uninvited. Savory, for instance, has a reputation as the "bean herb." Younger seedlings spaced at intervals when that crop is planted will help protect the vegetable. Basil helps tomatoes overcome both insects and disease. Set seedlings about 1 foot apart in the row alongside plants. Mints such as spearmint, peppermint, apple mint, and lemon and orange mint (bergamot) do a good job of keeping pests from the whole cabbage family—broccoli, cauliflower, brussels sprouts, and the like.

Other bug-repelling herbs include tansy, a fernlike plant that keeps Japanese beetles off grapes and cane fruits; rue, a hardy perennial that has bitter blue-green leaves very offensive to pests and helps dispel them among vegetables, flowers, shrubs, or trees; oregano, effective near vine crops; pennyroyal, a strongly aromatic herb; and lavender, a soft-gray-foliaged plant with a vigorous, cool scent that grows well in rock gardens.

## Breeding More Resistant Beans

More help is on the way, too. At Cornell University, workers have discovered that some bean plants resist damage by leafhoppers better than others because their leaves are more thickly furnished with tiny hooked hairs that snare and hold the insects. The hoppers stop eating and reproducing and soon die. As a result, breeders are at work in a new direction toward bean plants with more hair, and therefore fewer leafhoppers and thus more beans at harvest time.

And a study at the Agricultural Research Service lab in Corvallis, Oregon, has shown that plants under stress give off larger amounts of ethylene gas than what healthy, normally functioning plants give off. Insects appear to be aware of such indicators of tissue decay. Bark beetles, for instance, attack sick trees, which apparently release gases that the beetles sense and hone in on. Keeping a plant in good health, therefore, is a prime means to avoiding insect damage.

*June 1977*

*Marigolds and nasturtiums have wide reputations for their ability to discourage both root pests (nematodes or eelworms) and such aboveground insects as aphids and asparagus beetles.*

# A Catchy Approach to Pest Control

*Timothy White*

A s an entomologist, I get a lot of questions about insect traps. Do they work? For many pests, the answer is yes. Trapping for control is practical when the insect is causing indirect damage (not feeding on the fruit or desirable part of the plant) and a low level of damage is tolerable. Sometimes, the trap may not control the pest but will signal its arrival in the garden, allowing you to use other controls more effectively.

A good trap should be easy to construct, cheap, simple to clean, reasonably weatherproof, as selective as possible, and, of course, attractive to the intended prey. This final characteristic depends on how well the trap mimics something in the insect's daily life: a food source, mating attractant, resting or egg-laying place, and so on. A good example is the commercially available Japanese beetle traps that rely on both color and odor attraction.

Traps are the best bet against apple maggots, aphids, yellow jackets, earwigs, codling moths, and more.

## Control Traps

Traps for control attempt to reduce the pest population by trapping large numbers of pests at or before their damaging period. Here are my favorite ways to trap the following pests:

**Earwig**

- *Apple maggot flies* like to lay their eggs on apples. Red 3½-inch wooden balls coated with Tack Trap and hung in open areas of apple trees will capture adult females as they search for egg-laying sites. Tartar Red Dark enamel (Sherwin-Williams Company) has been the most attractive red paint in extensive tests in Massachusetts. For full dwarf trees (9 feet or less), two traps per tree should be plenty, while six to eight may be needed for full-size trees on seedling rootstock. Once hung in the trees, they should be recoated every two weeks. Try thinning the Tack Trap with Varsol thinner (available at hardware stores) to make brush application possible.

**Apple maggot fly**

- *Codling moths* will flock to a pot of 2 parts vinegar to 1 part molasses. Hang one from an apple limb, and you'll catch dozens of moths. Clean out moths and replenish the liquid to maintain odor attraction.

- *Earwigs* are active at night and will chew irregular holes in most crops but prefer loose heads of lettuce, Chinese cabbage, and flowers. Since they like to congregate in confined, dark spaces during the day, lure them with pieces of corrugated cardboard placed near susceptible crops. After a few days, gather the cardboard in midafternoon and burn.

- *Sap beetles* (black with yellow markings, ⅓-inch long) are drawn by smells from fermenting berries, melons, squash, tomatoes, and peaches. Frequent, thorough picking will keep them out of the garden. But if they invade, place a half-filled soup can of vinegar near the crop. Fruit flies in summer kitchens and around wine-making also can't resist a one-way trip into this trap.

**Sap beetle**

- *Aphids* apparently cue in on the yellow component of the pale green growing tips of most plants. They can even be found congregating on yellow pieces of laundry hung outside. Bright yellow floor tiles or painted fiberboard (10-by-10-inch) coated with Tack Trap or petroleum jelly and placed on stakes near susceptible plants will catch enormous numbers of aphids and can slow the population boom long enough to allow predators to exert con-

**Aphids**

trol. U.S. Department of Agriculture researchers have shown that a similar sticky yellow panel (5-by-72-inch) suspended several inches above the plants in a greenhouse bench will also eliminate greenhouse whitefly.

- *Yellow jackets* could be voted the most unwelcome summer and fall picnic guest, even beating ants. If you can find their subterranean nest, you can stop them. Press a cone-shaped emergence trap made of window screen over the hole on a cool night. Place a clear plastic shoe box over the cone. The workers will leave the nest, enter the trap, and be unable to either leave the box or reenter the cone. In a week or two the colony will die. Stuff rags and dirt around the trap's base to prevent escapes, and check the trap every few nights.

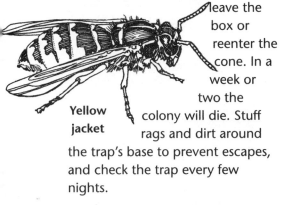

**Yellow jacket**

**Slug**

- *Slugs* and *squash bugs* go into hiding every morning. If you can catch these nocturnal pests in their daytime retreats, a determined application of your heel may be all that's needed. Provide these shelters by laying boards near affected plants, and inspect them in midday. Repeat daily.

## Monitoring Traps

The key to success in many commercial pest management programs is knowing when a particular pest is active.

- *Codling moth, cabbage looper, San Jose scale, peach tree borer, corn earworm, several leafrollers,* and dozens of other insects can be monitored by pheromones, imitations of the female insect's scent. These ultrapowerful attractants (one ten-millionth of an ounce will draw males from half a mile) have been commercially synthesized and are available both alone and in trap setups. Some companies now make reusable traps, but due to the extreme sensitivity of pheromones, the same trap should be used for the same pest each year, since enough pheromone is absorbed by the trap itself to make it attractive.

- The *plum curculio* is dark brown and ¼ inch long with a prominent snout. It's present in all tree-fruit crops from just before to a few weeks after bloom. If the orchard is near wooded areas, it can devastate the crop, causing early drop so little fruit remains at harvest. White (8-by-10-inch) sticky cards hung chest high (one per tree) will catch the first immigrants. Then jar the limbs over a bedsheet or tarp twice daily to remove the beetles from your trees. To increase attractiveness,

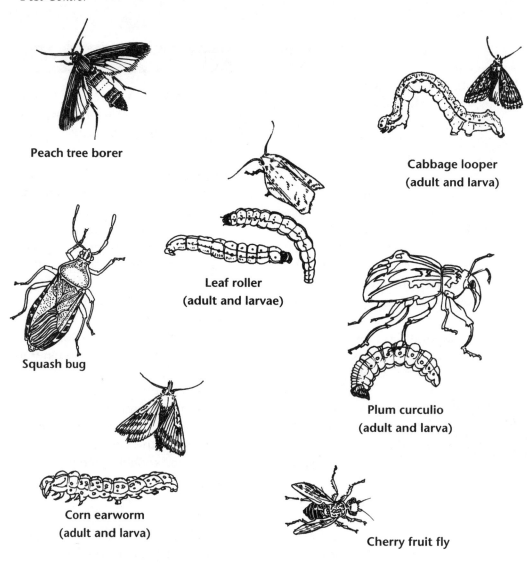

**Peach tree borer**

**Cabbage looper**
**(adult and larva)**

**Leaf roller**
**(adult and larvae)**

**Squash bug**

**Plum curculio**
**(adult and larva)**

**Corn earworm**
**(adult and larva)**

**Cherry fruit fly**

hang a small vial of Avon Apple Blossom perfume beneath the card, its top covered with aluminum foil that's been pinpricked to release the odor slowly.

- *Cherry fruit flies* and *immature apple-maggot flies* can be monitored with red sticky balls. For very early detection, use the sticky yellow panels and attract the flies while they're still maturing and feeding on aphid honeydew. They're attracted then to the same cues as the aphids, but once mature, they'll ignore the panel for the red ball. Hung in mid-May in cherry trees, the panels will reveal the presence of the cherry fruit fly. For either fly, hang the traps on the south side of each tree at the edge of the orchard to catch the first immigrants.

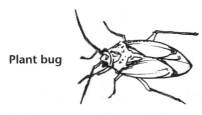

**Plant bug**

- *Plant bugs* as a group, and the *tarnished plant bug* in particular, are active around bloom in orchards and can be detected using a white 8-by-10-inch sticky panel hung from an outer branch 2½ feet off the ground. Tests in Massachusetts have shown that the panel should not reflect ultraviolet light, so use a gloss white paint to create this mimic of apple-bud reflectance. European apple sawfly, whose larvae cause the meandering scar on fruit, can also be monitored using this trap.

In all cases, where you place the trap is very important, especially where the attraction is visual. Clear away foliage and shoots for 18 inches around a trap to ensure high visibility. The trap should always be placed in or near the crop to be protected or monitored, since the crop itself has a strong attraction to the pest. When the attractant is a scent, care must be taken not to contaminate or mask it with other strong odors.

Whatever the trapping situation, you must first understand the pest's behavior, then attempt to include your trap, as unobtrusively as possible, into its daily routine. To think like your intended prey will help in designing an effective ruse.

*May 1983*

**Rising above Sowbugs**
I've had a constant battle with sowbugs over my strawberries. No matter what mulch I used, they usually got eight out of ten berries—until this year. I had accumulated a lot of plastic berry baskets, so I cut a hole in the bottom of each just big enough to thread a blossom cluster through. I place a basket upside down over a plant and gently pull the flower stem through the hole. The berries develop off the ground and out of reach of the sowbugs.

*Johnnie Aven*
*Carrollton, Texas*
*January 1987*

**Sowbug**

# Creating a Haven for Beneficial Insects

## Michael Lafavore

Growing as many kinds of plants as you can is the key to keeping them in your garden.

If you want some tips on how to plant your garden, take a walk through a wild meadow and see how Mother Nature plants hers. Does the vegetation grow in rows, each type of plant clustered in its appointed place? Not likely. In nature, a complex profusion of different plants grows together. Plants, animals, and insects coexist, and the environment is fairly stable and balanced. No one species is allowed to reign.

Nature keeps the populations of the insects we call pests in check by providing natural enemies, the ones known to us as beneficial insects. That's well-understood. But few of us fully appreciate the vast number of potentially beneficial insects that inhabit the land around us. It's not only the handful we read about so frequently, but dozens, perhaps hundreds, of kinds of insects.

You'll find many of the beneficial insects native to your region in Mother Nature's meadow, especially if the meadow includes the edge of the woods, a running brook, and perhaps a bit of marsh. By comparison, how many of those insects are in your garden? If you're growing strictly corn, beans, and tomatoes in the midst of an acre or two of close-cropped grass, it will be only a few. If you have flowers, fruiting trees and shrubs, and herbs along with your vegetables, perhaps near a weedy hedgerow, you will have more. The number will increase with the diversity of the planting you create.

The mere presence of pests like aphids isn't enough to lure predators to your garden and keep them there. Beneficial insects need places to breed, and most of them need other sources of food.

Take, for example, the huge family of minuscule wasps that parasitize several kinds of pests, from aphids to Mexican bean beetles. The adults lay eggs on the body of the pest, and when the larvae hatch out, they consume the host. The egg-laying adults need nectar for food to continue breeding and producing eggs and for

*With a little encouragement from you, tiny wasps will protect your plants from bigger pests. Don't destroy tomato hornworms you find covered with the white, cigar-shaped cocoons of parasitic wasps—the wasps will hatch into a new generation of trouble-free pest control for your garden.*

seeking out the pests. They need other plants for rest and shelter. These essentials may be provided by trees for one species, flowers for another, herbs or weeds for still another.

## Weeding Out Pests

One scientist who has done a lot of research on the positive role of weeds in garden ecology is Dr. Miguel Altieri, an assistant professor at the University of California's Division of Biological Control. One study he conducted in Florida proved that damage to corn by fall armyworms was higher in clean fields than in plots where the corn was interplanted with cockleburs, dandelion, and other weeds. He cites numerous studies showing that interplanting vegetables with weeds can significantly lower pest damage. As far back as 1936, four times more parasitized codling moths were counted in orchards that were uncultivated than in those that were clean.

"A weed is simply a plant whose virtue has not yet been discovered," says Altieri. "When we plow down a field of weeds, we may be destroying a habitat for beneficial insects. We're chasing out all the good bugs and leaving the garden to the pests."

There are a number of theories as to why weeds have such an effect on pests. In addition to providing homes for beneficials, scientists believe that weeds may produce odors that confuse or repel pests. The weeds' smell may also attract the beneficials. And there is evidence that many pests find crops with their eyes. They actually see the plants highlighted against bare soil. A border of weeds can camouflage the garden and keep pests away. Weeds also serve as home for neutral insects, which can serve as alternate food for some predators.

Altieri and his colleagues aren't suggesting that we let weeds have their run in our gardens. But letting selected weeds grow in certain places can help to create a better ecological balance. Take goldenrod, for example. It supports more than 75 species of beneficial insects. And over 30 beneficials call the common pigweed home.

The approach Altieri advocates is for gardeners to allow weed strips to grow every ten rows or so, or to leave weeds in ditches or to let a weedy border grow up around the garden. Flowering weeds such as dandelion, wild carrot, lamb's-quarters, goldenrod, and evening primrose seem to be particularly effective. Allow the weeds to grow until they begin to shade your vegetables, then cut them back to about 1 foot high.

Red and white clover have also proven to be refuges for numerous beneficial insects. Altieri suggest growing two or three "islands" of clover near the garden, then mowing them one at a time over the season to force the insects from the clover into the garden.

Planting herbs in and around the garden can also help control insect pests. Mint, for example, is believed to repel cabbage butterflies, ants, black fleas, and aphids. Rue, savory, basil, sage, lavender, thyme, garlic, and tansy are also said to repel many pests. Most of these have flowers that are potentially valuable nectar sources for beneficials, too.

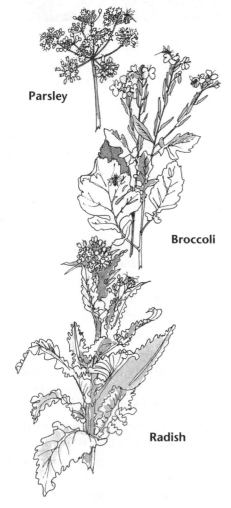

**Parsley**

**Broccoli**

**Radish**

*If you'd rather avoid growing weeds to woo beneficials to your garden, let more desirable garden plants do the job. The flowers of parsley, broccoli, radishes, mustard, and mint are appealing to beneficial bees, wasps, and flies. Just let a few plants flower, and you're in beneficial business.*

## Beneficial Companion Plant/Insect Interactions

| Companion plants | Pests | Factors involved |
| --- | --- | --- |
| Grapes with blackberry, raspberry, and Johnson grass | Corn earworm, boll worm, Pacific mite | Alternate prey for predators |
| Cotton with ragweed family and sour dock | Tomato fruitworm | Increase of predators |
| Cabbage with winter cress, horseradish, peppergrass, and mustard family | Aphid | Increase of predators and parasites |
| Collards with ragweed | Yellow scale, Western striped flea beetle | Chemical interactions |
| Brussels sprouts with wild oats, knotweed, lamb's-quarters, cole, mustard, and common nightshade | Cabbageworm, aphid | Increase of predators and parasites |
| Brussels sprouts with lamb's-quarters | Whitefly | |
| Brussels sprouts with knotweed | Armyworm | |
| Brussels sprouts with radish | Cabbageworm | |
| Beans with wire grass and goose grass | Leafhoppers | Chemical interactions |
| Peaches with strawberries | Strawberry leafroller, Oriental fruit moth | Increase of parasites |
| Tomato with cabbage | Diamondback moth | Chemical repellency or masking |
| Corn with peanut | Corn borer | Increase of spiders |
| Tomato with cotton | Flea beetles | Chemical repellency |

## "Weed Juice" to Halt Pest Damage

You don't have to grow weeds near the garden to get some of their beneficial effects. Studies at the University of Georgia found that when a blended mixture of wild amaranth leaves and water was sprayed on soybeans, it attracted more *Trichogramma* wasps, parasites of the corn earworm. Apparently the "weed juice" stimulated the wasps' appetites and brought them to the soybean field. Similar results were obtained with the use of wild geranium leaves.

To make weed juice, blend 1 ounce of leaves or stems with 1 quart of warm water. Apply the spray to your crops, then repeat every two weeks.

Herb extracts can be sprayed on crops to repel insects, as well. In a test conducted at the Organic Gardening and Farming Research Center, eucalyptus extract sprayed on potato plants halved the number of Colorado potato beetles. A nasturtium spray was similarly effective.

## Intercrop Barriers

If you don't want to grow weeds or herbs right in the garden, simply intercropping your vegetables will hamper pests. Insect pests tend to spread more easily and remain longer when crops are grown in pure stands. So alternate the rows of vegetables, making sure that one crop doesn't shade another. Disease can spread unchecked through entire sections of the garden if one kind of plant predominates there. But intercropping can check its spread as well.

Your garden's location can also be a factor in pest control. By planting near the border of a forest or meadow, you can benefit from the edge effect. The numbers of beneficials are higher around the edges of these diverse environments. Tall weeds, trees, and shrubs may also prevent some pests from being blown into the garden by the wind.

When we grow our highly domesticated vegetables in neat, weed-free rows, we are ignoring nature's model. Scientists like Altieri are beginning to develop models of how this new, better-balanced ecology can be created in our landscapes.

For the gardener, the keys to this new approach are observation and experimentation. Look at nature around you, and learn about the mixes of plants that thrive on their own and the societies of insects that operate among them. Try to recreate some of these mixes or similar ones in your garden. The garden needn't be a jumble. Create islands in the garden and the lawn. Convert part of the lawn to meadow. And develop borders that are a blend of useful fruiting and flowering plants and those stately strangers you may have been calling weeds.

*March 1981*

# Baking Soda Fights Fungi

*Yutaka Tatsuoka*

Sodium bicarbonate has long been known as an instant cure for heartburn. Now scientists at the Institute of Physical and Chemical Research, with laboratories near Tokyo, Japan, have come up with a new use for the popular antacid. They have shown that it is also effective in preventing attacks of fungi that infest cucumber and muskmelon plants, particularly those grown in greenhouses.

Sodium bicarbonate also gives off carbon dioxide, which is essential to photosynthesis.

The institute hopes to put the new finding into extensive use in two or three years with the cooperation of government-run agricultural experiment stations scattered throughout Japan.

Yutaka Arimoto, a research staff member, was working on extracting a fungicide from mandarin oranges when, quite by accident, he found that the sodium bicarbonate solution he was using to carry the fungicide could itself control the fungus.

An alkaline environment discourages the growth of most fungi, according to Tomomasa Satomi, senior engineer at the institute. He suspects that the slight alkalinity of the sodium bicarbonate solution (pH 8.3)

> This homely household product works best on cucumber and bean fungus.

was responsible for suppressing fungus development in mandarin oranges, as well as cucumber and muskmelon plants.

Vegetables grown in a greenhouse are susceptible to various fungus diseases. The institute formed a research team and concluded that sodium bicarbonate is as effective as any conventional agricultural chemical in fighting fungus diseases of cucumbers and beans.

It was 64 percent effective against *Helminthosporium* leaf spot in rice, 93.5 percent against cucumber powdery mildew, and 49 percent against rice rhizopus. It was also tested on seedling blight, bacterial soft rot disease in Chinese cabbage, cowpea

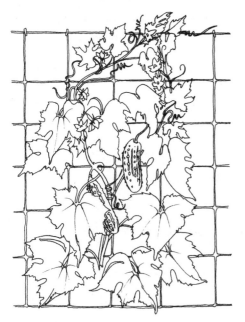

*A baking soda solution of 1 teaspoon of baking soda in 1 quart of water helps control the powdery mildew that plagues your pickles.*

gray mold, cucumber anthracnose, cucumber scab, grape ripe rot, *Alternaria* leaf spot in apple, and peach brown rot, but the results were not as encouraging.

To verify the results on a nationwide basis, agricultural experiment stations in Kochi, Saitama, Miyazaki, and Nara prefectures were asked to join the research project. Effects of fungus diseases of muskmelon, strawberries, eggplants, as well as cucumbers, are being investigated.

Sprayed on plants as it is, sodium bicarbonate will not easily stick to the leaves. It should be dissolved in water, and a tackifier (like starch) should be added to the solution. A spray containing from 0.2 to 0.4 percent of sodium bicarbonate should be applied once a week or so.

Sodium bicarbonate is a very benign chemical. A sodium bicarbonate solution decomposes into water, carbon dioxide, and sodium ions. Carbon dioxide is one of the essential raw materials needed when a plant produces nutrients through photosynthesis. In a greenhouse, carbon dioxide tends to be lacking, so much so that some growers supply it artificially. Carbon dioxide from sodium bicarbonate may help promote the growth of greenhouse vegetables.

*September 1978*

# Get the Right Hoe for Your Weeds

## David Tresemer

**W**hen you say "hoe," most people think of a 5-inch square of sheet metal attached to the end of a pole. It is a versatile tool for moving stuff, particularly toward oneself. It is especially good for mixing cement, and at least half of the neighbors' hoes I have tried out have had remnants of cement at the juncture of the blade and handle. I suppose this cement may have had something to do with my friends' outlook on weeding with a hoe—they find it hard work and dread it. I am more apt to blame the design of the tool.

How to choose a hoe to suit your weeding style.

*The author's favorite hoe features a socket for easy handle repairs and good-quality steel that holds a sharp edge well.*

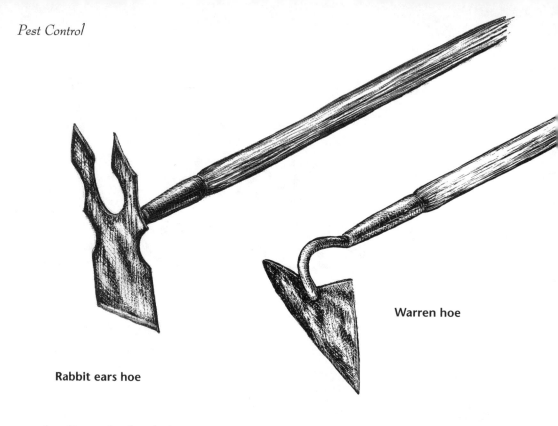

**Warren hoe**

**Rabbit ears hoe**

*The rabbit ears hoe dates back to Roman times. The blade design has its roots in digging hoes, not in weeding hoes.*

*The pointed head of the warren hoe makes it useful for shaping rows and furrows and hilling plants.*

Most modern hoes seem designed for chopping and digging rather than slicing weeds. The angle of the blade to the handle is close to 90 degrees, and the blade is square and heavy. When it's lifted a few feet in the air, it hits the ground with a wallop. The best have eye sockets for the handle to fit through. Cheaper spot-welded versions tend to break after heavy use.

One popular version of digging hoe I call the rabbit ears hoe. The single edge on one side is balanced by a pair of sharpened blades on the other side, like two mattocks. Other versions have just the rabbit ears—they sometimes have three or four teeth and are called potato hooks or simply cultivators. A third kind of digging hoe is the heart-shaped warren hoe, which is particularly good for dragging through loosened earth to form a furrow for potatoes.

A weeding hoe is quite different from a digging hoe. The blade is lighter, with a longer and sharper cutting edge on a narrow blade with rounded shoulders. (It is *not* good for mixing cement!) The angle between blade and handle is acute. Use the hoe while standing erect, with both hands holding the handle, thumbs pointing upward. The handle, also lighter, is longer, about shoulder height. The idea is to move this knife parallel to and just beneath the surface, thereby cutting the weeds at their root crowns.

The best time to hoe is when the weeds are only a few inches high or less, about the size of alfalfa sprouts. Then you can move quite rapidly down the aisles in the garden, the blade slicing just beneath the surface. (Later, when crop plants are larger and the soil warmer, a good mulch will do the job.) Move along with the line of the edge slightly angled to the direction of travel to avoid bulldozing the soil. By gently twisting the handle, you can work between the plants in the row without damaging stems or root systems.

There are three reasons why I prefer a weeding hoe and this approach to weeding. First, weeding takes up a lot less of my summer if it is done frequently when the weeds are just sprouted, rather than later when they must be hacked to be discouraged. Second, the weed seeds below 1½ inches of soil are left dormant, while the seeds in the top layer are sprouted and finished off early in the season. Third, few people can stoop without straining muscles, and there's no sense crippling myself pulling weeds when I can use a weeding hoe while walking down the rows.

My favorite weeding hoe comes from Holland. It is forged, not welded; has a socket, not a tang; and has a hardened steel blade which will take an exquisite edge. It is closest to what is called an onion hoe in this country, but it excels in many other crops as well.

Another sort of weeding hoe that is sharp and can be used standing is the scuffle hoe (a corruption of the Dutch name for this tool, *schoffel*).

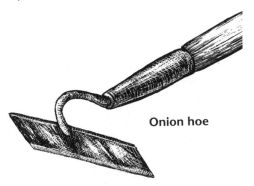

**Onion hoe**

*The onion hoe's blade has a slim profile for working close to plants and a good angle of attack. Kept sharp, it makes short work of weeds.*

**Scuffle (or *schoffel*) hoe**

*The scuffle hoe is meant to be shoved through the soil, cutting below the surface. The earth must be soft, or the blade will skip out instead of slicing in.*

Here the angle between the blade and handle is oblique, and the hoe is pushed, often with one hand. The idea is to achieve the right angle of thrust so that the sharp edge will glide along just beneath the surface. When it works, it is quite slick. It often doesn't, however, but dives in, then jumps up above the surface like a dolphin. For 6-foot-wide landscaped borders in which you don't want to walk, and for clearing beneath low-spreading plants, a sharp push hoe is the best alternative. For normal garden use, I prefer my weeding hoe.

One version of a push hoe oscillates so that when pulled back, the angle of the blade to the ground becomes just right. Pushed and pulled in short strokes for tough places, it attacks the weeds from all flanks. In cleaner ground, it can be pushed and pulled for long distances. The very best of these is a recent import from Switzerland. I call it a stirrup hoe because that's what it looks like. It is more expensive than American-made versions, but I have always been willing to spend a few dollars more for a durable, high-quality tool. The blade of the Swiss stirrup hoe is hardened steel that can be sharpened, and it's thinner than the American versions—it cuts rather than bulldozes. The part that governs the angle of oscillation is machined for accuracy, not stamped from sheet steel.

I once saw a Danny Kaye comedy in which he played a gallant swordsman. He cut through a group of candles, but they did not fall. His

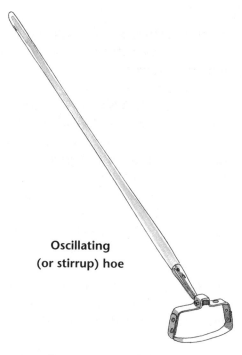

**Oscillating (or stirrup) hoe**

*The oscillating (or stirrup) hoe is an effective weeding tool. Its thin, sharp blade cuts on both the push and pull strokes.*

enemy sneered that he had missed, but Kaye confidently blew lightly and the candles toppled over. So too with a fine hoe. It may slice so finely that the weed is left standing, although the truth is that it has been cut at its crown and will wither within the hour. I had to learn not to be put off by this apparent ineffectiveness, since I, like most gardeners I know, wanted to see the evidence of my weeding labors in the form of moved earth and garden aisles that looked like storm-tossed seas. Now that I've learned the right way to use a weed hoe, I wouldn't change back to digging weeds for anything.

*February 1982*

# Chapter 9

# Extending (and Surviving) the Season

# Growing Plants in Hotbeds and Cold Frames

## Gordon L'Allemand

Expand your planting program, grow your own varieties . . . and enjoy yourself. These are just some of the advantages of using the hotbed and cold frame.

Here's how your gardening can *mean* and *return* more this year: Start your own plants in a hotbed or cold frame—and start 'em now for a head start on spring!

### Why Build Hotbeds and Cold Frames?

If you have even a fairly large vegetable garden and flower beds, you should learn to grow most of your own plants. You will save money, raise superior plants, get plants that are directly acclimatized to your locality, and you can produce a far greater variety of plants.

A great advantage in growing your own plants in hotbeds and cold frames is that you can send off for seeds from any part of the world and thus raise and experiment with cultivars and with new plants unobtainable from local seed men. Nurseries usually limit themselves to a few good-selling cultivars of plants. If you want to experiment with some hybrids or with new cultivars developed abroad or elsewhere in the United States, you should by all means learn to grow your own plants.

A very good man to tell us how to grow our own plants is Val Baima of Baima Farm, Grass Valley, California. Baima has eight acres, feeds his wife and himself the year around on produce from his farm, and sells locally and ships his dried fruits to all parts of the United States and abroad.

Baima makes his living from growing fruit and garden produce, and he is an experimental scientist as well— constantly purchasing new cultivars of vegetables and new strains from far places, also developing better strains from produce grown on his farm.

"What is the difference between a hotbed and a cold frame?" Baima begins. "If you want to grow peppers, tomatoes, eggplants, or any of the other heat-loving plants, a hotbed is best to grow them in. A cold frame has the same construction as a hotbed, except that there is no heat used inside it. In a cold frame you can propagate such cold-loving plants as cabbage, broccoli, cauliflower. Or you can use your cold frames to taper off and harden plants that have been moved into them from the hotbeds, to get them hardened between the hotbed and setting them out into open garden or field."

There are two types of hotbeds: One is heated by a great deal of fermenting straw or fresh manure (preferably horse or chicken) that has been placed in a pit 2½ feet deep. The manure is packed down to a depth of 18 inches and is well-watered to soak. Then you shovel into the pit 5 to 6 inches of composted soil or good, rich

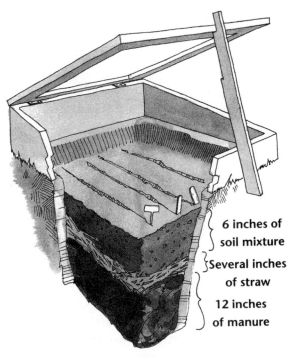

6 inches of soil mixture

Several inches of straw

12 inches of manure

*A thick layer of horse or chicken manure, moistened and topped with straw, provides the heat in a traditional hotbed.*

topsoil. This soil—which will make the seedbed—must be sieved fine.

The second kind of hotbed is made by arranging electric heating cables, 5 inches below the surface of the topsoil seedbed. No manure is needed for heating this type of bed. The coils produce a steady heat, day and night, while the manure is effective for a few weeks.

The electrically heated hotbed is much more expensive than the old-fashioned manure-heated hotbed. For the small to average gardener the manure-heated hotbed is best.

The frames and tops of hotbeds and cold frames are made the same

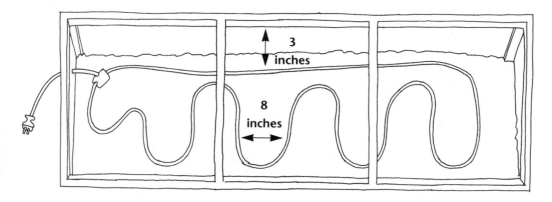

3
inches

8
inches

*A soil heating cable supplies steady heat to a hotbed.*
*Place the cable so it is 3 inches from the edge of the bed and its wires are 8 inches apart.*

way. A heavy frame of 2-inch-thick planking 1 foot wide should be made to cover the bed and to act as a base for the hinged or removable lid or top. Baima uses inexpensive glasslike Sun Ray cloth. It won't break and lasts a long time. For permanent frame tops you may use glass windows.

Planting the seeds: In the germinating hotbeds or cold frames, plant seeds plentifully, cover them lightly, and keep the rows 1 inch apart. You may later thin out to suit. In planting lots of seeds remember this: while most seeds will produce sturdy plantlets, others will be thin or weaklings. With plentiful planting you keep only the finest and sturdiest of the plants.

A *must* to remember: The grower must constantly watch moisture and heat with an eagle eye. You must not allow the heat to rise too high, or above 75 to 80 degrees, while the plants are small. If the growing beds get too hot—and there is no ventila-

tion—the hundreds of plants may easily damp off and die. To ventilate you simply raise the lids a bit. Leave lids closed at night.

## How to Build Hotbeds and Cold Frames

Use 2-inch-thick rough lumber for all frames. Have these planks from 12 to 14 inches wide, 10 inches above the surface of the ground. Always locate the beds in the warmest spot possible, your best southwestern exposure. No matter how cold or windy the day is— if the sun is shining—the beds will gather a wonderful warmth through their transparent lids.

Be sure to make one long side of the beds 2 inches lower than the other so water will run off. Hinge the lids on the high side. It's best to lay out the beds with their lower, longitudinal sides facing south. Just sink the southern edge of the board frame

2 inches or so into the soil. Drive stakes around outside the frame, and nail to frame walls for solidity. You are now in the plant-growing business.

## Seedling Care

Water the beds daily after planting. Use a fine can sprinkler and *tepid* water. Don't muddy the seed bed; just water it enough to be nicely damp. Once the plants have sprouted and are several weeks old—and there is the delightful feeling of their crowding one another—lift the lids more and more. As the growing season progresses and the bedding plants grow faster, there will be nice days when you should take the lids off and get the full benefit of the sun.

First transplanting: When your plants have grown to a size large enough to be handled, they are ready to be transplanted over into the cold frame beds. There they will grow rapidly and harden off so that the shock of final planting into the open garden won't hurt them.

Wet down the cold frame bed well before transplanting. Next, take out the little plants in clumps; place them in a tray or flat. Transplant these into flats or cold frames with enough space for growing larger. Allow these plants to grow several weeks at this second planting, or until all danger of frost in open garden or fields is past. I use a dibble to transplant. Plant the seedlings 1 inch apart.

Final setting out of seedlings into garden or field: When you are ready to transplant the seedlings to their final places in the garden, again wet down beds or flats well. When you dig up the plants, be careful to preserve the root systems with earth well-packed and undisturbed around them.

When you have your rows or beds ready in the garden, set out the new plants from the hotbeds or cold frames. Firm them in well in fertilized

*A cold frame makes an excellent spot for hardening off seedlings before transplanting them in the spring.*

rows. Then give them a good soaking, and they are on their way.

"This is the system I have used for 11 years to grow plants that have won me more than 800 prizes in California fairs for my vegetable and fruit displays," Baima points out.

## Defend against Damping Off

About the only things that can harm growing plants in the hotbeds or cold frames are overheating, drying out for lack of water, or being attacked by the fungus disease known as *damping off*. This damping off or "black root" or "wire stem" in the seedbed is caused by about a half dozen or more fungus parasites. They usually grow near the surface and enter the tiny plants at the point where they emerge from the ground. All of these fungus parasites require a high moisture content of soil and air for quick growth.

To prevent trouble from *damping off,* keep the air and surface of the seedbed as dry as is consistent with good growth of the plants. Getting the beds heated without proper ventilation and not allowing the moisture to escape is what causes damping off.

"One of the greatest pleasures of the gardener or flower grower," says Baima, "is to study seed catalogs or gardening and flower publications from other parts of the United States and other countries and find where you can buy seeds of promising new cultivars. Then send for these and raise them in your own seed beds.

"I have thus gotten a start with several fine new vegetables. One of them is South American garlic. This giant grows to 6 feet tall and has a massive garlic bulb often 6 inches in diameter, and each garlic clove is the size of a hen's egg. This new variety is much milder than our common garlic. I have a row of these plants—started in my own seedbeds—and will soon have enough to exhibit in California fairs."

*February 1958*

### Hay Frame

We have a large supply of baled wheat straw, so we decided to put it to use in our garden before the soil was warm enough to mulch. We built a three-sided hay cold frame with two layers of bales on the back and one on the sides to form a slope. We put bricks on the floor and back wall for extra heat-retention, and a sheet of plastic over the top and open side for protection. In the spring, when we set out our plants, we'll use the bales for mulch. Remember to place the bales so the binding twine is on the sides, not the ground, or it will rot and make moving the bales a real chore.

*Tom and Jan Jackson*
*Godwin, North Carolina*
*May 1982*

# Frost Protection for Spring Crops

I n just one night, a spring frost can wipe out the tender green growing results of weeks of indoor or greenhouse gardening effort. But the good gardener will persist in a certain amount of gambling in early spring so he or she can put fresh vegetables on the table as soon as possible. This report is designed to help you succeed in that effort despite uncooperative frosts.

## Know Your Microclimate

Make every effort to become used to observing *actual* conditions where you are, rather than accepting the prevailing opinion of *average* conditions. As we will see, a city or suburban yard, sheltered by old trees, is less likely to sustain severe frost damage than a nearby open garden. And when frost does settle, spots like the following are often spared: a corner of ground near the house, or an edge of the kitchen garden with a raised bed.

"Here on our farm on the south side of a mountain in the hilly northern end of York County in south-central Pennsylvania," writes Nancy Bubel,

With years of gardening experience to help tell what works from what doesn't, and knowing that you win some and lose some, growers from around the country offer you these methods for bringing in an early harvest despite frosts.

"we generally have somewhat cooler weather than the neighboring city of York. When the radio predicts 'possible scattered frost tonight'—*we know we'll get it!*"

In order to take advantage of your particular microclimate, you will need to spend a little time observing, experimenting, and recording what happens where and when. Then choose those spots that seem less vulnerable to frost damage to make your very early, chancy plantings.

From upstate New York, George and Katy Abraham write: "You can prevent frost damage by planting an apricot tree on the north or west exposure to minimize the frost. Also, grow the tree near a road or close to the house. The heat from the dark paving or brick building (even a wooden structure) is often enough to

prevent damage. Remember fruit trees need good air drainage; avoid low frost pockets where cold air gathers."

The Abrahams also note: "The so-called southwest injury found on the southwest side of maples, fruit, and nut trees is due to frost. It can be prevented by whitewashing or painting the tree trunk to reflect the sun's rays and thus prevent unequal heating and thawing of tissue."

## Prepare to Protect Your Garden

Just accept the fact, says one veteran frost fighter, "that there will be a few weeks in late spring when the patch will look a bit—'patchy.'" Stand ready to cover any and all tender seedlings with whatever is handy and plentiful when frost threatens. Wheel garden carts full of bottomless gallon jugs, berry baskets, flowerpots, coffee cans, and such out to the garden, and spend a few minutes night and morning covering and uncovering seedlings

*When a late frost threatens your garden, turn household items like milk jugs, baskets, and berry boxes into handy plant protecters. If you cover your seedlings with upended flower pots, be sure to put something over the drainage hole to keep frost out.*

*A simple paper cloche, known as a hot cap, is a lightweight plant cover that gives protection from a few degrees of frost.*

when the threat of frost looks serious. When using metal cans over tender plants like tomatoes, try to be sure that the leaves don't touch the metal. Those that do often get zapped by frost. Flowerpots make good insulators, but a really stiff frost will settle down through the drainage hole in the pot and hurt the plant.

The long lines of widely assorted plastic castoffs marking the garden row can sometimes look pretty bleak for a while, but this crucial period usually lasts only a couple of weeks, and the payoff is "an earlier vegetable crop than we might otherwise have been able to achieve."

Mulch is probably the best-looking insulation against frost, and if you have enough of it around, you can quickly tuck it around and over your plants to protect them. Wooden berry boxes and half-bushel baskets look neat and do an effective job.

Out in North Lima, where the wind blows out of Canada straight across the Ohio flatlands, John Krill keeps a supply of "cheap 9-by-12-foot clear plastic drop cloths handy in case an unexpected frost threatens." The Krills find this procedure beats other means of quickly protecting tender plants like cucumbers, melons, tomatoes, and peppers. Thrown over the plants in late afternoon, the plastic traps heat and thus defeats the frost.

The Krills dig deep holes for tomato plants which soak up heat during the days and pass it along to the surrounding soil. They also make it a policy not to stake their tomatoes until "at least ten days after the latest frost date." Stakes would get in the way of their big plastic covers, which they throw over an entire group of tomato plants.

On the other hand, Charlotte Waldron stakes her plants "firmly to support protective cover" in her Henderson, North Carolina, garden. For tall plants, she makes "wigwams of corn fodder by tying stalks in bundles with strong twine." Before a frosty night is due, she soaks the ground around the plants and stacks the bundles closely enough to cover the tomato foliage. The bundles are tied together at their peaks and also around their middles. When the day's "temperature has passed the danger point," she removes the bundles but keeps them nearby—just in case.

For tomatoes in wire cages she uses old burlap bags, split and sewn together, or old bedspreads "big enough to cover," anchoring their bottoms with books of hay or straw, rocks, and earth. For row crops, she builds walls on either side, working with bales of hay or straw, and covers them with roofing further supported by boards or "branches cut to size."

The Abrahams employ another trick to escape frost damage—covering their berry patch with black plastic film in rolls 12 to 32 feet wide and 100 feet long. The film is placed over the patch when frost seems likely, to absorb the heat rising from the ground. Temperatures outside the cover can sag to 28 degrees, but "underneath the film, just 3 feet away, it registers 38 to 40 degrees." Between frosts, the film is rolled or folded between the rows and held down with rocks or bricks. Keep in mind that clear plastic does not absorb and hold heat as well as black.

Still another trick used by the Abrahams is covering tender young transplants with milk cartons. They convert the empty cartons to "frost beaters" by cutting out their bottoms. The cartons are placed over the plants and thrust about 1 inch into the ground so that they don't blow over. The tops can be folded open during the day and then folded shut on the colder nights.

mean the difference between an 80-percent crop and a 20-percent one here in the Finger Lakes region."

Before they go to bed, they watch for a night when the sun sets in a cloudless sky, and the wind goes down with it. If it's around 40 to 50 degrees, the Abrahams can "smell frost in the air." So they put the sprinkler on the strawberry patch to save the crop. Next morning they're "not alarmed to see our plants coated with ice—we just keep the sprinkler on, and the plants come through in fine shape." The sprinkler is left running until all the ice is melted from the plants by the morning sun.

The same trick is reported by Nancy Farris, who does her gardening in South Carolina, less then 50 miles from the ocean and a bare 10 miles north of the Georgia line. It's hard to believe that frost can be a danger in such an area, but Farris reports that she turned on the sprinkler *before the sun hit the wilted foliage.*" As a result she saved part of several rows of beans which took some time to recover. The corn, though browned at the tips of the emerging shoots, was revived to send up new growth after it was doused with water.

## Use Your Sprinkler on Strawberry Beds

Your lawn sprinkler can be the answer for controlling frost in your garden bed and patches. The Abrahams report that, with strawberries, "it can

## Build Up Your Soils

Gardening at 3,300 feet in Oregon can be a trying but stimulating experience. Karen L. Carlsen reports that "I have learned to use each of the three distinctly different soil variations in my garden and how to correlate them to my spring planting schedule. For instance, a small area of light, ashy soil is the first to warm up and become workable, which allows me to plant the earliest crops of onion sets, spinach, chard, and a row or two of peas and carrots by mid-April."

About two-thirds of the Carlsen garden is composed of deep, fertile, loamy soil. Sowings of peas, carrots, beets, and other crops are extended into this area as soon as it becomes workable in April. Because of light snows into May, potatoes are never planted in her garden before May 15. She sets them 4 inches down so they are "protected from freezing nights as they begin their growth." As the first leaves emerge, she pulls the soil up to around the stems to give them some added protection.

At the far end of the Carlsen garden, the soil is a sticky clay, which is difficult to handle. With the addition of "tons of rotted barnyard manure, it has improved over the years" but is still the last soil to become tillable each spring. Consequently, it is the logical area in which to plant crops of limas, bush beans, corn, squash, and black-eyed peas.

Last but not least in her efforts to avoid frost damage, Carlsen has started a tight fencerow all along the northern uphill slope above the growing patch. "Not only will it provide food and shelter for the birds, but it will also break the downhill rush of cold air which so often nips my garden on cold summer nights," she predicts.

## Develop a Sixth Sense about the Weather

We have already noted that the Abrahams can "smell frost in the air." "This is not a quick trip," cautions Nancy Bubel. "It takes time and attention to develop a sensitivity to the air, the sky, the wind." The Bubels don't pretend to be very far at all along this road. But here are a few weather signs that they think are worth noting:

1. Frost is often likely during the last week before a full moon. Don't ask why—no reason is given!

2. If the sky is clear and the air is calm and still with no breeze blowing as dusk falls . . . watch out for frost!

3. When temperatures dip to 40 degrees by early evening, it's entirely possible that they'll plummet to the freezing point by the early hours of morning.

## Kelp Spray Increases Frost Resistance

The Bubels report using seaweed spray on their vegetables, but have no firm conclusions as yet about its effectiveness. However, they have contacted people who are enthusiastic about the method, while reports that have reached us are very convincing.

How can seaweed help ward off frost damage to a plant? All plants need trace elements as well as nitrogen, phosphorus, and potassium in order to put on healthy, productive growth. Apparently, the addition of as little as ½ part per million of certain vital elements can benefit the plant considerably.

According to E. Booth of the Institute of Seaweed Research, writing in *The Grower* (November 27, 1965), experiments indicate that it is sometimes impossible for plants to synthesize the necessary components of growth when the temperature is too low. Kelp is not only a rich source of trace minerals, it also contains alginic acid and other substances known to chelate metals, thus making some of the trace elements more readily available to the plant. In fact, some studies on seaweed-treated plants have revealed that the total amount of certain trace elements in a given plant was greater than the amount of that element formerly present in the untreated plant and the unapplied seaweed. Something in the seaweed helped to make formerly "tied up" soil elements available to the plant.

There is still a great deal that we don't know about the interaction of kelp and treated plants, but it seems reasonable to conclude, as Booth does in his paper, that seaweed helps the plant to compensate for the inhibiting effect of low temperatures by supplying, in ready-to-use form, those vital elements of growth that the plant would otherwise be unable to make for itself.

The funny thing is that the Eskimos have been doing this for years, in their far-north short-season gardens, although it was not until the 1940s that their use of kelp for frost protection was recorded.

If you live near the coast, you can collect seaweed for your garden and even make your own spray solution. Most gardeners, though, will find it more convenient to purchase a kelp concentrate for use on their gardens. Granular kelp may also be applied to the soil, but the foliar spray is more rapidly absorbed. Frequent light applications of the kelp are more effective than occasional heavy treatments.

*Contributors to this special frost protection report include Nancy Bubel (Pennsylvania), Doc and Katy Abraham (New York), John Krill (Ohio), Charlotte Waldron (North Carolina), Karen Carlsen (Oregon), Nancy Farris (South Carolina), and Managing Editor Maurice Franz.*

*March 1977*

# Some Like It Cool

## Michael Lafavore

I f you've ever spent a blazing August afternoon working in the garden, you know how oppressive the heat of the summer can be. After a while, the top of your head begins to broil, and the only escape is the nearest shady spot.

Your plants can't escape, although they may need a break from the sun, too. Unprotected, many heat-sensitive plants will wilt away or bolt under the midday sun, victims of heat stress and moisture loss. For every 10-degree rise in temperature, a plant's metabolic rate doubles. And the quicker that rate, the more moisture is lost through the leaves.

Lettuce, celery, spinach, cabbage, and other salad crops do much better when they are grown in partial shade. Onions and peas can become bitter when overheated by the sun, and radishes tend to become stronger-tasting and woody when they are grown in hot weather. Even heat-loving vegetables such as tomatoes and peppers can get too much heat and sun.

In Boron, California, where it's not unusual for temperatures to top 115 degrees, organic gardener Albert Coiner keeps curved sheets of corrugated aluminum and fiberglass panels on hand to shade his

> Shading devices can help keep your heat-sensitive plants happy all summer.

plants during the sizzling afternoons. He lets his eggplants, tomatoes, and peppers get the morning sun, then sinks the shading devices into the ground near the plants for cooling shadows in the afternoon.

Shingles, boards, house screens, cardboard, and even rolls of snow fencing can be used for shade. Stick them into the ground so that they shade, or partially shade, your plants. You can also use a stick or bricks to prop them up above the vegetables. Don't sink stakes too close to the plants, though, or you may damage the root systems and cause more harm than good. Collect all your shading materials early in the summer so you're not looking for things to use as your garden wilts on a blistering August afternoon.

Many garden supply stores sell special shade cloth that ranges in density from 25 to 70 percent. Ordinary cheesecloth works well, too, and is cheaper. Whatever you use, sew curtain rings or eyelets into the corners and along the sides to prevent tearing. The rings can be slipped over nails or hooks attached to stakes placed along the edges of your vegetable bed. Don't put the cloth up until noon or so, and be sure to remove it on cooler afternoons to allow the plants their quota of sun. On very hot days, lightly sprinkling the top of the cloth with water will help bring down temperatures underneath even more.

Young plants may require special care when transplanted into the garden on sunny days. Because part of their root systems has been lost in the transplanting process, they are unable to absorb as much water as before and should be shaded to avoid wilting and lessen transplant shock. If the plants are small, shade them for a few days, checking them regularly for signs of drying out.

If you've got a weekend or two to spare, why not try building a lath house to shield your vegetables. Use 2-by-4s for sides and beams and 1½- to

*As spring warms into summer, cool-weather crops such as lettuce and cabbage will grow better and be less likely to bolt (go to seed) if you give them some protection from the hot sun. Cool your crops with shade cloth, supported by a wood, wire, or PVC-pipe frame.*

*The shifting shadows created by a piece of lattice give plants a break from the heat while letting them have enough sunlight to remain productive.*

2-inch laths spaced one width apart. The lath should run north to south so that each plant gets alternating sunshine and shade. In spring, cover the lath house with polyethylene sheeting and use it as a mini-greenhouse.

Your cold frame can also be converted for year-round use by replacing the top with a lath frame or screen. The shading, along with the cold frame's insulation, should keep temperatures inside cool even on the warmest days.

In Saudi Arabia, where growers face a constant battle against the effects of the burning sun, vegetables are planted in the shady rows between date palm trees. You can practice the same method of intercropping on a smaller scale by planting corn or sunflowers near vegetables that require shading. Try shading early beets with late potatoes, and quick-maturing lettuce with brussels sprouts or tomatoes. Heat-sensitive plants can also be planted on the east side of buildings so that they catch the morning sun but are shaded in the afternoon. And if you grow vegetables in containers, simply move them under a shady tree for a few hours on hot days.

A little bit of shade will help many plants through the hottest part of the summer, but be careful not to overdo a good thing. All plants need *some* sun, so never leave them shaded for more than a part of each day. And keep an eye out for plants becoming leggy, a sign that they're not getting enough sun.

Another caution: Never use plastic, clear *or* black, to shade plants. These materials may keep some sun out, but they'll also keep heat in and defeat their own purpose.

For extra protection from the sun, combine shading with deep mulching. Both will prevent soil moisture from evaporating and help your plants through the dry season.

*August 1980*

179

# Frost-Proofing Your Garden

*Anthony DeCrosta*

I t's possible to keep frost at bay for weeks after the first frost date. Here's how.

First, regard frost dates as only general guidelines for planting. Trust your own experiences, and try not to think about frost in a regional, state, or even county perspective. You may have frost pockets that get hit two weeks or more before the elevated parts of your property.

Frosts are more likely in open country than near towns and cities or large bodies of water that tend to soften temperature extremes. If you live on the north side of a hill, you'll experience cooler temperatures, earlier frost dates, later thaws, and less sunlight than the south side. According to James Jankowiak of Lake Villa, Illinois, drained, dark soils are less liable to unseasonable frost than heavy clays, wet soils, or light-colored ones. Planting close to the foundation of a house, shed, or barn—especially on the south side—will help protect crops from chill damage, too.

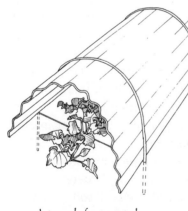

*A tunnel of corrugated fiberglass, pinned down by wire hoops, forms a row-sized greenhouse over plants to protect them from frost. Drape clear plastic over the open ends.*

To encourage the soil to warm up fast in the spring, pull all mulches back from the planting bed—bare soil warms up more quickly. Then as soon as the ground is warm, mulch to your heart's content.

Seedlings coming along in cold frames need special attention. Close the sash as freezing temperatures approach. If the frost is severe, bank the outside of the frame with soil or litter and place burlap bags over the glass panes. When the temperature rises above 32 degrees, you can allow some air in by raising the sash on the side of the frame opposite the direction of the wind.

Whenever temperatures start slipping, cover the plants. All coverings should first keep the severe cold off as much as possible and then help the plants gradually warm up afterward. For young plants, bottomless glass jars, hot caps, and waxed paper rolled up into a cone shape and fastened with a paper clip work well. To protect whole rows or a raised bed, construct a tunnel of sheets of 6- to 8-mil polyethylene plastic on a wood, plastic, or metal frame.

## Just Add Water to Ward Off Frost

If a sudden frost is expected, spray all plants—including budding fruit trees—with water. The water not only protects vegetation from frost injury, it also protects it from injury due to too-rapid thawing. Wet the leaves and stems thoroughly—don't just give them a light misting.

"As water on the plants freezes, it releases heat, which will help protect plant tissues," explains Dr. Paul H. Li of the University of Minnesota's Department of Horticulture and Landscape Architecture.

Spraying water on fruit trees and vegetables will protect them against damage from a frost of only one or two degrees. A more severe frost will kill the plants. Once buds are formed, fruit trees are de-acclimated and can be hurt by a sudden slight frost.

Be on guard for spring thaws, which can be dangerous to trees. In the spring, the tops of trees begin to shed water, which their frozen roots can't replace. At this time, trees can die from dehydration. Try to shade any uncovered plants with burlap until the ground completely thaws.

Learn to read weather signs, especially in autumn. "A really warm spell near the approach of the first average frost date can be followed by a quick drop in temperature," says Jankowiak. "Other signs of possible frost are clear days, with deep blue skies."

If you can nurse your tender crops through the first or second mild frost, you can usually expect an extended growing season—certainly enough time to ripen a few last tomatoes and squashes on the vines, and to bring in a few extra pounds of beans and corn.

Mulch is an important heat preserver. Although plants covered with snow generally have a better survival rate in subfreezing weather than exposed plants, don't rely totally on Mother Nature. A thick organic mulch will protect perennials through the winter. Mulch perennials with early growth and then cover with berry boxes, flats, flowerpots, and even cardboard boxes, until the possibility of frost has ended.

Ice-laden branches, or those covered with frozen snow, should not be touched. Shaking the limbs will prob-ably break them before it dislodges ice.

In summary, keeping a keen eye on the weather in your own microclimate, physically protecting your plants from cold air, and avoiding the urge to shake ice off of your frozen trees and shrubs will help keep Jack Frost from getting his frozen fingers on your garden.

*December 1980*

## How Frost Is Formed

At night, when the earth doesn't receive any of the sun's radiation, it loses heat to the atmosphere. If enough heat is lost, the surface temperature drops below freezing.

On a night when the humidity is high and the air temperature equals the dew point (the temperature at which the relative humidity equals 100 percent), moisture condenses and forms dew. If the air temperature dips below freezing but still equals the dew point, a visible "white frost" occurs. If the air temperature is above the dew point, but below freezing, no visible frost forms, but vegetation can still be damaged by the cold. This condition is often called a "black frost" because injured crops turn very dark.

Almost all freezes and a large proportion of local frost follow the passage of a cold front and the subsequent influx of polar air. There are exceptions, however. In California, heavy frosts can follow an invasion of polar air but without any local indications of a passing cold front.

*Anthony DeCrosta*

# Chapter 10

# *Seed Starting and Beyond*

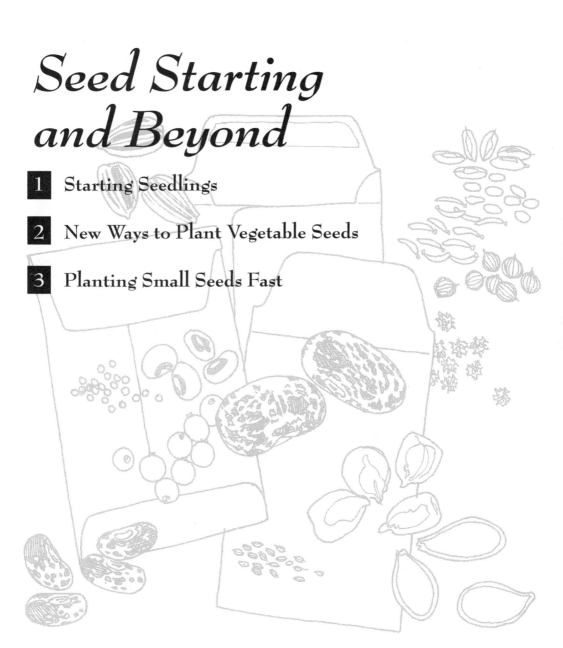

1  Starting Seedlings

2  New Ways to Plant Vegetable Seeds

3  Planting Small Seeds Fast

# Starting Seedlings

Here's some advice on how you can get an early start in the garden for the coming year. Start your plants indoors now and have them ready for transplanting to the outdoor growing sites when the ground is ready to take them.

Don't wait until April or May to begin your planting this year. You can start now. Many vegetables, such as onions, tomatoes, peppers, cabbages, cauliflower, and celery, along with tender flowers like marigolds and zinnias, should be started indoors. This article gives you step-by-step instructions.

A 3- or 4-inch-deep wooden box, 12 by 18 inches, known as a flat, is the best container for starting seeds. Be sure the soil surface is level before seeding, as this will ensure an equal distribution of moisture when watering.

*Fill your flat with seed-starting mix and moisten it before you plant. Soak the mix well and let it drain, then soak it again to ensure that it's thoroughly wetted.*

Sow your seeds into shallow furrows in the top of the mix. Don't sow too thickly, or you'll have a hard time separating your seedlings to pot them up.

Cover seeds lightly with sifted soil, fine sand, or vermiculite no deeper than three times their diameter. Mist the flat's surface, then cover with clear plastic.

Tiny seeds require only a very shallow furrow, while larger seeds should have a deeper one. After planting, cover seed with a depth of soil no more than two or three times its own diameter.

If burlap is used to cover the flat, look under it frequently and remove at any sign of mold. The covering should come off permanently as soon as plants appear above ground.

When plants develop their first leaves, they should have as much light as possible. Flats should be placed in full sun during the day; turning the flat every day or two helps the seedlings develop. Temperature at night should be about 60 degrees.

Seed for the larger onion and early cabbage varieties may be started indoors as early as January. Tomatoes, peppers, and eggplant cannot be planted in the garden until soil is thoroughly warm. Start their seed a month or more later, depending on the last frost date in your area.

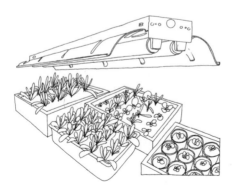

If you don't have a sunny windowsill for your seedlings, use fluorescent lights to give them the 16 hours of light they need each day. Keep the lights as close to your seedlings as possible without letting them touch to keep the plants from stretching and becoming spindly.

*February 1959*

# New Ways to Plant Vegetable Seeds

## Richard V. Clemence

You can improve your planting technique—and results—with these truly surprising ahead-of-season ideas for starting seeds!

Seed planting by the "usual" directions doesn't always work best. I've experimented and discovered some nonconformist methods that bring better germination, a faster start for young plants, and less trouble or risk for the gardener. What's more, these ideas add to the returns from a small vegetable plot—and subtract from the time and effort required to make sure of these returns.

How deeply, in fact, should seeds be planted? Seeds that are kept damp will sprout in the open air. Is the objective in planting merely to ensure that the seeds stay moist? Or is it to get them down to the level at which their roots should develop? Or just what is the idea?

When I was a boy, it was understood that peas would not grow well in hot weather. The reason was believed to be that the roots were affected by the heat, and growth thus retarded. The preventive measures, however, were another matter. In my youth, the approved practice was to dig a deep trench, place the seeds in the bottom of it, and after filling the excavation, wait for the peas to emerge. This naturally took a long time. But the gardener was assured that the scheme would keep the roots of his peas far down in the cool earth, well-protected from the sun's evil influence. Many thousands of cubic yards of soil were accordingly moved, and many crops of peas were successfully grown despite the considerable handicap.

Most vegetables have astonishing powers of survival, and ingenious abuses are frequently mistaken for special secrets of success. As far as peas are concerned, most gardeners now know that the roots will penetrate just as deeply into the soil if the seeds are planted near the surface as they will if buried far underground. But how near the surface should peas or other seeds be planted?

Reflection suggests that there is a rather simple logic to planting. To begin with, the seeds are to be placed where the plants are wanted, which means in "hills" or rows. Next, the seeds need to be anchored somehow, to keep them from blowing away, and from being washed out by heavy rains. It is also important to place seeds in close contact with the soil, to keep them moist for quick sprouting, and to give the roots immediate encouragement as they start to grow.

## Don't Cover Your Seeds

The closer to the surface seeds can be decently planted, the sooner their sprouts will appear, and the more quickly the crop can be grown. This idea is consistent with natural processes, too. The seeds of wild plants fall on top of the ground, and though most of them may fall in uncongenial surroundings, those that land in suitable places have no difficulty in germinating and sending their roots far into the earth. In contrast to conventional practice, logic would lead us to infer that seeds should be planted on top of the soil, and not under it at all.

I arrived at this theoretical position some years ago, and I was reluctant to prove it in practice. A few hesitant experiments were so promising, however, that I was encouraged to continue, and the results support the theory very strongly indeed.

I shortly discovered that my first successes were due to favorable weather conditions that cannot be relied upon once in a decade. Cloudy skies and occasional gentle rains will start seeds scattered on the surface of the ground in an astonishingly short time. But high winds, a hot sun, or heavy rains will virtually ensure failure. The problem, then, is to keep your seeds in place and moist until they germinate. After that, they develop as rapidly as their quick start would imply. The solution I have found after many tests certainly produces better and much faster results than do traditional methods.

To secure perfect germination in record time, all you need is some peat moss and a sprinkler. I recommend fine peat moss and a plastic "hose" sprinkler, but others may do almost as well. Coarse peat moss, however, tends to form a crust when exposed to the weather, and some sprinklers throw strong streams. With reasonably good equipment, you have only to do the following:

1. Mark a row with stakes and string over the exposed soil, and scatter your seeds on the surface.

2. Fill a large basket with peat moss, and walk down your row of seeds, shaking the moss onto them as you proceed, and employing your feet to step on the mixture of seeds and moss, pressing them firmly together. (A board or roller will also work.) At the end of the row, you return by the same route, stepping on the spots you missed before, and leaving a perfectly planted crop behind you.

3. The function of the sprinkler is merely to guarantee results. The peat moss needs a good wetting to keep the seeds damp until they sprout, and rain may well be forthcoming at the proper moments. The sprinkler, however, removes all doubts.

   This system of surface planting eliminates rotting, blowing, and washing of seeds and gets nearly every "viable" specimen started at once. No rain short of a cloudburst can move the seeds, for the peat moss absorbs water like a sponge. At the same time, the smallest sprouts reach the air and light immediately, and decay can hardly occur. Finally, sun and wind cannot dry or move your seeds, if you

*Topping seeds sown on the soil surface with fine peat moss and using a perforated hose "sprinkler" in the newly planted bed will produce excellent germination results with little effort.*

have a sprinkler ready for use. And the time and labor of planting are also reduced to a minimum.

## No-Row Gardening

In surface planting no furrows are made, of course, and the question thus arises as to how you get seeds like lettuce, carrots, and beets laid in single straight rows. The answer is that you don't. On the contrary, you aim at spreading them over a space about 1 foot wide, using your marking string merely as a guide for one edge of the row. You thereby get many more plants into a given area than you can by other methods, and when you thin your crops, you save time and effort again. You can thin wide rows nearly as fast as narrow ones, and space your plants in both directions in one operation. After thinning carrots, for instance, you will have rows four or five carrots in width rather than one thin line of plants.

I find that many gardeners shrink from the thought of rows more than one plant wide. But there is certainly no good reason why a plant should require more space from north to south than from east to west, or vice versa. Narrow rows with wide aisles between them merely waste space in the home garden. They have been copied from commercial practice, which requires space for the operation of machinery. Broad alleyways in the kitchen garden are about as logical as six lanes of cement in the driveway.

Seeds like cucumber, melon, and squash may be surface-planted in "hills." As the word may suggest to some, though not to me, a hill is a shallow depression in the soil, an improvement on the genuine mound

once used. The depression is usually made by filling a small excavation with compost or manure, spreading a little soil on top, and stepping on the area to press it down. In surface planting, you can prepare a hill in this way, or if your soil is rich enough, you can simply scatter some seeds in any convenient place. Then shake on peat moss, and press the moss and seeds well together against the soil. Again, the sprinkler provides insurance of quick results.

You can economize your time and strength by scattering your seeds rather carelessly and thinning hills to preserve only the most promising plants later on. If you conduct the thinning by clipping off unwanted plants, instead of pulling them out by the roots, you will not retard the growth of any of the specimens you choose to save.

Surface planting has real advantages over more common methods. It can be used successfully with nearly all sorts of vegetable crops, with only one important exception. In planting such crops as corn and pole beans, it saves trouble in the end to take pains enough to place the seeds in exactly the spots they should occupy and to make sure that they stay there. The easiest way of doing this is to push each seed slightly into the soil with your fingers. Since they are not lying loose on the surface, peat moss is not needed to anchor them, and it is no better than any other good mulch for holding the moisture.

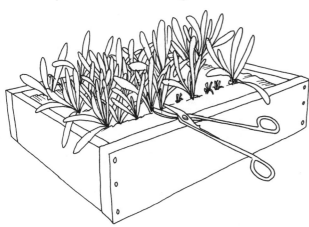

*Whether you're thinning seedlings in a flat or in the garden, snipping off unwanted plants, instead of pulling them, protects the roots of their neighbors from injury.*

*December 1959*

# Planting Small Seeds Fast

*Vic Sussman*

Try these three techniques for speedy sowing that produces good germination and a minimum of thinning.

Have you ever tried to thread a needle with your mittens on? That's how clumsy I used to feel when sowing small seeds. Either I spread them too thick and got a jungle of Lilliputian plants with roots entangled, or I planted too thin, getting a spotty array of seedlings. Another difficulty with tiny seeds is the fragility of their sprouts. Bean, corn, and squash seeds produce husky shoots that can burst through caked soil. But the tender filaments of smaller seeds must be covered with care lest they be smothered by heavy or crusted soil.

But good things come in such finicky little packages—carrots, spinach, lettuce, turnips, cabbages, parsnips, mustard, onions, and various herbs and flowers—that it was certainly worth developing some strategies for handling a handful of such tiny objects with a lot of control and finesse.

The goal is to find a way to sow small seeds in a regular pattern, one that produces the number of seedlings you need but not so many that thinning would be a nightmare. Thinning is like weeding. It's a tedious task that represents a waste of valuable seed. As you sow, direct your energies toward producing a mature plant from each seed that falls. You'll prob-

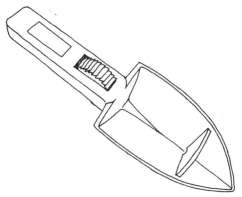

*The Seedmaster and other seed-sowing tools make it easier to plant tiny seeds without sowing them too thickly.*

ably never do it, but if you have to thin only one seedling out of two, you'll be way ahead of the game.

The common advice to "eat the thinnings" is hogwash, for the most part. I find the thinning and washing of tiny lettuces or carrots too laborious for the amount of food it yields. Thinnings are worthwhile in the kitchen only when the plants are about half-grown. If your first carrot thinning can begin when the roots are as big as your little finger, you've mastered the art of sowing just the right amount of seed and covering it evenly with the right amount of soil.

## Try Narrow Furrows

My preferred method for planting large numbers of tiny seeds in my 4-foot-wide beds is to sow in narrowly spaced furrows and cover them with sawdust. The traditional method for planting lots of seed quickly is to broadcast. Getting an even stand of seedlings by broadcasting requires skill in tossing out the

seed and skill in covering it, while producing a random arrangement of plants that can be hard to weed. At the other end of the spectrum, some experienced intensive gardeners now recommend precise placement of the seed in an equidistant grid. I've found this tedious. Using closely spaced drills is a good compromise. It lets me plant seed quickly and achieve spacings that are close to equidistant. It's easier to cover seed evenly when it's in a drill of uniform depth, and it's easier to control the weeds when most are in a line between the rows of seedlings.

Sowing tiny seeds evenly in furrows can be tricky, though. Tearing the corner off the seed packet and tapping seeds out has never worked for me, so I use a gadget called the Seedmaster Seeder (Gurney's Seed and Nursery Co., Yankton, South Dakota, is one source of this handy

*To space fine seeds like lettuce in a flat, moisten the point of a pencil in a bowl of water and touch it to a seed. The seed will stick to the pencil until you touch it to the planting mix in the flat.*

can pour a packet of seed into it, sow, and then easily pour the leftover seeds into the packet without spilling them or getting them stuck to my fingers.

Another method that works well with small seeds is the pinch-and-drop technique. Here you drop clusters of seeds every few inches instead of scattering them randomly down the furrow. In planting spinach, for example, you'd drop three or four seeds every 3 inches. Later, all you need do is remove two or three excess seedlings from each group.

tool). The Seedmaster looks like a miniature trowel with a special ratchet thumbwheel built into the handle and a series of tiny ridges that hold back the seeds near the tip. Clicking the thumbwheel jiggles the seeds, causing them to separate and jump forward out of the trowel. It's easy to control the rate at which the seeds tumble out. I also like this gadget because I

### Plant Seeds with Damp Knees

A friend of mine has a novel way of seeding by pinch-and-drop. You know how kneeling in moist soil leaves damp spots on your knees? My friend, who plants carrot seeds in clusters (four seeds, 3 inches apart), touches a

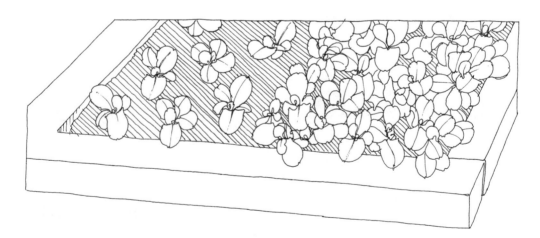

*When you're planting in blocks or beds of all one crop, broadcasting is a quick way to get seeds into the garden bed. Work on your sowing technique to get even seed distribution and to avoid a lot of thinning work later on.*

damp knee with his index finger. Then he lightly touches the seeds in his other hand. Four or five seeds attach themselves to his moistened fingertip, and he deftly flicks them off into the row at the correct spacing. Most of the small seeds can be planted in pinches, but you should not try this with beets. Each beet seed will produce several plants, so it's best to space individual seeds 3 inches apart.

My experience convinces me that sawdust is the ideal covering for all small seeds. I use fresh sawdust, straight from my workshop, and I've found it to be a blessing, especially in dealing with fussy germinators like parsnips and parsley. The ¼-inch layer

### Burlapped Carrots

After two years of bad germination left me with no carrots and sparse parsley, I tried covering the seedbeds with burlap bags. Each cut-open bag measures about 3 by 4 feet. I laid rocks on each corner to hold the bags down during high winds. During rainy weather I took the burlap off but replaced it as soon as the sun came out. I did do some hand-watering during long periods of hot, dry weather. After the seedlings were ½ inch tall, I removed the burlap for good. Believe me, it's a pleasure to thin seedlings again.

*Robert Legge*
*Etlan, Virginia*
*April 1983*

of sawdust that I use holds moisture, resists crusting, stays in place, and ultimately adds organic matter to the soil. Another benefit is that sawdust is cheap or free and safe to use. Extensive field tests have shown that raw sawdust will neither acidify soil nor create a nitrogen deficiency when used as a *mulch*. Fully decomposed sawdust can be safely tilled into the soil and is an excellent conditioner.

I sow my seeds, water with a misting nozzle on a hose, scatter sawdust, and mist again, saturating the material. I mist every day until the sprouts break through. Once I see the sprouts appear, I stop watering so the plants will develop deep root systems as they search downward for moisture and nutrients.

I begin thinning once the seedlings have developed their first true leaves, and I thin ruthlessly, striving to keep plants at their optimum spacing. I weed just as thoroughly, going over the beds every day or so.

Once my seedlings are up a few inches, I can safely mulch the bare ground between the narrow rows, and most weed problems are over for the season. The fresh sawdust slowly decomposes as the plants mature. By harvesttime, it's aged sufficiently to be turned under.

## Test Your Broadcasting System

Occasionally, broadcasting has a place in my bag of tricks. When pressed for time, it is the fastest way to get the seeds in the ground. But it's crucial to do a careful job of it, or you'll lose the saved time in thinning. Broadcasting is the best way to plant green manures, too.

To get the knack of broadcasting, I set up a practice area in my living room, spreading a white sheet on the floor so I could see the seeds as I tossed them. I used carrot seeds, scattering them at various rates, trying for a regular pattern of coverage with seeds falling 1 or 2 inches apart. This took some practice. Tiny seeds can be difficult to see against the earth, but my living room rehearsal gave me an intuitive feel for broadcasting. I cover broadcast seed with sawdust, too. I hold a shovelful over the bed and sprinkle it as evenly as possible.

Knowing the germination rate of your seeds is always important, but especially so if you're going to broadcast them. It's easy to overseed, either because you get into the pleasant rhythm of sowing or because you toss a little extra on "just in case." Knowing the germination rate will make your seeding more precise, minimizing subsequent thinning. For example, if I'm sowing carrots with a tested germination rate of 75 percent, I deliberately seed in a sparse pattern. But if the rate is 50 percent, I throw out some extra seeds to compensate for the lower viability.

Here are some other techniques I use for dealing with small seeds:

- The germination of parsley and carrots can be speeded up by pouring boiling water over the seeds after sowing them in rows. This drastic treatment softens the tough seed coats.

- Lettuce seeds germinate best when exposed to light. Sow seeds, and then water them, but don't cover them for several hours or more. Then cover lightly and mist daily.

- Do you have trouble seeing tiny seeds when sowing them in rows? You can make the seeds more visible by lining your rows with ribbons of toilet tissue. This quickly decomposes after being covered with moist soil.

- Beet seeds will germinate more rapidly if soaked overnight before sowing. The damp, swollen seeds will be harder to handle than when dry, so mix them with fine sand before sowing.

- Sowing radish seeds in with slow sprouters like parsnips is an old but worthwhile technique. The fast-growing radishes break up the soil surface, easing the way for the more delicate sprouts to come. You get two crops from the same area.

*May 1981*

# Chapter 11

# *Tomatoes*

# Spotlight on Tomatoes

*Roger W. Smith*

One of the richest sources of vitamins A, B, and C is the common tomato. Because of its food value and ease of culture it ranks among the most important plants available to the home gardener.

The origin of the tomato is obscure. We know that its name came to us from the Mexican word *tomatl,* but until a comparatively recent date, it was believed to be poisonous and disease-producing. Nowadays, however, we understand its great food value and appreciate its importance.

If you grow your own tomato plants, you will find the reward well worth the effort. One ounce of seed can produce about two thousand plants. With a couple of generous packages of good-quality seed, you could produce as many as three hundred plants.

## Starting from Seed

In February or March in a sunny southern window, arrange some sort of window box. Almost any small wooden box filled with fine, loose soil and having reasonable drainage will serve as a seedbed. Tomato seed germinates best at about 70 degrees, which is approximately room temperature. The seed should be evenly spaced and not planted deeper than ½ inch.

The young plants should appear in from eight to ten days, and for the next two weeks they should be watered from the bottom. The surface of the soil in the seedbed should remain

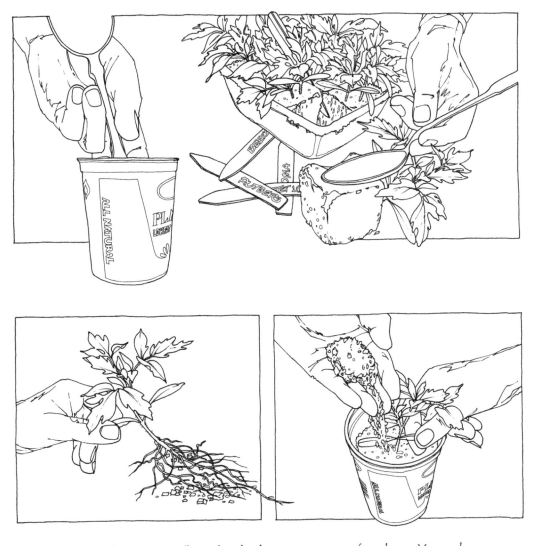

*Transplant tomato seedlings when they have one or two sets of true leaves. Move each seedling into its own container, using a spoon or other tool to lift its roots out of the planting flat and to lower them into a hole in the plant's new home. Hold a seed leaf to support the top of the plant, rather than grasping the easily crushed stem.*

as dry and sunny as possible to reduce the danger of damping off, a condition fatal to seedlings and brought about by the growth of soilborne organisms flourishing because of excess moisture.

To water from the bottom, place the box containing the seedlings in a pan containing shallow water and allow it to remain there until the soil has absorbed the moisture it requires.

As soon as the seedlings form one or two true leaves in addition to their seed leaves, they should be transplanted. The tray into which they are transplanted should be capable of holding individual containers about 3 inches deep. These individual containers may be berry boxes, paper cups with the bottoms removed, paper boxes, small flowerpots, cans with holes in the bottom, and so on. Each plant should be moved to its own container, and the containers packed in the tray with soil to prevent too rapid drying out.

The objective is to give each seedling about 3 inches of space each way and to keep them growing rapidly. When the time comes for moving the young plants into the garden (about seven weeks from the time the seed was sown), this can be done in such a way as to cause the least possible disturbance to the roots and the soil surrounding them.

The tray containing the young plants should be kept at a rather low temperature in a cold frame or unheated room in order that the seedlings may become stocky rather than spindly.

## Moving Your Seedlings Outside

Although tomato plants will bear fruit in from 48 to 86 days after they are planted in the garden, they are essentially warm-weather plants. They require an open, sunny, well-drained location.

The soil should be porous and fairly light and should contain a fair amount of humus. If the soil in your garden is quite heavy, that is, containing a large percentage of clay, you will find that you can improve its texture by the addition of peat moss or sand. But for plant food it is necessary to apply a generous quantity of humus from a well-made compost heap. The addition of composted material will also bring very sandy soil to a satisfactory condition.

Avoid choosing a poorly drained spot. Any part of the garden where rainwater tends to form a pond is a very poor place for tomatoes. Many diseases of tomatoes are associated with poor drainage, including bacterial wilt, stunting, and fruit rots.

You will find also that air circulation is quite important. Tomatoes thrive in open locations where the free movement of the air is not hampered by the surroundings. Most leaf-blighting fungus diseases and fruit decay are prevalent in locations where poor air circulation exists.

So if you keep in mind the fact that the tomato likes well-drained, porous soil and plenty of well-composted humus, sunshine, and air, there is no reason why you should not grow tomatoes that will be the envy of your neighbors.

Perhaps the most desirable method of growing tomatoes for the home gardener is the pruned, stake method. More plants can occupy a given space when you follow this method, and the difficulties of cultivation are greatly reduced.

After all danger of frost is past, set the tomato plants deeply and about 2 feet apart each way. Drive a 5-foot-long stake into the ground alongside each plant. Tie the plant to the stake with soft yarn or small strips of old cotton clothing. It is best to make the tie tight around the stake and loop it loosely around the stem of the plant just beneath a leaf node. This prevents injury to the rapidly growing stem.

If paper containers have been used, the plants can be set in the prepared place without removing the container. The less shock the plant has to endure, the more quickly it will continue its rapid growth.

However, plants will overcome the shock of transplanting more quickly if supplied with a good starter solution. To make one, mix 2 parts water with 1 part sifted compost humus. Allow the

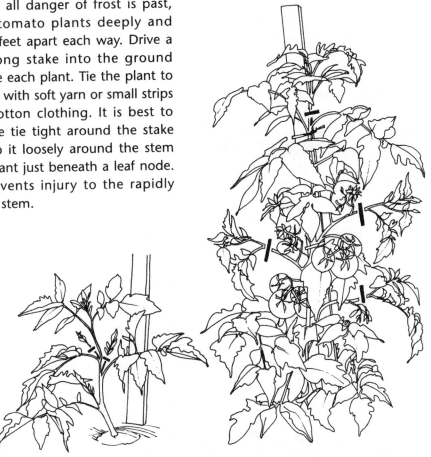

*Place stakes next to your tomato plants when you transplant them to avoid damaging the roots later on. Shortly after transplanting, begin pruning out suckers to produce a plant with two main shoots. As the plant grows, loosely tie it to the stake with strips of fabric or soft yarn. Keep side shoots pruned to about 6 inches long; pinch back top growth to control the plant's height.*

mixture to settle. Apply this solution to the hole in which the plant is to be set and again after the plant has been firmed and settled in place.

It is sometimes necessary to give young plants protection against the damage of late frost. This is easily done by using inverted baskets or paper bags over the plants during unusually cold nights.

Using the pruned, stake method, it is necessary to pinch out the side shoots so as to produce two main shoots, which are tied to the stake. If you follow this method, you will have larger tomatoes and will have no trouble keeping them off the ground.

## Nonstaking Method

Many gardeners find it necessary to allow their plants to grow without staking or training. If you do this, your total crop will likely be about the same, although the individual fruits will be smaller.

If you decide to use this method, it is best to set the plants about 4 feet apart each way. Before the sprawling branches bend to the ground, spread a layer of clean straw, dried grass, or similar material around each plant to keep the fruits off of the ground.

## Choosing the Right Tomatoes for You

Out of so vast a variety of tomatoes from which to choose, to which should the home gardener give preference? When he selects his two packages of seed, which two cultivars will give him the best results? What should be his first aim in choosing?

Generally speaking, it is best to use only wilt-free-certified cultivars like BREAK O'DAY, PRITCHARD MARVEL, MARGLOBE, and many others. In this way you eliminate one of your chief enemies, tomato wilt.

From disease-free stock there is indeed enough from which to choose—the giant OXHEART (each fruit often weighing around 2 pounds), the tiny CHERRY tomatoes, the great WHITE tomatoes (practically acid-free), the bright yellow TANGERINE and YELLOW pears (excellent for salads and marmalades). The many cultivars of tomatoes that are available form an unexcelled galaxy of colorful fruit forms.

Early strains are usually more satisfactory for the gardener than the late kind. But if the summer is long in your locality, you might use the late cultivars to advantage.

The late cultivars can be grown from seed planted in a cold frame and then transplanted directly to the garden, instead of using the seedbed-container-garden routine.

In some localities it is practicable to plant the seed directly into drills in the garden. The seedlings are then thinned until they stand the necessary distance apart. The advantages claimed by the adherents of this method are that the plants are much stronger because they root naturally in the place in which they are to grow, that the work of transplanting is avoided, and that the plants undergo no shock and its following setback caused by transplanting.

## Using Your Harvest

During the summer the vines should provide a steady supply of fresh fruit for family use. Later, when the crop reaches its peak, you will find it best to preserve much of it for future use. Tomatoes and tomato juice can be preserved in any of a number of ways. Whichever way you choose, you may be confident that the material will be a valuable addition to your family diet.

## Using Green Tomatoes

After most of the tomatoes have been gathered, but before the first killing frost, you will find a large number of green and still-growing tomatoes on the vines. This not inconsiderable crop should be gathered and stored. The smaller green tomatoes may be used for the making of relishes and the like.

*Frost doesn't have to mean the end of your tomato harvest. Before frost comes, harvest fully developed, unripe tomatoes and bring them indoors to ripen. Separating them into groups by stage of ripeness makes it easy to find those that are ready to eat and any that are spoiled.*

The larger green tomatoes may be wrapped individually in newspaper and placed about three layers deep in open crates or boxes. These crates of wrapped tomatoes may be stored in any warm place and will ripen without the aid of light.

## Mark Your Plants

Perhaps, as the vines grow and their fruits hang heavily on them, you will notice several plants that produce fruit that especially appeals to you—some striking difference, better flavor, thicker flesh, finer color, larger vine—some quality you admire. You wonder about the possibility of saving seed from these special plants for use next year. This is easily done.

But before you begin you will find it best to consider the individual plant as a unit rather than the individual fruit. The seed of an occasional large fruit found upon a vine that produces only inferior fruit will, as a rule, produce plants bearing fruit equal only to the inferior fruit. But if the vines you select show vigorous growth, good leaf color, and heavy sets of uniform fruit, then the chances are that the seed will produce plants having these superior qualities.

You will find it convenient to mark any plant selected for seed. Tomatoes are self-fertile and do not cross to any great extent, so you will not have to worry much about the distance of the selected plant from some inferior one.

## Gathering Seed

The tomatoes selected for seed should remain on the vine beyond the edible stage, but not so long that decay sets in. If only a few seeds are

### Earlier Tomatoes

I've devised a cloche that lets me pick my first tomatoes two weeks earlier than before. Prior to the last frost, I set out the plants and stake them. Next, I slip a plastic dry-cleaning bag or a heavier 4-mil plastic over each stake, tying or stapling the plastic above the plant. The bottom of the plastic is weighted down with soil. If hard frost is predicted, I wrap newspaper around the plants under the plastic for added insulation. The plastic can easily be rolled up to provide ventilation on sunny days.

*Charles G. Bartman*
*Louisville, Kentucky*
*April 1987*

to be collected, it is a simple matter to halve the fruits, remove the seeds with the thumb, then wash and dry them.

For large quantities, the fruit is picked, placed in a wood or earthenware vessel, and mashed. Water is added in a quantity equal to the mash and stirred vigorously. The resulting pulp should be held at about 70 degrees and allowed to ferment for three or four days, being stirred now and then.

## Fermenting Steps

This fermentation will cause the good, heavy seed to settle to the bottom,

**Tomato seeds and pulp**

**Fermenting mixture**

**Seeds drying**

*Ferment tomato seeds to save them for planting next year. Scoop pulp from the tomatoes you've selected into a container and add an equal amount of water. Place the jar in a warm spot and stir the contents once or twice each day. Add water to double the mixture when most of the seeds have settled to the bottom or when you see bubbles rising in it. Stir well, then skim debris off the top. Repeat stirring and skimming until only good seeds are left in the bottom of the container. Rinse the seeds and dry them on a screen.*

where it will remain when the pulp, inferior seed, and water are poured off. This fermentation is also nature's method of eliminating many seed-borne bacterial diseases.

The heavy seed should then be washed in clean water and spread out thinly on paper. It should be kept out of direct sunlight but in a place where it will dry rapidly. When the seed is dry, it should be stored in envelopes or paper bags and left in a cool, dry place.

Perhaps, during the long winter months, you remember the specially selected seed you have stored. You shake the envelopes or paper bags that each contain no more than a pinch of tiny, scalelike seeds weighing almost nothing.

Another summer comes along; the tomato seed you saved proves almost 98 percent fertile and disease-free. The seedlings flourish. And as you watch another crop of tomatoes coming on, you notice that every vine, almost every fruit, bears a close resemblance to the ones you chose last year.

Almost every fruit has that peculiar quality that you yourself selected. You realize that you have developed your own particular strain, one specially suitable to you and your locality. You wonder if the type of tomato you have developed should be given a name. You have learned to grow tomatoes.

*January 1954*

# Building the Japanese Tomato Ring

*James Grady*

> This ingenious structure will give you more delicious tomatoes in less space.

Looking for a way of growing tomatoes that makes maximum use of limited space, conserves water, and offers easy frost protection? Then the Japanese tomato ring may be just what you're seeking. It's a system of growing tomatoes in a circle, the center of which is filled with rich organic matter. This arrangement encourages the tomatoes to send their roots into the ring searching out this excellent source of nourishment. The tomato vines are simply tied to a wire meshing constructed around the perimeter of the circle. After the initial cost of the materials, you will have a structure that will last for years and require little or no maintenance.

Spade up an area with a diameter of about 7 feet. Within this circle trace out another circle with a 5-foot diameter for the wire ring.

Chicken wire can be used, but I find the welded wire mesh used in cement works makes for a more permanent and durable structure. About 16 feet of this mesh will be needed, and it will stand 5 feet high. Although it will stand by itself, I find that 18-inch sections of metal coat hangers serve as effective anchors. Bend the hanger in the center to produce a croquet wicket effect, and then loop it over the bottom rung of the mesh before driving it into the ground.

Next, take some screening and line the inside of the mesh to the height of 18 inches. This helps to retain the organic matter, which can now be placed within the completed structure. I begin with a layer of well-composted manure about 1 inch thick, followed by a layer of compost.

To get started, fill the ring with organic matter to a height of about 6 inches. After your tomatoes are off and running, you add another 6 to 12 inches of soil and compost. I also sprinkle granite dust, phosphate rock, and cottonseed meal lightly between each layer. Keep this material moist at all times.

Plant your tomatoes at 2½-foot intervals around the outside of the ring. As the plants grow, tie them to the wire mesh with strips of yarn or cloth. By restricting growth to two main branches, I was able to produce vines up to 11 feet long by training the vines up the 5 feet of structure and back down again as often as necessary. Since the ring is so compact, it is easily protected from frost by covering it up on threatening nights.

*June 1976*

*About 16 feet of wire mesh forms a 5-foot-tall ring that supports tomatoes around its perimeter and holds organic matter to nourish them.*

# Tomatoes in June

*David Freifelder*

*Cherry tomatoes from his deeply rooted plants have appeared on the author's table as early as June 22 and as late as Thanksgiving Day.*

The tomato season in the Northeast is disappointingly short, so 13 years ago, I began experimenting with new methods of growing tomatoes for harvest before the usual August dates. I've developed a simple technique that yields fruit of early-season tomato cultivars before the end of June and midseason tomato cultivars by early July—extending my Boston growing season by five to six weeks.

Most seed packets recommend planting seeds indoors eight to ten weeks before the date of the last frost. For New England, this means planting in late March. Instead, I plant my seeds in the last week of January. I have used BURPEEANA, BIG EARLY HYBRID, BIG BOY, and RED CHERRY cultivars. I put two seeds in each Styrofoam cup half-full of pure compost. The seeds germinate in about one week, and I remove the weaker seedling. The containers sit either in a sunny window or a few inches away from a 15-watt fluorescent light.

When the plants are 3 to 4 inches high, the roots will be crowded because of the small amount of soil in the cups, so I then transfer each plant to a 5-inch flowerpot. Place ½ inch of soil in the pot, put in the plant, and fill the pot with soil. That results in burying about 2 inches of the stem. New roots (adventitious roots) grow out from the stems, and a large root ball is formed.

By mid-April the plants are about 10 inches tall and pot-bound. I transfer each plant to a 10-inch pot. Again, place the tomato plant as deep as possible, put a 3-foot stake in the pot, and place it in a sunny window. By May 1, my plant is usually 2 feet tall and has many flowers. If it is too tall, I pinch the growing tip, and growth begins farther down the stem.

For the first week of May, I put the plants outside to get one or two hours of morning sun, then shade for the rest of the day. I bring the plants in each night unless the temperature is expected to remain above 60 degrees. During the second week, I increase the exposure to sunlight until, by May 15, they are ready to be planted in my tomato patch. By this time, there are small tomatoes on the plants. Removing the plant from the pot is difficult because of its height, but if the plant has been staked and tied, it can be done safely.

I set the plants in the ground in an unusual way to bury more stem and force more roots. I dig a trench 1 foot deep, 1 foot wide, and 2 feet long. A 6-foot stake is erected at one end of the trench before I put in the plant. The root ball is then laid on its side at that end of the trench. The plant is cut away from the pot stake

## Cagey Tomatoes

Extend your tomato season three to four weeks by making each plant a mini greenhouse. By using wire cages wrapped in clear plastic film, your tomatoes will be protected from early frosts, cool temperatures, and drying winds. When the weather turns hot, remove the plastic; the cage will support vines and fruit.

Hardware and building supply stores carry the ten-gauge concrete reinforcing wire with 6-by-6-inch mesh in 5-by-150-foot rolls—enough for 25 cages. (You might share a roll with a gardening friend.) While 5 feet may seem too tall a cage, by the end of the growing season, your tomato plants will fill the cages to the top.

Take a 6-foot length of the wire and wrap to make a 24-inch-diameter cage. Remove the bottom horizontal section of wire and push the cage into the ground. Next, wrap 5-by-6-foot, 2- to 4-mil polyethylene plastic film around the outside of each cage. Secure with duct tape or string.

Once night temperatures remain above 55 degrees, remove the plastic wrap. It can be used later to protect plants from fall frost. You can also make smaller cages to improve growing conditions for peppers, eggplants, and cucumbers.

*John Schabinger*
*Roseville, Minnesota*

## Hot Tomatoes

Tomatoes are heat lovers. But when it gets too hot, blossoms abort and drop off. No fruit will set until temperatures moderate. Daytime temperatures consistently above 90 degrees and night temperatures above 75 degrees will cause tomato plants to drop their blossoms. In the South, that can mean long stretches with no tomatoes.

Dr. Ray Volin of the Homestead Florida Research Center recommends several tomato cultivars that produce well in the heat. The WALTER tomato is very adaptable to variations in temperature. It is resistant to two strains of fusarium wilt but is not verticillium wilt–resistant. The FLORA-DADE is verticillium wilt–resistant and produces a firm fruit. FLORAMERICA is an award-winning multiple disease-resistant and widely adaptable hybrid tomato that produces large fruit. Burpee's BETTER BOY is another good choice for sunbelt gardeners.

Dr. Bill Sims of the University of California at Davis recommends the open-pollinated CASTLEMART tomato and the hybrid ROYAL FLUSH for gardeners in southern California. Both varieties set fruit in hot temperatures.

In southeast Texas, the Beaumont Research Station reports that gardeners have success with SPRING GIANT, TERRIFIC, and HOMESTEAD tomato cultivars. Other hot-season tomatoes are TAMU CHICO III and IMPROVED SUMMERTIME. Researchers recommend that gardeners make sure that any tomato seeds and plants are VFN (verticillium-fusarium-nematode) resistant because these three afflictions of the tomato are always problems in hot climates.

*Candyce Merkle*
**Organic Gardening**

and carefully and gently bent up the new stake. The trench is filled with a mixture of compost and soil, then watered in.

My tomato plants grow very rapidly. My record early harvest date was June 22 for cherry tomatoes and June 25 for BIG EARLY hybrid. Every year, I have early tomatoes before July 1, and the midseason plants always bear before July 8. All of the plants bear heavily, and my 12 plants (3 cherry, 4 early, and 5 midseason) supply my family and friends with tomatoes for the entire season. This past summer, a cherry tomato plant on my sunny patio continued to bear until Thanksgiving.

My plants have developed such enormous root systems that they grow

*By starting his tomatoes early and repotting them as they grow, the author makes the most of New England summers and produces an extra-early crop of tomatoes.*

extremely high if unchecked. Some years ago I allowed one to climb a nearby hedge, and it reached 10 feet by the beginning of September! Now I usually allow two or three suckers to grow from the base of the plant to keep the height in check.

*February 1981*

## A Hairy Solution

If you'd like to put more nitrogen in your gardening but have been put off by the high cost of nitrogen supplements, there's one source of this nutrient that's readily available in even the smallest town. It's free for the asking and is 12 to 16 percent rich in nitrogen. It's human hair.

I have long-standing arrangements with two local barbers. My approach is to supply each barber with a feed sack or garbage bag, pick up the contents regularly, and bring him a few garden goodies in summer. Most barbers are glad to save themselves a few bucks in garbage bags, and they are tickled to see the hair go to good use. Both my sources are quite entertained at how I appear regularly to pick up my clippings.

Hair is an essential part of my organic approach. I add it to compost piles, spread it on the ground before applying mulch, and put it in planting holes and under fruit trees. Our tomato yield is 30 pounds per plant. My two in-town barbers appreciate my remembering them with a few of what they affectionately call "those hairy tomatoes."

*Bob Schwarz*
*Reader, West Virginia*
*November 1986*

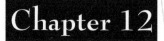

# Chapter 12

# Sunflowers, Sweet Corn & Such

# *Those Sensational Sunflowers*

O ver the years, the sunflower has become a popular symbol of organic living—something beautiful, natural, and versatile. With a little effort, these sunny giants can reach 15 feet. More than ornamental, they can make a natural fence, provide garden shade, and produce nutrient-rich seed for snacks, oil, and bird food. After the harvest, stalks and leaves can be composted to enrich garden soil. Sunflowers have become economically important, too. A major oil and seed crop, they're grown on over 2.8 million acres in the United States alone.

Here's how to grow golden giants!

## Something for Everyone

Sunflowers are real renaissance plants. They're easy for kids to grow, and the spectacular flowers and abundance of seed make them an ideal introduction to gardening. Children love harvesting and snacking on the delicious seeds. Mature sunflower seeds are highly nutritious, an excellent source of high-quality protein that contains every essential amino acid. At 8.7 grams of protein per ¼ cup, just ¼ cup of sun-

flower seeds will provide a child with 20 to 25 percent of his daily protein requirements. They're also a fine source of vitamins, except for vitamin C (which you can get by sprouting the seeds).

The sunflower is native to America. Native Americans grew them long before the arrival of European explorers.

*Old-fashioned sunflowers, with their dinner plate–sized heads, brighten the garden and yield the nutritious, gray-striped seeds people love to snack on. Heart-healthy sunflower oil is pressed from the smaller black-hulled seeds some cultivars produce.*

Sunflower-seed bread was an American Indian specialty! The Europeans were so impressed with the plant that they took seed back, and now sunflowers are favorites in China and Russia. Sunflower oil is derived from Russian-type oilseed and is 70 percent polyunsaturated, a higher percentage than soybean, corn, or olive oil, which means less cholesterol in our diets. And the seeds yield 40 percent oil, compared to soybeans' 20 percent.

## So Easy to Grow

Growing these sun-worshipers isn't difficult. Just choose a cultivar that will give you the size and type of seeds you want. *Helianthus annuus,* the common garden sunflower, is the easiest to grow, reaching heights of 10 to 12 feet. MAMMOTH, a popular cultivar, matures in about 80 days. It's the tallest sunflower and has the largest seed head, with big, meaty, striped seeds. GREY STRIPE, MANCHURIAN, and GIGANTEOUS are other top-notch cultivars. They mature in 83 to 90 days. SUNGOLD, a shorter seed-producer, grows to about 6 feet. Seeds from these standard large sunflowers (available from many seed companies) are of good quality and are suitable for fresh eating, baking, and grinding for sunflower meal.

If you're going to press your own sunflower oil, you'll need seed with a higher oil content. PEREDOVIK, a Russian-type oilseed, matures in 110 days. One pound of seed will give about 3 ounces of oil. Because this variety is open-pollinated, you can save seed to plant next season. SUNBRED (also 110 days) is another oilseed variety.

Check your soil before you plant—it should be loose and have a near-neutral pH, about 6.0 to 7.5. Sunflowers need lots of nutrients and moisture for optimum growth. Add compost, manure, or other humus sources and ground rock fertilizers to enrich the soil. Or try a mixture of 2 parts cottonseed or soybean meal to 1 part phosphate rock and 2 parts granite dust. Apply 3 pounds per 100 square feet.

*Once your sunflowers are fully dry, rub them against a piece of wire mesh stretched over the top of a bucket to free the seeds from the flower.*

Sunflowers are hardy. They can be started about two weeks before your region's frost-free date and can withstand early light frosts at the end of the growing season. Depending on the cultivar, you'll need from 80 to 120 days before the first hard frost, so check your calendar, and plant accordingly. Sow seed about ½ inch deep in rows 2 to 3 feet apart. Weed regularly, and mulch to keep down competition so that your sunflowers get a good start. Water thoroughly as needed, especially during dry spells. You can prevent wind or storm damage by staking the tall cultivars when the heads get heavy.

## Off with Their Heads

It's time to harvest when the back of the ripe sunflower's head is dry and brown, without a trace of green. However, if you leave sunflowers to field-dry, the birds may harvest them. The heads can also shatter and drop that precious seed on the ground.

To foil birds and prevent loss from shattering, you can cover sunflower heads with netting, cheesecloth, or paper bags. Or cut off the heads when the seeds are full size and put them in a dry, well-ventilated place (like an attic). Leave a foot or two of stem on the heads to hang them from for drying.

*April 1981*

# Cold-Country Corn

## Samuel R. Ogden

Short seasons and a late spring don't stop this Vermont veteran, who tells how he wrestles the rugged climate to grow sweet corn aplenty.

Not much thought goes into having enough time to grow a crop as enjoyable as sweet corn—unless you happen to live where the weather makes it tricky. Then, as "fringe-area" gardeners do with other vegetables or fruits, you start figuring the number of frost-free days you can hopefully count on. And you start hunting for cultivars requiring the shortest time span to mature. (Seedsmen and horticulturists have consistently been breeding improved strains for the frigid sectors.) One more thing—you start learning little knacks and maneuvers that help produce a good harvest. So, I'm glad to share some of my corn-growing experiences along the fringes of climatic possibility.

Up here at Londonderry, Vermont—an upland valley at an elevation of 1,400 feet—the air drainage is such that places around us, but higher above the streambed, have an advantage over us amounting to a week or more on either end of the season. In this latitude (43-plus degrees) the nights are seldom hot, and thus several desirable vegetables such as lima beans and melons will not reward the time and labor invested in them, even higher up on the hills.

*Sweet corn germinates best when the soil
temperature is at least 60°F.*

Nevertheless, there are compromises to be made among the frost-tender kinds—and one of the most satisfactory of these is sweet corn.

## Just 85 Days to Go

During the 1969 season, the last frost of spring took place on the morning of May 27 (and this was a real freeze); the frost-free period ended on August 22, a span of 85 days—which is about the average length of our growing season. There have been better years and worse. In fact, in several years since my garden has been on this same spot, there has been a frost in every month of the 12.

Of all the quickly maturing varieties of corn, most are hybrids. The fastest-growing of these that I could locate was a strain sold by Harris Seeds of Rochester, New York, called ROYAL CREST, the package of which proclaimed that it matured in 64 days. As it turned out, this was an optimistic claim; the actual elapsed time was 71 days. My corn plot last season contained 384 hills, which were planted 28 inches apart in each direction, with three, occasionally four, stalks per hill. Each hill had a round-pointed shovel of earth removed, which was replaced with fine well-rotted, granular compost.

Two hundred thirty-two of these hills were planted to ROYAL CREST, the first time I had used this variety. The balance of 152 hills was planted to SENECA CHIEF, likewise being planted for the first time. Both varieties are yellow-kerneled corn, and I started to pick SENECA CHIEF, which purports to be a 78-day corn, I believe, on the September 4, just two days after the ROYAL CREST was all gone. That was 88 days after it was sown, another example of catalog optimism—at least as far as our climate is concerned.

Both varieties had been planted on the same day, June 6. At this point I must admit to an error of calculation: I could perfectly well have planted a week earlier. As a matter of sound practice, it is better to plant early—for to be caught by frost on the front end is apt to be less damaging than on the tail end. Fortunately, the frosts that hit us first on August 22 and thereafter were not severe and were followed by growing weather, so the maturing of the corn was not seriously interfered with. But it could have been disastrous.

## "The Best Corn They'd Ever Eaten"

The growth of both varieties was excellent, the ROYAL CREST stalks averaging 7½ feet with reddish stems and tassels. SENECA CHIEF went about ½ foot higher with yellow stems and tassels. The quality of the ROYAL CREST ears was very fine for an early variety, the first ears running about 7 inches in length and well-filled to the tips. The tag end of the pickings were smaller, but all held good, sweet quality, and the crop averaged four ears per hill.

SENECA CHIEF still produces as of mid-September, and in my opinion it is the best variety that one might hope to raise in this climate; although it is not one that the gardener can safely count on. Its ears are larger than the 64-day corn, and the kernels are extra sweet and tender. In

fact all who tasted this corn vowed it was the best they had ever eaten. Gardeners around here seem to prefer the mixed white-and-yellow varieties to the all-yellow ones, and of these the 78-day BUTTER AND SUGAR appears to be the favorite. By now, though, I have tried most of the varieties that one could hope to bring to maturity in this climate, and in my opinion SENECA CHIEF is the best of them all. Records aren't complete yet, but it is perfectly clear that its productivity is higher, along with its superior quality. I am sure the plants will finish up at about six marketable ears per hill.

There is one other difference between the two varieties that must be noted, and that is while the growth in both instances was all that could possibly be expected, ROYAL CREST was hit by two pests, one an insect, the other a fungus, although in neither instance was the damage enough to materially affect the crop. There were corn borers in a few of the ears, and I found three stalks af-

*Start checking your corn for ripeness about three weeks after silks appear. Pierce a kernel with your thumbnail. The corn is ready to eat when milky juice spurts out.*

fected by smut, the first time either of these enemies had visited this garden planting in a number of years. There was no sign of either infestation in the SENECA CHIEF.

## Feed the Soil— Move the Crop

As a matter of sound practice, a crop of corn should not succeed itself the next year on the same ground. My garden is composed of four plots, each separated from the others by greensward, and the corn is rotated between them from year to year. Normally each one of these plots receives four yards of rotted barnyard manure every year. But this past fall the deep snows came before the manure could be delivered, and in the spring the ground was too soft, so I had no manure. Fortunately, I had been building a pile of organic material that I did not choose to put in my regular compost piles, and this had been going on for several years. There were cornstalks, old baled hay, lawn clippings, shredded bark, and so forth in this pile—and at the bottom of it, here was as fine a compost as one could hope for. However, since there was no way to sort it out, I had it dumped on two of the quarters in its entirety, raking off the coarse material after the piles had been spread. There was enough compost in my regular piles to cover the other two sections, and so for the first time in 35 years, the garden received no fer-

tilization except that which straight compost could give it—and I must say the results were phenomenal.

The corn quarter was one of those which received the rough compost, with a shovelful of fine compost added to each hill. (I should say now, that this last wasn't really necessary, but at planting time I could not be sure.) The corn was up in five days, and nothing interfered with its growth from that day on. The whole plot received its first hoeing by the Fourth of July, and then two more before the stalks were too high to permit further cultivation. So, the corn grew apace and was the marvel of the countryside—all even in height, dark green and broad in leaf, standing in ranks so closed that nothing showed but a solid cube of healthy vegetation, which eventually became tinged on top with the red and yellow of blossoms.

## Cucumber Vines Climb the Corn

For several years now I have put corn and cucumbers together. There is a strip of soil between the first row of hills and the garden path on each side of the plot. In these strips I have planted cucumbers, having great success with them and no resultant disadvantage to the corn. I keep the runners of the cucumber vines turned in so that they penetrate into the garden and do not clutter up the paths. One of the varieties I planted last year, Harris's CHINESE CUCUMBERS, is a great climber—and many of these vines actually climbed the cornstalks. (These cucumbers, incidentally, are very mild and tender, rather more spiny than standard types, producing long, slender fruit that grows to an extraordinary length. Visitors to the garden were amused to see long, green objects, as much as 20 inches in length, hanging down from the cornstalks—objects that upon examination turned out to be cucumbers!)

In summing up, I would say that cold-country corn is perhaps less productive than crops grown where nights are hot and humid, and that the requirement of rapid maturity excludes from the range of choice, varieties wherein the ears are larger and the kernels possibly sweeter. But in my experience it would be hard to beat SENECA CHIEF. However, in this climate, this variety took 88 days from planting to picking, so it's far from being a sure thing. Thus I hedged my bet by planting more of the less acceptable 64-day corn. Nevertheless, I shall be sowing SENECA CHIEF again this spring when planting time comes around, and if the weather seems propitious, it will be a week or more earlier than last year.

*March 1970*

*Interplanting sweet corn with vining crops such as pole beans or cucumbers makes better use of your garden space without reducing either crop's productivity.*

# Gardening, Health, and Garlic Go Together

## James Jankowiak

There's more to garlic than planting cloves in spring, pulling bulbs in the fall, and eating this aromatic vegetable in highly seasoned Italian dishes in the winter. Let me introduce you to a few of the subtleties of this multiple-use crop.

Not only is garlic good food, it's also good medicine and a top-drawer garden pest control. European and Middle Eastern peoples are great garlic eaters for more than

> A true enthusiast doesn't let garlic's strong aroma stand between him and healthful eating.

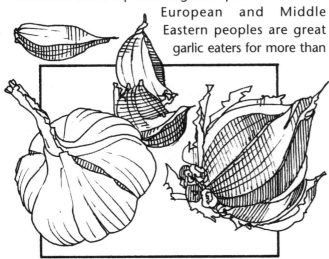

*Plant your garlic in the fall, around Columbus Day. Don't plant cloves from supermarket garlic—they may have been treated to retard sprouting.*

culinary reasons. Somewhere in remote antiquity their forefathers discovered that many disease-carrying organisms can't exist in garlic oil. Today we know that garlic's essential oil contains a substance with natural antibiotic properties. And a little goes a long way. For example, an old technique of treating the common cold is to rub garlic on the bottoms of the feet at night. By morning the patient will have a hint of garlic on his breath—proof of the penetrating power of its oil.

Garlic on the breath—certainly an unpleasant odor to anyone but another garlic eater—is the main reason this health-giving member of the lily and onion family has lost favor in this country. (There is an old-time way around this problem, which I'll mention later.) But medical researchers have figured out a way to deodorize the healing properties in garlic. Now it's used without objection for the treatment of stomach disorders.

## Take Two Cloves ...

I've heard that eating a couple cloves of garlic a day for a month will kill off harmful intestinal bacteria and promote the growth of beneficial varieties, and I believe it. Both my wife and I have escaped dysentery in our foreign travels with garlic, and we've been in some pretty doubtful gastronomic situations. In the same foreign lands, before I became a garlic eater I always had stomach problems.

But my observations are nothing

new. Dioscorides, a Greek physician who traveled with second-century Roman legions, specified garlic for intestinal disorders. Less ancient sources claim a garlic clove every two hours coupled with ½ cup of yarrow tea will break up a cold or mild flu in 24 hours. Again, I've tried this simple remedy and it works.

Garlic works on garden plants, too. The famous garlic-oil-cayenne-pepper spray is a safe homemade alternative to toxic chemical pesticides. Garlic is also good for roses. It makes a good general-purpose insect repellent and has a controlling effect on diseases like downy mildew, early tomato blight, bacterial bean blight, and other such maladies.

I use live plants tucked away in odd corners of the garden as repellents, being careful only to keep them away from beans and peas, which for some reason just don't grow well near garlic, onions, and shallots.

Speaking of growing, here are a few of the finer points for getting a garlic crop.

## Grow Great Garlic

Bulb and clove selection is most important. There are three major types of garlic: white or silverskin, red or Italian, and elephant. Elephant is big like its name and makes a better vegetable than it does a seasoning or medicine. Of the other two, whites are earlier-maturing and bigger, have a shorter storage life, and are most prolific. But reds, though they take a couple weeks longer to mature, last much longer in storage and have a more powerful garlic flavor. They're my favorites.

Pick the biggest bulbs. You can buy them by the pound at many groceries or preferably from gardening and seed companies. These little packages in the supermarket with two or three garlics are far too expensive. Of the biggest bulbs, take only the outside cloves for planting and use the rest for cooking or eating. The outside cloves are the largest in the bulb, and as you save and plant them each year, you'll develop your own strain with inner cloves bigger than the outer cloves on most store-bought garlics. If you've ever had to laboriously peel tiny garlic cloves, you'll know what a blessing a large strain is.

I sprinkle a liberal amount of bonemeal in my garlic bed along with the usual heavy application of well-rotted manure or finished compost. This helps my plants grow stronger and mature earlier.

Here in north coastal California I plant cloves 3 inches deep in 12- to 15-inch rows, spacing them 4 inches apart. I start in mid-November and continue through February. The growing season is long but cool and slow, and winter frosts are few and light. My main keeper planting is in January. Where the ground freezes, you can plant as soon as the soil thaws. Garlic can stand moderate

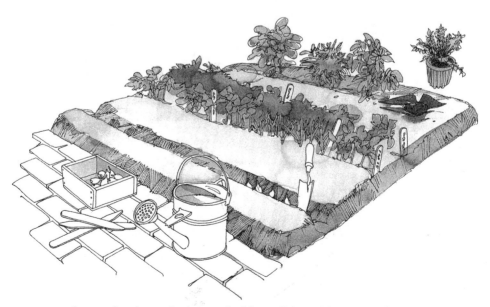

*For best results, plant garlic cloves in the fall in well-drained, humus-rich soil. At harvest time the following midsummer, save the biggest cloves (usually the outer ones) from your garlic crop for replanting. By selecting the largest cloves each year, you'll develop your own bigger strain, with fewer tiny, hard-to-peel cloves.*

*Braided garlic makes an attractive and convenient kitchen decoration.*

hook are both a pleasant rustic decoration and a culinary convenience in the kitchen.

## Good News for Garlic Breath

If you're enthused about garlic and its multiple uses but still worried about a garlic-on-the-breath problem, here's the old-time solution I mentioned earlier: Plant parsley. After eating garlic or any garlic dish, chew on some fresh parsley and much of the garlic odor will disappear.

And good garlic growing to you.

*September 1974*

frosts and even a snow cover.

Garlic likes a moist but well-drained soil. A high humus soil and a good, thick mulch applied when the shoots are 8 inches high will assure you a big bulb crop if you keep up on your watering. Failure to provide enough moisture will give tiny bulbs or single, undivided clove-bulbs.

When the growth dies back, I stop watering to give the plants a chance to mature. Any top that doesn't turn brown and fall over, I kick over. When all the plants have died, I pull up the bulbs and let them cure in the sun a few days with the tops covering the cloves. Then I braid and store in a cool, not-too-moist place.

Some people clip the tops and roots, then store the bulbs loosely in boxes, but I find braids hung on a

### Perpetual Peppers

Four years ago, I had a green pepper plant just loaded with small peppers when a killing frost was predicted. I couldn't bear to lose the peppers, so I dug up the plant, put it in a 12-inch pot, and brought it indoors. Today my green pepper "tree" is alive and well—and I've had peppers from it each winter indoors. Each fall I cut back the longest side shoots, which seems to encourage the plant to flower and bear better.

*Lorene C. Nelken*
*Clinton, Iowa*
*November 1981*

## Chili Peppers for Health?

More chili peppers are produced and eaten in New Mexico than anywhere else in the United States—a whopping 55,000 tons a year. And that region of the Southwest has the lowest death rate from heart disease and cancer. Some medical investigators believe that's more than just coincidence.

Chili apparently has the ability to help lower the consumer's blood fat level and reduce his chances of heart attack, Dr. Lora M. Shields of New Mexico Highlands University has reported. She also found that those persons who eat chili-rich Mexican cuisine have a longer blood coagulation time, which might spell the difference in the occurrence of a stroke or heart attack.

Chili peppers are also a phenomenally rich source of vitamin A. It's estimated that an average serving of some Mexican food can run well over one hundred thousand units of that nutrient. Imagine countless small farms and family garden patches raising fresh chili peppers for local consumption, and you begin to see that vitamin A deficiency should never be a major problem in New Mexico.

The red chili is also a natural preservative, according to a report from the New Mexico State University of Las Cruces. It acts as an antioxidant and retards the oxidation of meat and fats. Chicken, beef, and pork casseroles can remain in frozen storage much longer and still retain their flavor when they contain chili.

*John Feltman*

# Just Enough Lettuce

*John Meeker*

*A spring sowing of lettuce is ready for harvest well before tomatoes need more room to grow.*

T he average packet of lettuce contains ¹⁄₁₀ ounce, or about 2,000 seeds. That's enough to make a row of lettuce 100 feet long—roughly 150 heads of lettuce every two to three weeks.

Probably no one ever plants a whole packet of lettuce seed, but a lot of gardeners *do* overplant. After several seasons of suffering lettuce feast and famine, I learned how to keep lettuce coming without overdoing it. What worked for me were weekly sowings of just a few lettuce seeds in pots. By sowing religiously every week, I have a steady supply of lettuce. And I give my seedlings ideal growing conditions by planting first in pots or flats rather than sowing directly in the garden. My transplants are strong, they're free from insect damage, and they don't need thinning, so I know every plant will be productive. The weekly potting-up—10 to 12 seeds and some rich, well-drained potting soil— takes less than 15 minutes.

In summer, these pots of lettuce seed need a plastic cover to prevent moisture loss. You can put them outdoors in filtered light—direct sun can be fatal. In early spring and late fall, they can take direct

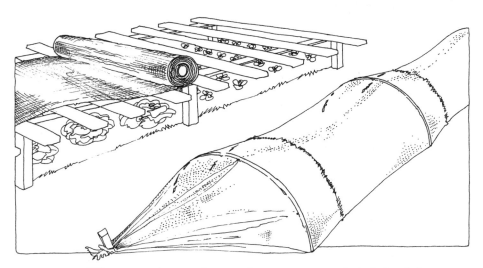

*When summer heats up, keep your lettuce crop going with shade from lath, snow fence, or shade cloth to protect the plants from the afternoon sun.*

sunlight. They also need to be protected from sudden cloudbursts, which can wash out the seed. In cool months, the pots can be placed on stones or cement walks where the sun's heat will radiate into the pots at night. In cold climates, pots of lettuce can be put in cold or hot frames. Or put them indoors on a windowsill, where, again, they need to be protected from moisture loss with a plastic cover.

From sowing time to transplanting out into the garden takes roughly three weeks to a month (in cool weather). That's a month of saved garden space for other vegetables. To save more space, I plant lettuce with vegetables that take longer to mature. Lettuce fits well among young tomatoes, eggplant, cucumbers, corn, melons, squash, and beans. Flower beds are good spots for tucking away a lettuce head or two. I also put some of my weekly lettuce crop on the outside of a double row of climbing peas, with good results. Strawberries, onions, carrots, beets, and celery are some crops that won't grow well with lettuce, mainly because the faster-growing lettuce shades the companion crop so it gets leggy and poorly formed.

With diligent sowing and transplanting, I have just enough lettuce—not too much and not too little.

*June 1982*

# Chapter 13

# Don't Forget Flowers!

# A Wealth of Flowers

## Doc and Katy Abraham

Every year the price of flower plants gets higher. You could switch to perennials—you pay a little more, plant once, and the blooms come back year after year. But annuals have other virtues that few perennials can match. They flower fast, and most of them bloom all season. The best solution is to raise your own plants from seed.

People prefer to buy plants that are in full bloom, so that's the way nurseries raise them, unfortunately. The bought blooms soon drop, as the plant—too long in the pot, with a small, fertilizer-dependent root system—struggles to overcome transplant shock. For prolific flowering all season, you need a plant that's never been stressed—one that's young, stocky, and just forming buds at the time you set it out. To get this kind of plant, however, you'll probably have to raise it yourself.

We've been growing flower (and vegetable) plants for 45 years, and we grow thousands each season, mostly for our own yard and for friends. And we have learned a few tricks that give us healthy flower transplants year after year and save us a lot of time.

No-fail seed-starting tips for petunias, marigolds, impatiens, salvia, portulaca, alyssum, and zinnias.

*Annual flowers such as these marigolds, salvia, zinnias, and alyssum will brighten your garden all summer long. You can't beat the brilliance and abundant bloom of an annual bed. And you can't beat the price of homegrown plants.*

For almost everything we grow, we use two kinds of containers and two kinds of soils. Germinating seedlings have very different requirements than growing plants do. For germination, we prefer shallow containers that allow us to scatter many seeds close together—flats or something like them. We sow the seed fairly thick because we will soon transplant the seedlings to larger containers. This saves us space in the germinating area and greatly cuts down on the amount of special soil we use. To prevent damping-off in the young seedlings, we make our own version of the peat-lite mix. We blend 1 part *milled sphagnum* peat with 1 part perlite and 1 part vermiculite. The ingredients are free of the disease-causing organism, so there's no need to pasteurize the mix.

Immediately after planting, seed flats get bottom heat. A heating pad is worth every penny of its modest cost. Germination is faster and more uniform. For all the flowers discussed here, 70 to 72 degrees is excellent for germination. To retain moisture, we put the flats into clear plastic bags. But at the first signs of sprouting, the plastic comes off and the flats are moved to a cooler area.

When the seedlings are well-established but still quite small, we transplant them into containers with enough room for them to grow until it's time to put them outdoors. We like market packs (4-by-8-inch containers made of plastic or papier-mâché) or cell packs that hold 12 plants (plastic trays with six to nine compartments). These we fill with a much cheaper and more nutrient-rich medium: 1 part compost to 1 part builders' sand (not play sand), 1 part topsoil, and 1 part vermiculite or perlite. Because the plants are no longer very susceptible to damping-off, we don't pasteurize this mix, either, and have had no problem with disease.

Each kind of flower, we've discovered, has its own little quirks. Here are the details you'll need to grow seven of our favorites from seed.

**Impatiens**

*Start your own impatiens from seed. You'll get healthier plants at a fraction of the cost of buying them from a nursery.*

## Impatiens

There's no need to cover impatiens seed. It needs light to germinate, and the pores in the planting mix are like the Grand Canyon to the minuscule seeds. Most of them fall well below the surface. We find impatiens do better if we include a little sand in the peat mix. After we fill the flat, we sift a thin layer of pure peat over the surface, then we scatter pinches of the seed as you would sprinkle salt over food.

After ten days under plastic on the heating cable, look carefully for the first flush of tiny green leaves. When they appear, put the seedlings in a cooler place that has plenty of light. Fifty to 55 degrees at night is not too cool. When the seedlings grow to about 1 inch tall, transplant them. Although they may not have more than their seed leaves and two true leaves, do it at this time. The older the plants get, the harder they take the transplanting. Hold the seedling by one leaf, not the stem, and put one plant in each cell of a six-pack tray.

## Petunias

The secret of growing petunias is never to let them become crowded, and never let the roots dry out. Their seed is very small, and we plant them the same way we do impatiens, eight weeks before the last frost. If anything, petunia seedlings like cooler temperatures than impatiens. We

**Petunia**

*Tiny petunia seeds pay off with big,
showy flowers.*

move them off the heating pad as soon as the seeds are up. We transplant them when they are still quite small, under 1 inch tall.

If petunias get dry, the stems become woody, and they never seem to recover enough to bloom freely. Plan your planting so you don't hold them in containers very long. If your petunias do get woody or you must buy some that have been in pots too long, cut them back drastically before transplanting, then keep them well watered and well fed.

## Marigolds

These flowers are considered easy because they can take abuse like becoming root-bound or drying out. Coddle them like any other, however, and you'll be happier with the results.

For the large, hedge types, allow ten weeks between seeding and setting out in the garden. Some of the

newer cultivars, however, will begin to blossom much sooner. Sow the dwarf marigolds eight weeks before your last frost date. Lay the seed on the surface of the soil in the flats, then sprinkle on enough sphagnum peat to keep the seed moist. With bottom heat they'll be up in five to seven days. Move them to a cooler area right away. Transplant them to the larger containers when they're 1½ inches tall.

## Portulaca

If you've got a bone-dry spot, this is the flower to plant. We skip the flats because portulaca comes up so quickly. Many people sow it directly in the ground, where it will self-sow year after year. But we like to raise transplants—we find they make planning and planting a bed easier. The improved cultivars offer more brilliant colors.

Six weeks before the last frost, we fill cell packs with germinating mix and put three or four portulaca seeds in each cell. The seeds like darkness, so we cover them with sifted sphagnum peat, cover the packs with plastic, and put them on the heating pad. Later we plant the seedlings directly outdoors, without separating or thinning them.

## Sweet Alyssum

This is a hard one to transplant successfully. Even if the plants are only 3 inches high, they generally drop all their leaves and take a long time to recover. The answer is to set them out young and disturb the roots *very* little.

Alyssum is pretty cold-hardy. You can put it into the garden two weeks before the last frost. Four to six weeks ahead of time, start the seeds—directly in the cell packs. And as with portulaca, put a pinch of three or four seeds in each cell, and let them grow in a clump. Cover the seed with a sifting of milled sphagnum. Transplant the seedlings outside when they are about 1 inch tall. Once the plants are up, they like 60-degree temperatures at night and about 70 degrees during the day.

## Salvia

Salvia is a joy to transplant. We sprinkle the large seed on the top of the flat and cover it with a *fine* dusting of peat. Without the peat, the seed would dry out, but don't put on too much because salvia needs light to germinate. It will sprout in 10 to 15 days. Allow eight weeks from sowing to planting outdoors around the last frost date. Move the young plants from the seedling flat to the larger containers when the plants are about 1 inch tall. They should have two true leaves and another set just appearing.

## Zinnias

You don't need to start zinnias early. They'll sprout in four or five days and shouldn't grow in containers longer than four weeks. If you set out stocky young zinnias on the last frost date, they'll soon outdistance bigger transplants that have had confined roots.

We sow the large seed a bit sparsely on the soil surface in the flat and cover them with ⅛ inch of peat. Then we move them to cell packs within a week after they sprout.

We feed young plants very little. The seedlings are in our peat mix, which is poor in plant nutrients, a very short time, and the seed itself contains all the nutrients a seedling needs. The compost-soil mix we transplant into is rich in plant food. Generally we feed only once, with a weak solution of fish emulsion. If the leaves become a bit pale, see if a feeding helps.

We wet the planting flats by subirrigation. Set them in a shallow pan with 1 inch of water in it, and leave them until the soil is thoroughly moist. They shouldn't need any more until after the plants are up if you cover the flats with plastic. Let tap water rise to at least room temperature before you water your plants. It is usually quite cold in the spring and will chill the seedlings. (Evaporation also keeps the soil cooler than you might think.)

Raising flowers from seed is really very simple. Most crucial to success are good soils and good timing. Because we raise so many, we use a greenhouse, but most gardens could be stocked with flowers from a cold frame. A frame will provide plenty of light and heat if you bring the plants in at night.

*January 1983*

# How to Plug In Fall Bulbs for a Brighter Spring

## M. C. Goldman

Set out some fall-planted bulbs to welcome spring with a dazzling blast of color—from the earliest crocus through the latest tulips.

Look at a bulb. Examine it. Even with a wild imagination, you're not likely to picture the rich, stately flower that rises from it at the crack of spring. Yet it does—and even gardeners who've witnessed that transformation over countless seasons still gaze in awe at nature's startling artistry.

Best of all, the hardy bulbs that so boldly announce spring's arrival across the cold north and wide midsection of the continent are delightfully easy to grow. Simple to plant, they'll thrive in just about any soil and adapt to less-than-ideal conditions readily, despite their look of delicate grace.

Once planted, a bed or border of hardy bulbs demands very little attention. With faithful regularity, they keep reappearing year after year. Only crowding or separating bulblets for larger blooms or more plants makes digging any of them up necessary. Some gardeners—like Ruth Stout, now 96 years old—never bother. Her row of tulips has stayed happy and productive for 25 years. My own fence line of iris and tulips has remained undisturbed for over a dozen seasons—and blossoms just as lovely every spring.

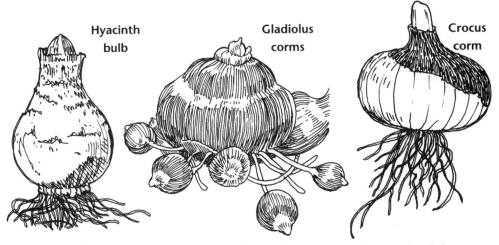

**Hyacinth bulb**  **Gladiolus corms**  **Crocus corm**

*Whether you're planting bulbs, corms, tubers, or rhizomes, start with top-sized stock that is solid, heavy for its size, and free of moldy spots.*

## What's in a Bulb?

Most gardeners confer the name *bulb* on the whole group of plants that grow from bulbous underground parts. Botanically speaking, though, some of them are also corms, tubers, or rhizomes. A true bulb is not a seed, but a flower or plant in miniature, an embryo surrounded by scales that hold all its nourishment. Sometimes, next year's plant is inside a tight layer of food-packed material, as in a tulip bulb, a daffodil, or an onion. Some bulbs, like lilies, are scaly and looser. A hyacinth bulb is like a single big bud.

On the other hand, a crocus or gladiolus starts from a corm. That's a solid mass of storage tissue with several growing tips on top. Roots grow out from around the edge of the flat, platelike bottom. The plate shrivels over the summer, and new corms emerge on top, with little ones called cormels forming at the edges.

A tuber consists of another solid mass of storage tissue, but minus the base plate. Both shoots and roots sprout from eyes, or growing points, around it. If you plant an old potato tuber, for example, it shrinks and disintegrates, then new tubers form on the roots of the new plant that comes up. Dahlias do the same thing, and so do tuberous begonias. Perennials that grow this way are generally called tuberous-rooted.

Finally, there is the rhizome, such as found in irises, cannas, and many others. It's a thickened underground stem. That's why rhizomes of iris, for instance, are planted horizontally, with some of the stem remaining aboveground. Also a storage-tissue type with eyes, a rhizome's roots grow from the lower surface, while flower stalks and leaves come from the upper stem side.

No matter what you call them, however, now's the time to plan and act. The recipe to brighten your garden calls for just a handful of bulbs, a little effort, and a pleasant fall afternoon. Keep in mind that the hardy bulbs—those that push impatiently through melting snow and thawing earth to trumpet a new season—need about two months of low temperatures (about 40 degrees) for their roots to grow and buds to develop. You can plant them any time from mid-September to November, depending on frost dates where you live. Set out even later—as long as the ground isn't frozen solid—these bulbs will still blossom, although they will not perhaps be as large.

## Plant Bulbs Right

Good drainage is the one "must" for bulbs. They'll take almost any sort of soil other than sticky clay, and they'll put up with less food or sun than most plants. But they refuse to have their roots standing in water. Improve soil by deep-digging, working in generous amounts of organic matter—compost, well-rotted manure, leaf mold, or peat moss and sand—to overcome sluggish drainage.

*Don't* add fresh manure around bulbs at planting time. If you add peat moss, mix 1 pound of ground limestone or dolomite through each bushel of dry peat before working it into the soil to neutralize the acidity. No additional lime is advisable because the large majority of bulbous plants thrive in a slightly acid soil.

More than other plants, bulbs need adequate amounts of phosphorus

and potash to develop bright flowers with strong stems and to mature firm, heavy bulbs for the next season. Ground bonemeal makes an excellent fertilizer because it releases a good share of phosphate and a small amount of nitrogen slowly (too much produces excessive leaf growth and poorer flowering). Team it with some wood ashes or potash rock for a complete feeding. Add both bonemeal and wood ash or ground rock potash at a rate of about 5 pounds each per 100 square feet.

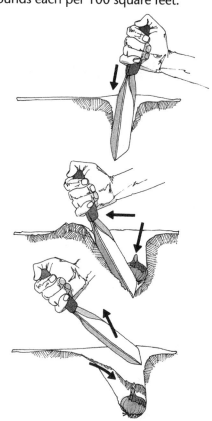

*To plant small bulbs quickly, drive your trowel straight down into the ground and push it away from you. Drop a bulb into the space you've created, then pull your trowel out. The hole will fill itself when you remove the trowel.*

To set out bulbs, use a trowel, first forking the soil well below the planting depth. Of course, bulbs are planted right side up, which is sometimes a puzzle for beginners. Look for the small roots at the base of the bulb. The upper part is usually more pointed and forms a kind of neck. Crocus bulbs are so flattened, however, that you should always look for the dead roots on the base to be certain which is the bottom side.

As to how deep to plant, an old rule of thumb says 3 times the height of the bulb is about right. Plant crocus and other early-flowering kinds 3 inches deep and 3 inches apart. Most daffodils, tulips, and larger bulbs go 4 to 6 inches deep and the same distance apart. Measure the depth from the *top* of the bulb, not the *bottom* of the hole.

Mix compost in the bottom, then place bulbs, nose end up, and cover with topsoil. Gently tamp to firm soil so as to avoid air space under bulbs, and make sure there's good contact between each bulb and the soil, which encourages early rooting.

Lay a thick mulch of several inches of hay, leaves, straw, or other loose material over bulb plantings *after heavy frost* has frozen the top 2 inches of the ground. The mulch is not to keep the bulbs warm, but to prevent the damaging effects of alternate thawing and freezing, which can often heave soil—bulbs and all. When green shoots begin to emerge in spring, pull the mulch back. Later add a warm-weather mulch to keep down weeds and conserve moisture.

## Leave Those Leaves!

Once crocuses, daffodils, tulips, and other spring-flowering bulbs finish blooming, we tend to forget about them. However, that's when a little aftercare is important—since it is when they are producing and storing food for flowering the next season.

Never cut off foliage while it is still green and actively growing. Healthy, vigorous leaves are necessary for food production and development of the bulbs. Removing these leaves too early stops bulb growth and may keep them from flowering next season. Allow foliage to remain until it naturally begins to yellow and die.

Remove flower stems promptly after bloom has been completed. This prevents seed formation, which can take stored food away from the bulbs and reduce flowering for the next spring.

After the bulbs have lost their foliage and gone dormant until the fall, they may either be lifted and stored, or allowed to remain in place. Some types, such as daffodils and crocus, are best left in place unless large clumps need dividing.

Spring and bulbs belong together. If you've ever stared in envy at a neighbor's early splash of color, make this the fall you do something about it. Plug in some bulbs for a brighter spring!

*August 1980*

# Easy-Care Roses

*Eric Rosenthal*

Our six regional experts pick the 36 best trouble-free varieties.

Everyone likes the fragrance and beauty of roses, but no one wants the bother of season-long spraying to keep them healthy and in bloom. Luckily, this dilemma is no longer a problem. You can avoid the extra work and effort by growing low-care roses. Of the hundreds of selections available, you can select ones that stand up to disease and others that require only minimal pruning.

Rose experts, who call themselves rosarians, agree that virtually trouble-free, beautiful, and fragrant varieties are available in every region of the continent.

"Almost all roses are susceptible to disease, but some roses resist infection much longer than others," explains Don Ballin, president of the American Rose Society, which includes 20,000 rose growers. He takes the occasional claims heard for "disease-free" hybrids with a grain of salt. "Some varieties may be disease-free in one region but not in another," he says. For example, a disease-resistant rose might remain free of infection in Southern California, where climatic conditions reduce the probability of black spot, but not in the Northeast, where black spot can be virulent.

## Midwest

If there is one prototype of the modern low-maintenance rose, it might well be breeder Dr. Griffith Buck's CAREFREE BEAUTY, a shrub praised by rosarians everywhere. It is remarkably disease-resistant over a broad range, overwinters without protection under subzero conditions, boasts generous pink flowers all season, and can be planted as a hedge or stand alone as a specimen plant.

Buck, a retired professor of horticulture at Iowa State University, spent much of his career improving roses. "I was looking to develop cold-hardy roses but subconsciously selected for disease tolerance as well," he says. To imbue his hybrids with exceptional hardiness—this is the characteristic he believes most important for a low-maintenance rose in the Midwest— Buck used a species native to Siberia, *Rosa laxa,* which has survived temperatures of minus 85 degrees. "It is also quite tolerant of disease, but I really didn't know that at the time," he confesses. The Siberian rose's toughness has been imparted to many Buck introductions, including HAWKEYE BELLE (white with pink centers), PRAIRIE STAR (white with yellow centers), and SERENDIPITY (buff yellow). All are shrub roses, a group of plants noted for their durability and appealing untamed appearance.

Hybrid teas are popular for their large blossoms on long stems, and a few are fairly disease-resistant. Buck names PINK PEACE and PARADISE (lavender) as among the easiest hybrid teas to grow in the Midwest.

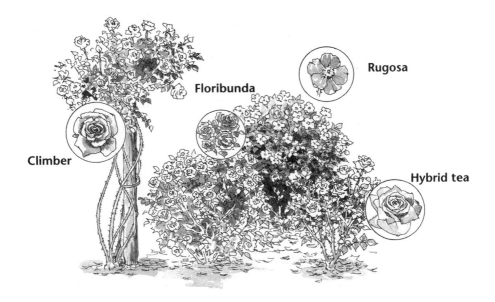

*The many species and cultivars of roses offer excellent easy-care choices for every garden.*

## Summer Pruning for More Bloom

Removing spent rose blossoms is always worth doing unless the hips—round seed pods that form on roses after blooms—that follow the flowers are part of a particular variety's appeal. Cutting off old blossoms diverts nutrients and energy from seed production back into more leaves and flower buds. In varieties that bloom repeatedly all summer, this removal is especially important for abundant bloom.

In general, cut back to a strong bud without removing any more leaves than you have to. The leaves are essential to power regrowth. Don't just snip off individual flowers. It's time-consuming and favors only the smallest buds.

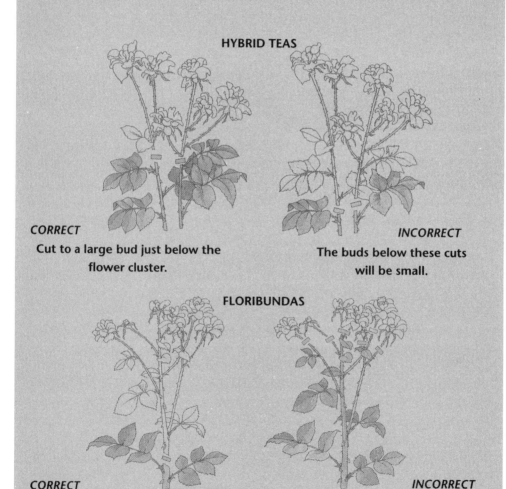

**HYBRID TEAS**

*CORRECT*
**Cut to a large bud just below the flower cluster.**

*INCORRECT*
**The buds below these cuts will be small.**

**FLORIBUNDAS**

*CORRECT*
**Cut to a strong bud just below the entire flower cluster.**

*INCORRECT*
**This time-consuming approach leaves ugly stubs above small buds.**

"Their disease resistance is above average," he says, "and without winter protection their canes die back to 3 or 4 inches from the ground, which is how you would prune them in spring, anyway." Equally resilient are ICEBERG (white) and SUNSPRITE (yellow), members of the floribunda class, which is characterized by large clusters of blooms on compact plants.

To help minimize winterkill, Buck urges gardeners in his region to plant roses deeper than is generally suggested, with the graft union placed 2 to 4 inches below the soil instead of at ground level. He also advises organic gardeners to spray regularly with wettable sulfur, which he describes as a threat neither to garden soil nor to the environment. Spray once a week from spring until the Fourth of July and every ten days thereafter.

## Northeast

Stephen Scaniello, rosarian at Brooklyn Botanic Garden's Cranford Rose Garden, singlehandedly tends over five thousand rose bushes, including nearly eight hundred varieties. Any that are undemanding enough to remain in flower into November make his list of low-maintenance plants for the Northeastern gardener.

One of the modern roses that provides him with the most blooms for the least effort is BONICA, the first shrub rose named as an All-America Rose Selection (1986), the highest honor bestowed on new introductions by the American rose industry. "In flowering, it took a full season before BONICA did anything," Scaniello recalls, "but then it really took off." The low, sprawling bushes can serve as a ground cover and are idea for controlling soil erosion on embankments. "But the plants also work as a low hedge, as an underplanting in formal beds, or fastened onto pillars like a climbing rose," he says.

As a class, floribundas are the most easygoing of modern roses, according to Scaniello. "In the Northeast, they may need some spraying against fungal diseases but don't require very careful pruning to remain productive, as do hybrid teas," he says. "Simply snip off dead flowers during summer and cut the canes every few years to within 6 inches of the ground in early spring." Exceptionally trouble-free are SIMPLICITY (pink) and SHOWBIZ (bright red).

Certain wild roses, also called species roses, need even less care. "Rugosa rose (*R. rugosa*) really is care-free—and the poorer the soil the better," Scaniello says. (The same is not true for all rugosa hybrids, he cautions, because some are susceptible to disease in the Northeast.) Rough-hewn and featuring reddish single blossoms followed by huge hips in autumn, rugosa makes an ideal shrub for seaside locations. Except for removing dead wood, pruning is rarely necessary. Also recommended are white-flowering Scotch rose (*R. spinosissima*) and its pink hybrid, STANWELL PERPETUAL, one of the few old-garden varieties that blooms in spring and summer.

Scaniello suggests frequent wa-

# Pruning Shrub Roses

It is a myth that shrub roses need no pruning. They do require far less pruning than hybrid teas, but you'll get more vigorous, more heavily flowering shrub roses if you give the plant some light attention with the pruning shears at the end of each dormant season.

At planting, prune minimally, removing damaged wood and creating an open framework. Your long-term pruning program should encourage strong new shoots that arise near the base of the plant by removing older, less vigorous wood that shades the new growth. The process is one of gradual renewal rather than radical removal.

*1. After the second growing season, head back overly long, vigorous shoots about 25 percent. Watch for strong shoots to develop near ground level.*

*2. When flowering has finished, remove spent blossoms, unless the rosehips are part of the plant's appeal.*

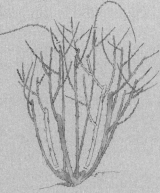

*3. During the third and subsequent dormant seasons, remove one or two of the oldest shoots to favor the strong new canes. Trim growth to maintain the open, upright shape you desire. Head back any excessively long shoots.*

tering and regular fertilizing for nearly all roses. He has gotten excellent results by fertilizing with fish emulsion every ten days from mid-March until late September. To minimize disease and insect problems, water early in the day so moisture can evaporate from foliage by evening, keep plants properly spaced and pruned for good air circulation, remove flowers as soon as they fade, and keep beds free of litter.

## Southeast

Dr. Charles Jeremias, a Southerner who has been growing old-fashioned roses for about 28 years, has a reliable approach to finding varieties that flourish with little attention. "When I see a deserted country home with roses that are still going strong, well, that's what I call undemanding."

A retired chemistry professor from Newberry, South Carolina, and a vice president of the American Rose Society, Jeremias says that old-fashioned roses are considered low-maintenance plants in the South when they are unfazed by black spot. "Infected old roses may lose their foliage, but, unlike many modern varieties, when they're left untended they recover and make a strong comeback," he explains. "In some cases, spraying with a fungicide does more harm than the disease." HARISON'S YELLOW (*Rosa* × *harisoni*), FATHER HUGO (*R. hugonis*) and others with fernlike leaves are particularly resentful of spraying.

Two old-species roses that, ac-

cording to Jeremias, need more space than attention are sweetbrier (*R. elganteria*) and chestnut rose (*R. roxburghi*).

Sweetbrier grows 8 feet tall and bears deep pink blossoms in spring, and huge clusters of showy orange hips in fall. Its apple-scented foliage is delightful all season. The original species is more disease-resistant than the hybrids.

Chestnut rose is unique in that its grayish bark peels like birch. Eventually becoming 6 feet tall and wide, the bushes bear lilac-ringed pink blossoms that unfurl throughout the growing season. Flower buds are covered with bristles like those on chestnuts. Deadheading to encourage additional flowers and some pruning are this rose's only demands.

Jeremias notes that he finds many alba roses (*R. alba*) relatively carefree. These large spring-flowering shrubs produce extremely fragrant blossoms in delicate shades of pink or white. His favorite cultivars include CELESTIAL and FELICITE PARMENTIER, a smallish alba that can easily be maintained at hybrid tea size with occasional pruning.

Among modern roses, Jeremias praises two dependable yellow cultivars, SUNBRIGHT, a hybrid tea, and SUN FLARE, a floribunda. He says he also likes PINK FAVORITE, an older hybrid tea mentioned by Buck, and he recommends CHANELLE, an older floribunda with semidouble, peach-apricot blossoms.

Many Southern gardeners prune their roses around March 1, about one to two months too late, says Jeremias.

"I prefer pruning in January or February," he says, "so that new growth will gradually harden and be able to withstand late cold snaps." He explains that when tender shoots are killed by cold, the canes from which they sprouted may also die.

## Northwest

Fred Edmunds has been growing roses all his life, first with his father, who was curator of the International Rose Test Gardens in Portland, Oregon, and later for his own nursery when he left college in 1950. He has grown over five hundred different roses.

"Varieties that are highly resistant to black spot, the curse of roses in this area, need far less care than others," Edmunds says. OLYMPIAD, a medium-red hybrid tea that was an All-America Rose Selection in 1984, has proved virtually disease-free, in his experience. "Dark reds are never disease-free, because there seems to be a linkage between this color and susceptibility to mildew, another problem around here," he says. White roses can be extremely resistant, though, and one of his top choices is a hybrid tea called PASCALI, a 1969 All-America Rose Selection.

Because there are so many pink roses today, any *new* pinks have to be outstanding in every way to succeed commercially, says Edmunds. One very much to his liking is COLOR MAGIC, a hybrid tea that combines beauty with resiliency. He also agrees with

rosarians in other locales on the reliability of yellow floribundas such as SUN FLARE and SUNSPRITE, and also of BONICA and rugosa rose.

"Winters in the Pacific Northwest are mild enough for some rose leaves to be evergreen, yet cool and wet enough to make this foliage a staging ground for fungal disease," he says. A preventive approach he likes is stripping off the foliage at the onset of the dormant season, then spraying plants once with Bordeaux mix (copper sulfate and lime) immediately after pruning when growth resumes in spring. "Personally, I never spray against insects because all of the destructive ones here have natural predators," he adds.

## Southwest

Where it's dry, conditions are unfavorable to black spot and rust, but not to mildew, considered that region's number-one enemy of roses. "Rose bushes with glossy foliage are the most resistant," says Thomas Cairns, a transplanted Scot who serves as a senior scientist with the U.S. Food and Drug Administration when not tending his garden of 1,300 rose bushes. "The thick waxy coating that gives some rose foliage a sheen forms a physical barrier between the leaves and the fungus," he says.

As an example, Cairns points to GOLD MEDAL, a deep yellow grandiflora rose whose glossy leaves are almost impervious to mildew. (Grandiflora roses, with their abundant clusters of fairly long-stemmed blossoms, combine qualities of floribundas and hybrid teas.) He also likes this plant's vigor—that is, its ability to send up rapid new growth from the area of the graft union, assuring continuous flower production and bushiness.

"Vigor and disease resistance are the two key factors in low maintenance," Cairns states. "I also look for plants which, by nature, have pleasing shapes and the ability to bloom repeatedly." His choice for the quintessential low-maintenance rose is orange PLAYBOY, a Scottish cultivar that found its way to Southern California, becoming among the region's most sought-after floribundas. "Along with its fabulous glossy foliage and vigorous growth, it remains a compact 3 to 4 feet high and flowers again and again when deadheaded." Other Cairns picks include deep-pink PLAYGIRL, as well as DEEP PURPLE and FRENCH LACE (white with pink center), all floribundas.

He doesn't recommend hybrid teas, because the normally small to medium-size bushes grow up to 8 feet tall in the region's mild climate. Keeping them well-shaped and within bounds usually takes frequent pruning. Where a tall climbing rose is desired, he recommends AMERICA, a pink cultivar that is vigorous and disease-resistant.

Hot, dry climates encourage spider mites, and Cairns uses a 4-gallon-per-minute mister at the end of an ordinary garden hose to knock the tiny pests from plants, spraying the underside of foliage once every ten days during the hot growing season. He also washes foliage from above to clean away dust particles on which mildew spores can become lodged. All wetting is done in the morning.

A group of overlooked roses that merits attention are the hybrid musks, vigorous plants whose growth habit falls between bush roses and climbers. In *The Book of Old Roses,* legendary rosarian Dorothy Stemler writes: "None of the hybrid musks I know intimately are susceptible to mildew, black spot or red rust, so they can be planted in out-of-the-way places, hard to reach with spray material. They bloom from early summer until frost, pushing up new shoots while in bloom.... You can prune or not, depending on how big you want them to be.... Fencing may be covered with them, they can be used as graceful specimen shrubs and even low bedding plants if kept pruned." Among Stemler's favorites were BELINDA (pink), WILL SCARLET (bright red), and BISHOP DARLINGTON (peach).

Clearly there is no shortage of low-maintenance roses for gardeners all across America. Try some of these, and as your skill and knowledge of roses grows, try some others, too. You'll uncover some beauties that will thrive under your conditions.

*April 1988*

# Something Wild

## Jeff Cox

Follow our steps for a colorful wild-flower bed.

**Beebalm**

*Beebalm (*Monarda didyma*) will attract butterflies and hummingbirds to a moist meadow planting.*

**W**ildflowers sow themselves easily in natural settings without our help. But to establish your own wildflower bed or meadow in your landscape, you'll need to do more than just toss the seeds where you want them to grow.

The first step is to find suitable native species that will thrive in your location. You can discover these by walking through a wild setting that is similar to your site. Visit a nearby forest or meadow and observe what is growing. Bring along a guidebook from your local library; the National Audubon Society's books are especially useful.

To ensure that your choices are appropriate, check the information published by the National Wildflower Research Center, 4801 La Crosse Boulevard, Austin, TX 78739. They can provide you with a list of recommended wildflowers for your state, along with basic cultural requirements and buying information. Also, check with your local extension service for any bulletins available on selection and culture of native wildflowers.

You also may want to try some common wildflowers that aren't true natives but that have become well-established enough that they perform like natives. Some examples are white yarrow, bachelor's button, and oxeye daisy, all of which emigrated three hundred years ago from Europe and Asia. Naturalized species such as these make great companions for native wildflowers.

A primary attraction of native species is their ability to successfully reseed themselves, says Elinor Crank, research horticulturist at the NWRC. "The problem with nonnative species is that they won't reseed, and by the third year there's not much left of them." Yet Crank says that at least four native species can be established in a low-maintenance wildflower garden in *any* location.

Wildflowers can be started from seed, which is widely available. Most are perennials that grow for two years or more before they bloom. Wildflower seedlings often transplant poorly, but researchers at the University of Massachusetts have found a workable method using wildflower "sods." When transplanted eight weeks after seeding, sods of black-eyed Susan, yarrow, and blanketflower showed 100 percent survival one year later. And oxeye daisy and evening primrose had begun to spread into adjacent areas. To create your own wildflower sods, see the illustrations on page 246.

Prepare a site for either sod or seed in the spring a year before planting. Use a shovel or spade to remove the surface weeds and grass from the planting site and in a 2-foot

**Calliopsis**

**Blanket flower**

**California poppy**

**Prairie gentian**

*Annuals and tender perennials like prairie gentian supply quick color in a wildflower planting while perennials are still getting established.*

# Wildflower Sod

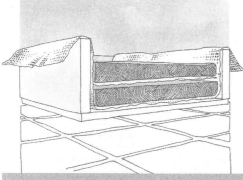

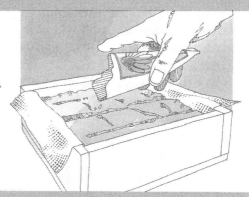

1. Line a flat with one thickness of cheesecloth overlapping the sides. Fill with 1 inch of potting soil, then add another layer of cheesecloth (non-overlapping) and more soil.

2. The sod method works best for perennials that grow in colonies; avoid wildflower mixtures. Sow during the time of year when the flowers would seed themselves in nature. Broadcast seeds evenly over soil. After sowing, sprinkle a fine layer of soil and firm gently. Maximum soil contact is desired. If soil is dry, water lightly.

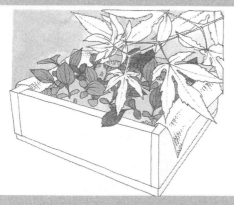

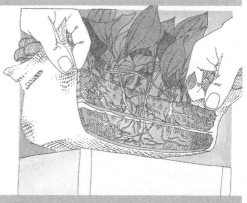

3. Set the prepared flat outdoors, but in shade. This will expose the wildflowers to appropriate temperature and light. Most wildflowers will sprout within 20 days.

4. When you're ready to transplant about three months later (or after five leaves), lift the sod out of the flat by the bottom layer of cheesecloth. The roots will be entwined with the cheesecloth, so plant with it attached—the cloth will decompose. Be careful when handling wildflower transplants to avoid damaging roots.

radius around it, leaving the adjoining areas undisturbed. Avoid tilling the area, as it may turn up many unwanted weed seeds, which can hinder young wildflower growth.

You'll need approximately ¼ pound of wildflower-seed mixture per 1,000 square feet of bed. Broadcast the seed, then rake lightly. Water the bed before sowing; keep it moist for four to six weeks after. When seedlings appear, gradually reduce watering. Because many wildflower seedlings resemble weeds, beware of pulling the wrong plant. Use a wildflower identification guide to identify your seedlings. Or start a few plants in pots for comparison. As soon as you can distinguish them, begin weeding out unwanted seedlings. Don't wait until the weeds are big enough to dominate the bed.

In trials at the Rodale Research Center in Maxatawny, Pennsylvania, head gardener Eileen Weinsteiger used five different methods to prepare wildflower beds. Three of the beds were tilled, and of those, one was planted with buckwheat and another with hairy vetch. The third was only tilled. The remaining two beds were not tilled, but one was covered with black plastic, while the other was mulched with 6 inches of straw. The best show of flowers with the least amount of weeds and grasses was produced by the latter two techniques. Started in 1986, the beds include perennials and some annuals that reseed. The plots are maintained with a single annual mowing.

**Oxeye daisy**

*Durable oxeye daisies (*Chrysanthemum leucanthemum*) thrive in poor soil and tolerate partial shade.*

Weinsteiger adhered to the seed packets' sowing recommendations, "although I am likely to seed more than what's recommended rather than less," she says. After planting, she watered lightly and placed a fine layer of straw on each bed to help retain moisture. Weekly watering during dry periods is suggested. Weinsteiger weeded minimally, only on an as-needed basis. "Most wildflower beds will need some hand-weeding each year, but you're better off without tilling initially," she says.

Timing your plantings is crucial because many wildflowers have strong preferences for spring or fall. For example, University of Nebraska researchers found that black sampson and butterfly weed grew best when seeded in fall, while prairie coneflower and purple prairie clover preferred spring. If you can't ascertain when a certain wildflower should be planted, follow nature's lead by sowing flowers at the time they would plant themselves when growing in the wild.

Another useful strategy for growing a wildflower garden is to anchor your bed with two native perennial species, plus a native biennial (resown in fall as needed). Then, add various annual species—including those from other regions that have a good chance of naturalizing in your area. Annual wildflowers may dramatically improve the visual appeal of any wildflower bed, though you should keep in mind that you will need to reseed them from time to time.

Elinor Crank advises novice wildflower enthusiasts to be patient. "With wildflowers, your results will never be instant," she says. "It may take years for your plot to develop a good balance of species." But the rewards are invaluable. Native wildflowers can become established in three to five years and will persist for decades. Woodlands studded with wild violets and irises will show new touches of permanent color within two years of planting.

*September 1990*

## Foraging for Flowers

With so many native wildflowers endangered, don't randomly collect them from the wild. And don't buy native plants that you suspect have been poached from the wild. Even commonplace wildflowers may disappear eventually if people can profit by digging them up. Legitimate wildflower growers specify that their plants are "nursery-propagated." Look for that phrase when purchasing plant material.

One positive way to collect native wildflowers is to rescue them from impending destruction, such as in new housing developments or at road construction sites. In many communities, local wildflower and rock-garden clubs organize "collection digs" whenever they learn of a doomed natural stand of natives. To contact these clubs, check with your local chamber of commerce. A list of wildflower and rock-garden societies also is available from the New England Wildflower Society, c/o Garden in the Woods, Hemenway Road, Framingham, MA 01701.

# Chapter 14

# Fruits and Berries

# Be Fruitful

*Mark Kane*

You harvest fresh vegetables all season long. Why not grapes, peaches, berries, and apples, as well?

The first fruit of the year is the strawberry, and the last, even later than fall apples, is the persimmon, which often still hangs on the tree, ready for eating, at the first snow. In between these two come apples, pears, peaches, plums, and the small fruits, a dozen or more if you count the many types of raspberry and blackberry and uncommon fruits like the pawpaw, fig, and kiwi.

*Don't let limited space limit your fruit-growing ambitions. An espaliered fruit tree produces ample yields for home use without taking up much room in the garden.*

If you garden in a northern state, you have no lack of fruits to grow. Those that survive a temperature of 20 degrees below zero include apples, elderberries, blueberries, grapes, currants, gooseberries, strawberries, pears, and raspberries. Farther south, the choice widens: blackberries, dewberries, peaches, plums, persimmons, apricots, muscadine grapes, and many others.

With such a variety of fruits to choose from, and a fruit season nearly as long as the vegetable season, how do most of us grow fruit? In fits and starts, I think. My part of Missouri has a season of 180 days, and a great variety of fruits will grow there. But for most gardeners I know, the season is full of fruitless blanks. For a few weeks, we get our fill of strawberries. When the strawberry glut passes, our yards are barren again until peaches come in. Harvests alternate with dearth, and we seem to spend almost as much time waiting for fruit as we do enjoying it.

## No Need to Wait for Fruit

The waiting isn't necessary. If you grow five or six kinds of fruit, rather than the usual two or three, the harvests can be made to fall closer together. And you can stretch the harvests until they overlap if you plant cultivars of each fruit that ripen at different times.

When you plant one peach, say the old standby ELBERTA, you get about two weeks of picking. The first week, only the odd fruit ripens. The second week, all the rest come in and your season is over. In a good year, a medium-size tree can leave you with a two-week supply in the refrigerator. But you could eat fresh-picked peaches for six weeks and more by planting just two other cultivars. The U.S. Department of Agriculture lists 65 peach cultivars that ripen before ELBERTA, and 18 that ripen after it. The earliest ripen eight weeks before ELBERTA, and latest cultivars four weeks after. Even near the northern limit of peach growing, you can plan for more than a two-week harvest. In the South, early peaches may overlap late strawberries.

Plant an early, middle, and late cultivar of each fruit you grow. At the least, you'll double the season you can expect from a single cultivar, and for some fruits, you'll do even better. Even when you're putting in just two plants, choose two different cultivars.

## Nine Weeks of Blueberries

Many blueberry cultivars have month-long harvests, but the blueberry season runs up to nine weeks. With one grape you can pick for about two weeks, if you don't mind eating tart fruit at first and shooing away the wasps toward the end of the harvest. But the grape season can run seven weeks or more. A spring strawberry will yield well for about two weeks.

Then the harvest wanes quickly. But there are many strawberry successions—one example is EARLIDAWN, MIDWAY, and VESPER—that yield for six weeks. In apples, when the ripe fruit clings to the tree for two weeks with little change in quality, the cultivar is said to hang well. Counting the occasional fruit that ripens early, such a cultivar may give you apples to pick for three weeks. Compare three weeks to the length of the apple season—the earliest summer apples in the central United States appear in mid-June, the latest in early November. That's 4½ months.

Even very small yards have room for some kind of fruit, though maybe not the apple that first pops to mind for most people dreaming up a fruit planting. In smaller yards, it is almost always better to look first to the berries—bushes, brambles, and vines. These require less space, yield early (some the second summer after planting), and are usually far less troubled by insects and diseases than are the tree fruits. It's easier to find room for berries because they are smaller plants, much more easily trained and confined than the smallest dwarf trees. Bushes don't cast shadows or interfere with head space like trees, and a row of them can be laid out to work well with a vegetable patch or flower beds.

## Create a Fruitful Landscape

If your yard seems too small for fruit, try landscaping with your planting. Blueberries and gooseberries are handsome shrubs that can stand alone or form a hedge. Strawberries serve as groundcovers. Dwarf fruit trees fit along a driveway or a property line. Grapes on an arbor make an inviting shade over a patio or against a wall.

You don't need much room to get considerable yields. Expect about 6 quarts of fruit from 2 square feet of strawberries. With three cultivars in single rows 8 feet long and 2 feet wide, you can pick 3 quarts a day for six weeks. A blueberry bush at maturity yields up to 15 quarts of fruit and occupies a 4-foot circle. A dwarf apple needs an 8-foot circle and yields ½ bushel or more of fruit.

The horticulturists have kept busy over the last 20 years and have given us new ways and new places to grow old fruits, and a new fruit or two as well. You should consider growing some of them. Everbearing strawberries are one development. Though they yield less than spring strawberries, their second season is well-placed and long—it starts a month or so after the spring strawberries end and continues through fall. A strawberry grower in Illinois reports an everbearer harvest in June, a two-week pause, and then more strawberries from July to October.

Fall-bearing raspberries, like everbearing strawberries, give two crops. You can also grow them just for fall fruit—and reduce disease troubles— by cutting all the canes to the ground after the fall harvest.

Though still not as tasty as the highbush blueberry, which grows best in the North, cultivars of rabbiteye blueberry are not far behind. Native to the South, the rabbiteye grows from northern Florida to North Carolina and has been reported to thrive in Southern California. Both blueberry types need an acid soil, mulch, and constant moisture. Give the highbush a soil that is high in organic matter by adding ½ bushel of peat or leaf mold to the planting hole.

Tender fruits are getting hardier and moving north. Some peaches now bear after winters that kill most cultivars. Canadians enjoy home-grown peaches after winters that reach 20 degrees below zero. And the kiwi, once considered a tender plant, has survived the same temperature in the New Hampshire plantings of plant breeder Elwin Meader. We may even see hardy citrus someday, thanks to breeding now under way with strains that stand temperatures well below freezing.

**Pawpaws**

*Pawpaws need cross-pollination to produce fruit. Plant at least two seedlings, a seedling and a named cultivar, or two different cultivars.*

## Pick the Best Cultivars for Your Site

Once you choose which fruits to grow, call your local extension service and ask about cultivars adapted to your area. Among the peaches, SPRING-TIME and FAIRTIME ripen a tempting three months apart, but you have to live in California to grow them. Many apples need a long winter chilling, and without it are slow to waken in spring. Southern extension services will recommend cultivars that need little chilling, like WINTER BANANA, OZARK GOLD, and MUTSU. Strawberry breeding is so specialized that the recommended cultivars are different in neighboring states. (Some cultivars, however, do well over a wide range.) For the less common fruits—the kiwi, persimmon, pawpaw, mulberry, and elderberry—the best advice comes from enthusiasts. A good place to find them is the North American Fruit

# Ripe for the Picking

Here are the fruit harvests in the Virginia area, where the frost-free season runs from April to November (as it does in Evansville, Indiana; Tulsa, Oklahoma; Salt Lake City, Utah; and Medford, Oregon). The harvest dates will be different in your area, but not the order of ripening—grapes follow peaches in Michigan and Mississippi, and strawberries are the earliest fruit everywhere. To the north, as the season shrinks, the harvests bunch together, or overlap more. Strawberries run into blackberries in Connecticut, but not in Louisiana. To the south, harvests are longer.

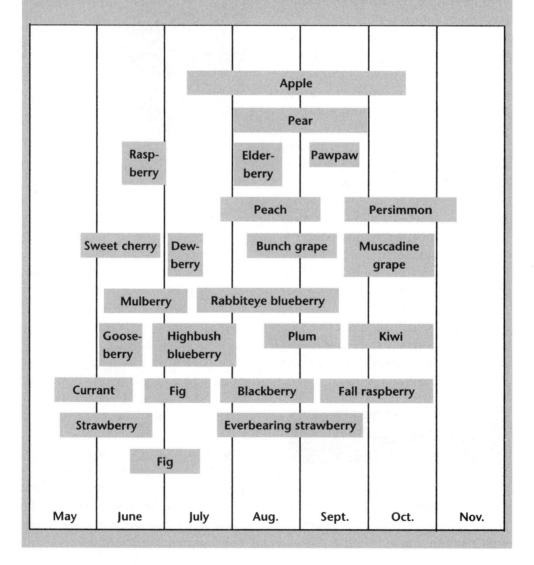

Explorers (NAFEX), a group of amateurs and professionals that exchanges information on all the fruits, native and exotic, grown in the United States. Membership includes a subscription to the group's quarterly publication, *Pomona.*

You can enrich the soil intensively in a small planting, giving each plant plenty of nourishment. You have time to visit the planting often, tying canes and thinning the fruit. Pruning takes less time in a small planting, and you're more apt to stay ahead of pests if inspecting and cleaning up the plants takes only a few minutes a day. With intensive culture, your fruits may yield twice what our chart shows.

Large numbers of plants are hard to keep picked at the height of the harvest, and the ripe fruit that gets left behind will invite pests and disease. Picking a small planting is barely

work. Two bowls of raspberries, which are quick to pick, is as fine a reward as a gallon of raspberries if you know that tomorrow you'll pick two more bowls.

So keep your fruit plantings moderate. When you use our chart of fruit yields to estimate how many plants you want, watch your appetite. You're more likely to get the fruit you plan for from a small, well-tended planting. A large one yields big crops only if you care for it.

You have a choice of fruits, room to grow them, and a season to enjoy them. So while you plan this year's garden, include fruit. Your plantings will mature in a few years, and you'll have the pleasure of fresh harvests all season long for many years afterward.

*January 1982*

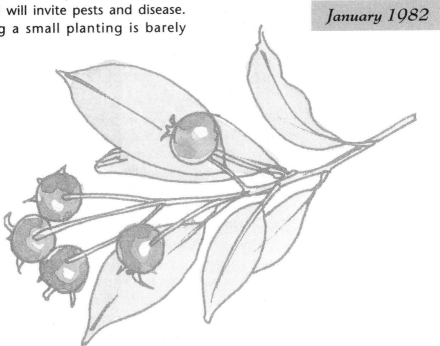

# Pollination Pointers for Better Fruit-Set

## Lewis Hill

Here are tips from a veteran nurseryman for a more productive harvest.

The year our raspberry bushes produced half their usual crop, the weather had been abnormally wet. Rains were frequent and heavy. The pollen that bees brought between rains was quickly washed off.

Prolonged rain during the blooming season is only one of the factors that can go wrong with pollination and interrupt the fruiting process of a plant. Without pollination, even if plants are healthy and growing well, they will produce nothing. And in the world of berries and fruits, honeybees, with some help from hornets and bumblebees, do practically all the pollinating.

Lack of pollination should be suspected if your plants produce lots of blooms but no fruit. And you can tell that no pollination, or poor pollination, has taken place if tiny fruits form on the trees and then soon fall off.

Most fruit trees need to be cross-pollinated—the pollen from one plant must be moved to another in order for it to bear fruit. If you have the only apple tree in the neighborhood, for example, it probably will bear sparingly, if it produces anything at all. If you have several fruit trees, but only one of each species, they won't bear fruit, either, since apples, pears, plums, peaches, and cherries can't pollinate each other. Two trees of the same cultivar won't cross-pollinate, either. Two NORTHERN SPY apples cannot pollinate each other, for instance, nor two BARTLETT pears, since they were cloned originally from the same tree.

## Apples

For proper cross-pollination, not only are at least two different cultivars of apple needed, but they also must be of different families. For example, MCINTOSH, MACOUN, and CORTLAND apples are too closely related to pollinate each other well. If you plan to grow MCINTOSH-related apples, you'll need to plant a completely unrelated cultivar, such as a WEALTHY. The same characteristic is true of certain other apple families, such as the DELICIOUS, the SPY, and the JONATHAN, each of which has many close relatives.

Although it sounds complicated, apple blossoms are usually cross-pollinated easily because in most neighborhoods there are two or more cultivars of apple trees growing within flying distance of bees. (Bees easily fly 500 feet while foraging, and 1,000 feet is not too far.) Wild apples growing in the vicinity of an orchard are often excellent pollinators, as long as they bloom at the same time as the trees you want pollinated.

We've found that crab apples are extremely good pollinators for other apple trees, and we planted several throughout our orchard for this purpose. Unfortunately, some of them, including our favorite, the DOLGO crab, often bloom a few days ahead of the larger-fruiting apples. Though the blooms usually hold until the

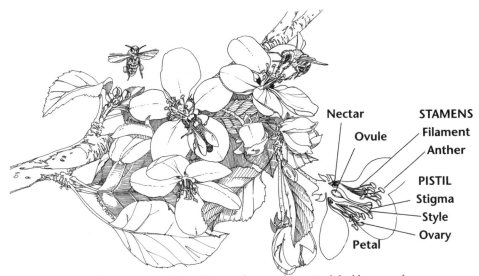

*Bees do 90 percent of the pollinating for most fruits. And the blossoms of most fruits require pollen from flowers of a different cultivar.*

others reach their peak, during some years, we've had hot weather and the DOLGO trees dropped their petals before they served their full pollinating potential. It is important that your trees have partners that will bloom at the same time.

Early blooming apples include CORTLAND, DOLGO, DUCHESS, IDARED, JERSEYMAC, JONATHAN, JULYRED, LODI, MCINTOSH, MILTON, PURITAN, SPARTAN, WEALTHY, and YELLOW TRANSPARENT.

Late blooming apples include EMPIRE, GOLDEN DELICIOUS, MACOUN, MELROSE, MUTSU, NORTHERN SPY, ROME, and SPIGOLD.

Certain apple cultivars have weak pollen and don't pollinate well with each other or with other cultivars. It is important to plant some good pollinators near the following apples: BALDWIN, GRAVENSTEIN, RHODE ISLAND GREENING, STAYMAN WINESAP, THOMPKINS COUNTY KING, and TURLEY.

## Plums

Pollination for plums is more complex than for apples. Though a few cultivars are self-fruitful, most need another cultivar as a pollen source. There are three distinct strains of plum: Japanese, European, and American. A European plum is only receptive to pollen from a different European cultivar. The same is true for the American types. But while different Japanese cultivars effectively pollinate each other, American plums are reported to be good pollinators for Japanese cultivars.

If you want crops that are consistently large, plant at least two different cultivars of the same nationality of plum. For instance, plant an EMBER and a PIPESTONE, both American hybrids. (Wild American plums will also pollinate American hybrids.) Or plant a GREEN GAGE and a YELLOW EGG, both Europeans, or a FORMOSA and a SHIRO, Japanese cultivars. Nursery catalogs usually tell which kinds are compatible if they list more than one grouping.

STANLEY PRUNE and FELLENBERG, both European plums, are self-fertile cultivars, which will bear fruit without mates.

## Pears

Pears nearly always need two different cultivars for proper cross-pollination. The BARTLETT and SECKEL cultivars will not pollinate each other, so you must plant a third cultivar to get fruit if these are the only pears in your orchard.

## Peaches

Most peaches bear well without a partner, but they often do better with another tree in the neighborhood. J.H. HALE and JUNE ELBERTA are not self-fertile, however, so they need another cultivar for good fruit-set.

## Apricots

Most apricots are self-fertile, but some bear better if two or more

kinds are planted. The hardier cultivars, such as MOONGOLD and SUNGOLD,
are best planted with each other for
good pollination.

## Cherries

All the sour cherries are self-fertile, so
only one tree is necessary. They will
not pollinate sweet cherries, however. Sweet cherries are not self-
fertile: Two cultivars are necessary.
BING, LAMBERT, and NAPOLEON will not
fertilize each other.

## Berries and Small Fruits

Cross-pollination is seldom necessary
for berries and small fruits, including
strawberries, blackberries, raspberries, and grapes. An exception is the
blueberry family. Two or more cultivars of blueberries should always be
planted for good fruiting. Hybrid elderberries and Juneberries also produce better if two cultivars grow near
each other, unless wild ones are
nearby.

## Weather

Pollination problems often occur
when trees bloom in the early spring,
before the few wild bees that survived
the winter are able to handle the
thousands of blooms that appear at
the same time. The early bloomers—

apricots, peaches, plums, pears, and
cherries—often suffer if spring arrives
late and is cold and wet, because neither the domesticated nor wild bee
colonies have yet had a chance to
build up their numbers.

Not only are there too few bees
in the early spring, but often the
cold, wet days limit their activities.
Many blossoms may come and go
without visits from the bees. And
even if they are well-pollinated, frequent rains can wash off the pollen
before it sets.

If a frost occurs at the end of
the blooming season, there is usually
no damage unless the temperature
gets extremely low. When a frost hits
before the blossoms are fertilized
by the bees, however, the tiny tube
from the pistil to the ovaries may
be damaged so the pollen cannot
move down it, and as a result, no
fruit will form.

So delay the blooming by at-
tending to the microclimate. Plant
early-blooming fruit or nuts on the
north side of a building or wind-
break. Avoid south- or west-facing
walls. A heavy mulch helps keep the
roots of the plants cool in the spring
and postpones blooming for a few
days, thus allowing the bee population to build up while the spring
weather improves. Mulch is particularly effective on strawberry beds—
by delaying the blooming time,
danger from spring frosts is less-
ened. And, of course, it suppresses
weeds and retains moisture while
feeding the soil.

## Help Your Trees

The best insurance for a serious orchardist is having a large bee population nearby. If neither you nor your neighbors keep bees, you can invite a beekeeper to place one of his hives in your backyard for the spring and summer. We have a good friend who parks some of his hives in our orchard to our mutual satisfaction—we get fruit-set, and he gets honey.

### Bagged Apples

If you have only a few dwarf apple trees, this technique will justify the time it takes by deterring apple maggot fly from destroying your fruit. When the apples are the size of small cherries, thin them to 5 inches apart. Then enclose each apple in a paper bag. First, slit the bag down about 2½ inches on each side and reinforce the cut edges with waterproof tape. Apply bags only on fruit growing on the side of the limbs where leaves grow beyond the fruit, not on the ends of limbs, where the fruit may not mature. Wrap each bag around the limb and staple securely. Leave them on until you pick the fruit.

*Virgil Spencer*
*Lancaster, Pennsylvania*
*June 1985*

If your trees persist in blooming early (before there are enough bees), or if cool, windy weather keeps the bees in their hive, or if rain washes out the pollen, you can always do the job yourself. Although it sounds like an enormous task to pollinate a fruit tree by hand, it is not difficult. You can collect the pollen yourself or buy it from supply houses.

If you collect pollen yourself, use a small, soft brush, such as an artist's paintbrush, and brush off into a dish the yellow powder on the stamens of each blossom. Then, with the same brush, dust flowers on another tree, marking the limbs as you go so you can tell where you've been. It will be time well-spent if it makes the difference between a crop of fruit and no fruit-set at all.

In large operations, collected pollen is sometimes spread by dusters. Some growers put it in their beehives so that the bees will walk through it as they leave the hive on their way to the trees.

There are other ways that you can aid in the pollinating process. If your fruit tree doesn't have a satisfactory mate in the neighborhood, borrow a few blooming branches from a friend's tree, and put them in a bucket of water under your tree or hang them in its branches. The bees will do the rest.

*October 1982*

# Grafting
# Made Simple

## N. Burglon

G rafting fruit trees is not difficult if one has an understanding of the basic require-ments of joining new growth onto an es-tablished tree.

If you've been envying a neighbor whose apple tree produces exceptionally luscious apples and would like some on your tree, here's a tip. As soon as the leaves have fallen, go over to him and ask if you might have a twig from the end of a branch measuring the span of a hand. While you are at it, you might as well take three or four such tips.

Take them home. Dig a little trench. Set them down into the trench to their necks. Tamp the soil down well, and let them go to sleep. That is what being dormant means.

The frost and the moisture in the ground draws the sap, if there is any, out of the twig. In the spring, when you first notice the pussy willows taking on life (March), go out and select a branch on your tree where you would like the new fruit to grow.

Find a twig the same size around as the twig that has been sleeping in the ground all winter. Snip it off on the slant. Be sure it is one clean, sharp cut. Cut a similar whack at your dormant twig. Try it on

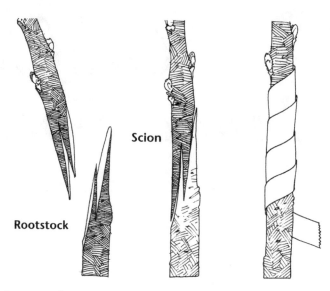

**Scion**

**Rootstock**

*A whip-and-tongue graft creates a sturdy graft union and increases contact between the rootstock and the scion. After making an equal-sized, sloping cut on both the twig you wish to graft and the branch it will go on, make vertical cuts into each to create the "tongues." Carefully push the two pieces together, so they interlock securely. Wrap the graft without covering the lowest bud on the scion. After a month or so, when new growth has started, remove the wrapping.*

the branch. Do the two fit each other exactly? No, they don't. Well, then keep cutting up the stem until at last the dormant twig fits the branch.

There is a thin, green-to-chartreuse-colored layer of living cells, known as the cambium layer, immediately under and protected by the outer bark. It is through the cambium that growth takes place and sap is transported from the roots to the twigs and leaves. It is the most important factor in grafting, as the piece to be grafted must grow into it or else the graft won't "take."

After the two cuts lie cheek to cheek, wrap string around the joint. Then melt some beeswax. Take a brush and brush it on the cut so that the gash is completely covered.

If you leave it this way, a fierce wind could come along and break the joint. So to ensure its holding, put some toothpick splices over the waxed portion, and wind it with string again. Remove the windings the first of May.

The twig you put in the ground is empty of sap. There is a vacuum in its veins. As the sap comes up into the vacuum, it knits up the cambium. Before long, the outer bark joins together, and year after next, you'll have some of your neighbor's apples growing on your apple tree. Try it. Put a different splice of a different cultivar on every branch. You'll have an apple tree that will amaze the neighborhood.

*September 1952*

# What's Wrong with Your Fruit?

*Ruth Rodale*

The apple tree in your backyard is definitely out of kilter. The new twig growth is dying back, the leaves are abnormally twisted, or fruits are blotchy and bumpy. What do you think of first? Codling moths and apple scab, I'll bet. Now take another look. Can you find any codling moth worms in the apple cores? Are the splotches just on the surface, or can you see hard brown spots inside? What you may have is a mild case of zinc deficiency, which can get progressively worse or through your help can be cleared up completely.

Possibly your trees have other symptoms of mineral deficiency. Potash or phosphorus may be low, or your soil may be too alkaline to allow certain minerals like iron and aluminum to become available. But the following list can perhaps solve your problem. These symptoms apply for all deciduous fruit trees.

## Nitrogen Deficiency

Examine the leaves of the old branches. With a lack of nitrogen, these older leaves turn a yellowish green, working toward the tips. You may also notice reddish or reddish purple discolorations. If nothing is done to relieve the deficiency, leaves become very small, and the twigs slender and hard.

## Phosphorus Deficiency

The young twigs develop a ghostlike hue: Stems show purple coloring and the leaves are abnormally small and dark green. Old leaves become mottled with light and dark green areas. Occasionally, bronzed leaves will show up on mature branches.

## Potash Deficiency

The key to potash deficiency is purplish discoloration and scorching of leaf edges. The dead spots will be found on mature leaves, but under continued deficiency, even very young leaves are affected. Peach foliage often becomes crinkled, and twigs are unusually slender.

## Magnesium Deficiency

The large, old leaves will display tan patches of dead tissue, not restricted to the leaf edges. Watch for dropping of leaves, first on old branches, then on twigs of the current season. Defoliation may be so severe that only tufts or "rosettes" of thin, small leaves are left on the tree.

## Zinc Deficiency

Both zinc and magnesium deficiencies are very much alike. Each of them can cause rosettes of leaves in the advanced stage. But without zinc, crinkled leaves are common, which are also chlorotic (rather washed-out yellow). In peach trees this is very true. With citrus fruit, very small, smooth fruit and pointed leaves are the symptoms. There may also be striking contrasts in leaf patterns— dark green veins and yellow tissue.

## Calcium Deficiency

Calcium and boron shortage will show up first on young twigs rather than the mature branches. Without calcium, dead areas are noticeable on the young, tender leaves at the tips and margins. Later, the twigs will die back, and roots are injured.

## Boron Deficiency

Immediately coming to mind should be internal cork of apples, which is the most most common boron deficiency problem. Early in the season, hard, brown spots with definite margins form inside the fruit. As the season progresses, the spots soften, become larger, and lose their definite outline. The leaves may be entirely unaffected.

In other cases, the young leaves can become very thick and brittle, then cause dieback of twigs. Some trees may also form wrinkled, chlorotic leaves.

## Iron and Aluminum Deficiency

With an overdose of lime comes an unavailability of certain minerals like iron and aluminum. These minerals may be right in the soil, but are held insoluble when the acidity is low. Look for yellow leaves with brown patches, and loss of flavor in the fruit.

## Correcting Deficiencies

When symptoms indicate that your fruit trees are suffering from a specific nutrient deficiency, select the appropriate fertilizers and amendments listed below to supply the missing element.

**Nitrogen:** Apply cottonseed meal, dried blood, raw bonemeal, fish wastes, legume hay, or one of the organic nitrogen commercial products now on the market.

**Phosphorus:** Apply raw or colloidal phosphate rock, bonemeal, fish wastes, guano, or raw sugar wastes.

**Potash:** Add granite dust, greensand, wood ashes, seaweed, or orange rinds.

**Magnesium:** Use dolomitic limestone or raw phosphate rock.

**Zinc:** Add raw phosphate rock.

**Calcium:** Apply raw pulverized limestone.

**Boron:** Apply raw phosphate rock (avoid lime; add acid organic matter like peat moss, sawdust, or ground oak leaves).

**Iron and Aluminum:** Add greensand (avoid lime; use the acid organic matter recommended under boron).

*June 1952*

## Golden Fertilizer

After getting a pet goldfish, I realized that I had a great source of houseplant fertilizer—goldfish water! Once a day, I move my fish to a bowl of fresh water that has been allowed to stand for at least 24 hours (chlorine is toxic to goldfish). Rich in fish manure and the uneaten fish food that becomes an additional source of nourishment for my plants, the water rivals commercial fish-emulsion fertilizers. It's also a great motivation to clean the fishbowl!

*Lynne Moose*
*Statesville, North Carolina*
*January 1984*

# "Our 10-Year Strawberry Bed"

## Helen and Scott Nearing

> Good fruit yields for lots more than the usual two or three seasons reward these veteran Maine gardeners who dared to try something different.

Experts advise setting strawberries in rows or hills rather than beds. The first-year runners and blossoms, they say, are to be picked off. Second-year plants should yield a big crop. If there is a third year, the crop will be smaller, hardly worth the trouble of weeding and fertilizing. "For impressive performance," wrote one *Organic Gardening and Farming* grower, "the same bed should not be used for more than two seasons."

Well, we used the hill system for years—plants kept 12 to 16 inches apart each way, three rows in a bed. All runners, except where needed for replacements, were pinched off, and after two or three years we dutifully replaced old beds with new plants.

Then about 12 years ago, we read a piece on strawberries in a Canadian magazine. The writer was praising a strawberry, the EMPIRE cultivar, that was doing well in Canada under a new method of culture. After picking stopped in July, all plants were mowed or cut off close to the crowns. With the old foliage went insect eggs, spores, and other pests. By September the plants had developed new, disease- and pest-free leaves. The writer also claimed that with this method, a strawberry patch would yield good crops for several more years than the usual two or three.

In the summer of 1958 we sent an order to Harris Seed Company for some RED RICH strawberry plants. Harris replied that they had no RED RICH, but that instead they were sending a berry they highly recommended. The name was EMPIRE. If not satisfied, we could return the plants.

We set the plants in a bed, 12 inches each way between them. The new plants were small, but they put out an immense number of runners, which we pinched off. The second year brought a good crop of large, delicious berries, borne high on long stems that kept them off the earth.

## Giving the Bed a Crew Cut

We liked these new berries and hoped to keep them for more than the usual two years—so we decided to try the Canadian cropping method. In July of the second year, we cut off every bit of foliage, down to the crowns. The bed, with this crew cut, looked pretty desolate by the time we had finished, and we wondered whether we hadn't made a mistake treating them so harshly. But by September a fine new crop of foliage was spreading all over the bed. We felt better and waited for spring.

The plants wintered well and put out a shower of white blossoms. Ripe berries grew abundant and were first-class for size, texture, and flavor. We

kept the patch weed-free with a heavy hay mulch in the 30-inch runway between beds. Pickers who wished to could sit on the hay and slide along as they picked on both sides of the runway.

The third summer, encouraged by EMPIRE performance, we used daughter plants to set two more beds on the hill system. But instead of 12 by 12 inches apart, we set the new plants 16 by 16 inches apart. They took hold well— and by fall we had two more beautiful beds of excellent plants. The first year, we did not cut back the foliage but

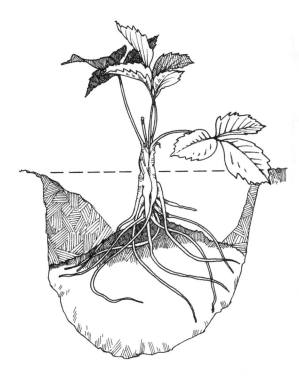

*Strawberry success starts with smart planting. Spread the roots of new strawberries out as you plant. Set each plant in the ground so that the middle of the crown is level with the soil surface.*

simply pinched off all runners.

In 1962 one of our three beds of EMPIRE berries was four years old; the second and third beds, two. That season, picking lasted from June 24 to July 29—more than five weeks—and berries were large, bright red, and of good texture and fine flavor. Each bed bore about the same number, with the four-year stand doing a shade better than the other two.

### Ginger versus Slugs

While researching and writing on pharmacognosy—the use of herbs and other natural substances for medicines—I discovered that ginger is an extremely potent snail and snug repellent, one that is not toxic to people, pets, or the environment. Perhaps this should not be surprising, considering ginger's sharp, burning taste. (Many of the spicy flavorings of herbal seasonings, such as ginger, serve to protect plants from insects.)

Spreading some of the powdered spice on the ground around plants creates a barrier beyond which snails and slugs will not tread. Salt and garlic, oddly enough, do not have the same effect. Try buying ginger in bulk at your health food store; it costs much less than at your supermarket.

*Mark Sunlin*
*Saratoga, California*
*April 1989*

### A Conference on Berry Strategy

At the end of the picking season in 1962, we held a conference. Plants in our oldest row had finished a fourth year. Since we had two excellent two-year EMPIRE beds, might it not be wise to get rid of the older section? We decided to try the four-year bed another season.

We clipped all foliage from the three beds and applied our usual mixture of cottonseed, soybean, and alfalfa meal, topped off with an inch or more of acid compost made of 3 parts compost, 1 part peat moss, and 1 part sawdust. The usual rich-green foliage sprang up by fall; then we mulched the plants over winter and had banks of white blossoms the following spring.

### Hay-Mulched Strawberries

Plants overwintered well, with few losses. The spring was cold, sunless, and dry—terribly poor strawberry weather. With some watering we got a good crop. The largest and sweetest berries came from our original bed, now in its fifth year. For volume of production, it held a slight lead over the others. Clipped back, fertilized, and winter-mulched, the old EMPIRE bed went into its sixth year. Again it finished ahead of the other two in quality and quantity of fruit—in a cold, foggy, damp spring and early summer.

## "Just One More Year"

By 1964 our procedure was a well-established routine: picking, cutting back foliage, fertilizing, mulching. After each picking season we decided to give our 1958 bed "just one more year." Each successive year's performance was so good that we decided to try again and again.

The year 1968 was a bad strawberry year—dry, foggy, sunless. Plants also suffered badly from winterkill, and we picked less than half a usual crop. Our original EMPIRE bed limped badly. (It was now ten years old!) The other two beds, now eight-year-olds, did better. Regretfully, we ended our experiment and pulled out the old row, ordered some fresh plants, and set them out in a new bed last September.

What had this experiment taught us? First: that the hill system, with plants 16 by 16 inches apart, will give a maximum yield of quality berries over a long period. Second: that with replacements here and there, a strawberry bed kept free of weeds and cut back severely can bear satisfactory crops for a decade. Third: that with EMPIRE plants, re-

### Padded Handles

For a more comfortable, blister-free grip on garden tools, slip ³⁄₄-inch plastic-foam pipe insulation over your hoe and rake handles. The insulation eliminates the need for wearing hot, bulky work gloves.

*Steve Sneeden*
*Salem, Oregon*
*February 1987*

moving the foliage after picking prompts a healthy new crop of leaves before the fall freeze-up. Fourth: that with adequate annual fertilization, a ten-year-old bed can bear a good crop of fine berries.

*February 1970*

269

# Berries Keep Producing!

*M. C. Goldman*

For nonstop good eating, get started with the plants that deliver the sweetest, healthiest yields in the backyard—strawberries, raspberries, blueberries, plus others—and do it year after year.

Good taste grows by the bucketful when you introduce berries to the backyard. More than that, these fruits fit right in when it comes to planning a well-balanced food supply from the garden. There's a nutritional bonus, too, since berries rank high in nutrients. A cup of strawberries, for example, provides as much vitamin C as the same amount of fresh oranges. Many of the berries help stretch the season by serving up bowls of ambrosial eating both earlier and later than other crops. They're also flavorsome prospects for fresh-freezing or canning as jams, preserves, and other stocking-up favorites.

Perhaps the biggest plus factor is that, unlike nearly all vegetables, berry plants are perennials. They become permanent garden residents, requiring little further effort and no further investment to keep producing yields of tastier homegrown fruit year after year.

Take strawberries, for instance, today's most popular fruit grown in home gardens. It's no wonder, either. With just average attention, these herbaceous perennials produce up to a quart or more of big, red, mouth-watering berries for every foot of garden row planted. Some return over 125 quarts to the 100-foot row—a lot of juicy eating in anybody's berry patch.

Of all the berries, strawberries are also the first to produce a big crop. Young plants set early this spring will bear well next year if blossoms are picked off the first season to conserve the plant's strength and encourage more growth.

To ready a new bed, dig up the area roughly, getting out sod, especially with grass, weeds, stones, and the like. Then fix a small place, about 2 feet square, for each young plant. The soil should be loose and rich with lots of dried or rotted manure or commercial cow-manure compost mixed

in. Bonemeal makes a good booster for annual feeding.

Set plants so that the crowns are not submerged; the base of the crown should rest at ground level. Keep plants about 3 feet apart to give the runners plenty of room to root.

Water well and mulch thickly with hay. (Rotting leaves or other plant material can be used, although they don't look as neat.) Keep adding more as the mulch decays. It will seem amazing (to the novice) that the soil beneath stays moist and gets soft and loose even though it may not have been dug up thoroughly.

The minimum worthwhile number of plants to start with is 25, say the veteran growers. The plants can multiply several times before the first harvest.

As for renewing plants, some experienced growers prefer setting out beds each season (it's less work weeding, they say), some alternate

*A mulch of hay or straw keeps berries clean and keeps the soil in your strawberry patch healthy. If you want runners to root, it's easy to tuck them through the mulch and into the moist soil below.*

rows each year, while others keep a three- or four-bed revolving production. Veteran Ohio strawberry-raiser Lucille Shade says she likes a four-bed system, "one producing for the first time, one for the second year, another for the third, and still another for the fourth and last time. It is this flat bed that I till under after the plants finish bearing around July 1. If you are able to keep weeds under control, a strawberry bed can last for a number of years, provided it is properly cared for and continually renewed. Starting a new bed each year doesn't have to cost you a cent. You can use some of the plants from your older patches," notes Mrs. Shade. Renew the bed by allowing about two new runners from each mother plant to carry over to the next year.

"I like to set out 25 new plants each year," she adds. "That doesn't sound like much, but most kinds will make new runners so fast that I end up with some 200 plants by the following spring. Multiply that by four beds and you can see why I have all the berries my family can eat, all I can get in the freezer, some to give away, and some extra for jam!"

Want an assortment? You can stretch the strawberry-picking season by having a different kind in each row or bed—early, midseason, late, and extra-late. And you can double the harvesttime from part of the patch by planting some everbearers, which fruit first in the spring, then again in late summer.

Several new strawberries in 1976 provided some good choices. One of them, TIOGA, starts producing a large flush of fruit in April and keeps it going to July. Highly disease-resistant, the early-bearing strain yields better, especially in California and other western areas. The firm, medium-size berries are fine for cooking, freezing, or eating right off the plate. TIOGA was introduced by Koppes Berry Plants, Watsonville, California.

EARLIGLOW, and introduction developed by the Maryland Extension Station, has been bred with strong resistance to red stele root rot, plus has a sweet flavor and high productivity. Test plantings have done well in the Midwest, Pennsylvania, Ohio, and Missouri, as well as Maryland.

AMERICAN SWEETHEART is a heavy-cropping everbearer from Dean Foster Nurseries in Hartford, Michigan, which also introduced the extra-early-spring TEMPTATION and the novel WHITE STRAWBERRY, which you might like to contrast with BLACK BEAUTY, a very dark red June-bearer.

Other strawberries to choose from: Among early and midseason types, CATSKILL, FAIRFAX, NEW EMPIRE, and the high-quality PREMIER rate consideration, as do late-bearers SPARKLE and NEW JERSEY BELLE. Check out everbearers such as CHIEF BEMIDJI, which survives 40-degree-below-zero temperatures; OGALLALA, with its flavor of wild strawberries; HONEY-LUMP, one of the sweetest; deep red SUPERFECTION; prize-winning OZARK BEAUTY; 60-day-maturing STREAMLINER; and old favorite GIANT GEM.

## Blueberries for a Lifetime

Ranging from little shrubs a few inches tall to bushes standing 10 to 12 feet tall, blueberries represent a clan of the *Vaccinium* genus—the ones that deliver those appetizingly deep-colored fruit clusters.

One of the unfussiest of bush berry fruits, blueberries will do well even on meadow-type soils that are often too wet for many crops, returning heavy yields as a result of the extra moisture. Highbush plants, properly set out and then given an annual feeding and a good mulch, thrive and produce for a gardener's lifetime. Used as fruiting hedges, the plants are attractive and productive, with good-looking red foliage in the fall. And they don't need the constant pruning of hedges like privet.

*Blueberries thrive in acidic, humus-enriched soils. To create a planting that's pleasing to the eyes and the palate, combine these attractive, easy-care shrubs with acid-loving ornamentals such as rhododendrons and azaleas.*

Depending on the cultivar chosen, blueberries may ripen anytime from mid-July (after the first raspberries) on through September. The harvest from any one cultivar lasts about a month. For better pollination and bigger yields, nurseries recommend planting two cultivars that bloom at more or less the same time.

The time to plant blueberries is when they are dormant—either in spring as soon as the ground is ready, or in the fall as soon as the leaves turn color and until the ground freezes too hard to be workable. Space plants about 6 to 8 feet apart—except for hedge use—so the sun reaches all parts of the bush equally for better ripening of fruit. Good drainage is important while blueberries are growing actively, so try planting bushes on the lower part of a slight slope, where they'll usually get ample moisture as long as there's enough organic matter in the soil to conserve it. Because they like both plenty of moisture and aeration, it's important to build up the soil's organic content.

## Success Starts with the Soil

To set out blueberries, prepare the soil a bit deeper than for most vegetables, and try to have 6 to 8 inches of humus under the plant. Soil pH should be between 4.5 and 5.0 and kept that way by applying acid organic fertilizers or mulches—never any lime. Work a top-dressing of acid compost or well-rotted manure into the soil. Peat moss, hardwood leaves, pine needles, and the like, decompose into an acid compost.

Next, ready a hole 2 or 3 feet wide at least 18 inches deep—large enough to allow roots to spread out flat rather than hang down deep. Plant the same depth as the transplanting soil line on the main stem, or just slightly deeper. Never let sun or wind dry out roots. Keep them protected while preparing your hole. When the soil under the bush is thoroughly moist, apply a mulch 2 to 4 inches deep around it, extending out beyond the drip line of the branches.

Mulches will smother most weeds, keep the underlying soil cool in summer, protect roots from late-spring freeze-and-thaw damage, and as they decompose, provide food for bushes over a long period. In fertilizing blueberries, it is better to err on the lean side than to overfeed, since you will produce beautiful foliage but little fruit if too much nitrogen is applied.

The best blueberry fertilizers contain organic sources of nitrogen, phosphorus, and potash in approximately equal amounts. Good sources of nitrogen include soybean and cottonseed meal, dried blood, fish meal, sheep manure, dried cow manure, castor bean pomace, bonemeal, corn gluten meal, and so on. An application of phosphate rock and granite dust once every three or four years is advisable to keep up the soil's mineral health.

Make three small applications of fertilizer in March, April, and May, instead of all at once, advises a leading blueberry nurseryman. A three-year-old bush should have about 3 handfuls spread around it in the area under the drip line and away from the main stem. As the bush grows, more can be applied, until at eight or ten years it will be receiving about 2 pounds.

Besides an acid soil, the blueberry's other prime requirement is a little pruning to cut out weak or dead branching or to remove thick twiggy clusters to let in light. Once in a while an old branch should be cut back to the ground to induce new growth.

Among the long list of hardy cultivars are BERKELEY, which produces one of the largest berries on vigorous, spreading bushes; EARLIBLUE, superior in size, color, fruit quality, and firmness and ripening very early; BLUECROP and BLUERAY, which follow in early-season maturing; HERBERT, one of the finest late cultivars in size and productiveness; and COVILLE, latest of all to ripen, with large berries and heavy crops. For the South and Southwest, where standard blueberries fare poorly because of heat and alkaline soil, the "rabbiteye" cultivars—TIFBLUE, MENDITOO, GARDEN BLUE, and HOMEBELL—take up the job admirably.

## Raising Cane— Fruits, That Is

Brambles, the common name for a group of shrubby plants of the genus *Rubus* (part of the rose family), make up the third type of berries. Included are

**Black raspberries**

*Raspberries begin ripening as the strawberry harvest wanes. By growing both crops, you can have fresh fruit to eat for nearly two months in early summer.*

the popular blackberries and raspberries, plus loganberries, dewberries, and several more. A raspberry crop follows strawberries, extending the fresh-fruit season by three to four weeks. A beginner would do well to start with 10 to 12 canes, and although harvests will be light the first two years, they'll reap heavy yields from then on.

Early spring or late fall is the best time to set out canes. Dig up the area, then simply prepare planting holes 3 to 4 feet apart each way, and put in the canes carefully. Raspberries are shallow-rooted, but should be planted slightly deeper than their original position. Firm the soil well around the roots, but don't cover the crown of the plant. The new canes emerge from this. Keep a distance of at least 3

feet between plants. Then mulch thickly with hay or leaves between the plants. A constant mulch about 6 to 7 inches deep will kill weeds or even sod beneath and eliminate the need for cultivation. Mulching also protects the shallow roots in winter.

## Drastic Cutbacks Produce Future Vigor

Cut the cane way back when planting. This may seem drastic, but the future results will be sturdier, more vigorous canes.

The brambles all produce their fruit on canes (stalks) that grew the preceding year, except for fall-bearing raspberry strains. It's important to understand that growth pattern clearly in order to prune plants correctly—which is the key to success with these berries. *Organic Gardening and Farming* Contributing Editor Gene Logsdon explains: "As soon as the crop of bramble berries has been picked, cut the canes off at ground level and remove them from the garden. They will have started to die, anyway. But of course you do not cut off the new canes, which will produce next year and which are growing right alongside the bearing canes."

Faithfully following this practice of cutting old canes out immediately, or as soon as possible after harvest, goes a long way toward controlling insects and diseases, which nearly always begin on old canes.

As for what plants to start with,

the most practical raspberries for the beginner are either standard one-crop red berry cultivars (harvested in July when few other fruits are ripe) or everbearing reds (July harvest with another smaller crop in fall on the tips of the new canes).

Some good raspberry choices available from many nurseries include BIG RED LATHAM, a hardy grower with large fruit; POLARIS, a one-crop northern cultivar bearing on dwarf canes; and TAYLOR, a tall, light-red-berried heavy producer. FALLRED, DURHAM, SEPTEMBER, and INDIAN SUMMER are all fine red everbearers ripening a late crop into autumn. HERITAGE, a winter-hardy two-crop strain holds its fruit well right up to hard frost. FALLGOLD and GOLDEN AMBER, excellent yellow everbearing cultivars, also produce until freezing weather sets in. ALLEN, BLACK HAWK, BRISTOL CUMBERLAND, and JEWEL are four of the reliable "blackcaps," or black raspberries. CLYDE is a promising performer among the purple raspberries (noted for their vigor and consistently heavy yields), which also include the one-crop SODUS and everbearing PURPLE AUTUMN.

HURON, a cultivar with large, glossy-black berries, ripens after midseason and is productive and hardy. Along with the late-midseason red SENTINEL are SOUTHLAND (adapted to middle and southern conditions), and SCEPTER, a large everbearing red that ripens about ten days before SEPTEMBER.

Blackberries, another of the bramble fruits, generally yield better than raspberries both in the wild and

*Expand your fruit possibilities even further by planting gooseberries (shown here), currants, and other attractive, easy-care berry bushes.*

the garden, although they are not always considered a high-quality berry for eating fresh. DARROW, which has proven far superior to other selections, produces berries that Gene Logsdon describes as tasting "very good indeed if you wait until they are dead ripe before picking them. When fully ripe, the berries almost fall off in your hand as you pick them. SMOOTHSTEM and THORNLESS are good yielders for USDA Plant Hardiness Zone 4 on southward, and, as their names indicate, they do not have thorns, praise be!"

Once you've established a basic planting, you might want to expand into some different berries for variety in both flavor and growing challenge. There are colorful boysenberries, red currants, huge gooseberries, loganberries, and old favorite elderberries. One thing for sure, you'll never want or need to be without your own homegrown berries—the plants that keep producing!

*February 1976*

## Chapter 15

# Special Events—
# Ruth Stout
# and Friends

# Sharing with the Birds

*Victor A. Croley*

Here's a man with highly unconventional ideas on co-existing with both winged helpers and gluttons in the garden—ideas that save crops, insect problems, and birds!

One spring thrill we always enjoy is watching a cock cardinal in a blossom-laden pear tree. The proud bird in his bright crimson feathers and jaunty cockade seems fully aware of the startling contrast he makes among the snow-white flowers, for he preens and yells at the very top of his voice: "Jeepers! Jeepers! Jeepers!" It is such a breathtaking moment that I can only stand and admire and echo, "Jeepers!"

Such delights are commonplace with all who share a garden with the birds. And with just a little forethought and care, the delights can be multiplied many fold.

In my own case, sharing was involuntary and un-intentional at the start. I was grubbing about the as-paragus bed on a balmy early spring day when I felt something brush against by bare head, followed by a sharp twinge. Looking up I discovered a tiny gray tit-mouse had been so desperate for nesting material he had plucked a tuft of hair from my scalp! I was out-raged at the boldness and by the fact that my hairline is fast slipping back and thinning out. I certainly have no hair to spare for a feathered robber's nest, so I snipped up some of the madame's embroidery silks

e wood to burn during the
her. The saucy Carolina and
rens immediately take pos-
orking around, under, and
through the pile to collect
, worm, bug, larva—even
ic insect eggs. They cease
ties only for a moment of
 scold me for taking a few
 their pile.

learned that bird courage
be in inverse ratio to their
by-throated hummingbird,
jewel in metallic green and
 half as big as a tiny tufted
 and yet I watched with
t when two of them dive-
crow that had approached
eir button-size nest. I am
ack marauder could have
a hummingbird at a single
instead he flapped away
eetops, cawing in terror
poking back.

had my own brief en-
h one of the midget bul-
ed it off to cowardice on
the crow. I was inspecting
owering bean vines when
ngbird, apparently feeling
encroaching on his private
made several warning
ously close to my head. I
ed up to find the bird
the air not 6 inches from
s wings almost invisible in
f their beating. For a long
It myself eyeball to eyeball
ble-sized atomic bomb. I
sage quickly and, realizing
v is a very smart bird after

all, promptly took myself elsewhere.

There are no English sparrows or starlings here in the deep woods, and I think it must be because they find living so much easier in town where, nearly every home has an overflowing feeder in the backyard. Their place is taken by a dozen varieties of native sparrows: song sparrow, chipping sparrow, fox sparrow, and others. In winter these ground-feeders are joined by flocks of juncoes and chickadees that only occasionally feel the need of a few sunflower seeds.

## Birds Help Keep Weeds and Bugs at Bay

At first I was somewhat uneasy about these ground-feeding sparrows, for I remembered what a nuisance the white-capped sparrow can be in Southern California and how quickly they could go down a garden row of emerging seedlings and make them disappear. Here, however, weed seeds sprout on warm days right through the winter and apparently they are more attractive, for although 26 types of sparrows have been observed in Arkansas—and I'm sure many of them have visited my mountainside—I have yet to discover any loss or damage from them.

Perhaps the most interesting bird we have is the white-breasted nuthatch. He is called the clown of birdland, and justly so. Our spacemen might have learned secrets of weightlessness from watching the nuthatch, for he defies the law of gravity and into short lengths and laid them beside the feeder. Then I donned my hard hat as an added precautionary measure.

I have since learned that titmice are among the boldest and tamest of wild birds. Only half as big as a minute, these feathered mites are lion-hearted and fear man no more than their arch-enemies, the household cat and the black snake. With a bit more patience, I am sure, they would take food from my hands, for they often swoop down to snatch a fresh sunflower seed from the feeder even as I am filling it. But I am not interested in taming birds, and I offer sunflower seed only as a supplement to their regular diet. Sharing is a cooperative proposition—in return for a small handout, some nesting material, and a few added nest boxes and gourds, I expect them to keep weed seeds, worms, and insect pests within reasonable bounds.

## Encourage Birds— Don't Pamper Them

Observing the elaborate feeding stations and diets some of my neighbors prepare and set before the birds, I wonder just what they expect. Our chickens and pigeons were wild birds not too long ago. Now with food, water, and shelter, they have become household pets requiring daily attention and care. Stuff them with fancy rations and pelletized foods and they will turn up their beaks at ordinary fare. You can't blame the birds. Who wants a hairy caterpillar or a wriggling worm

when yo
raisins, c
with a dr

No,
them—
their ke
vigor, ar
tended.
put out
sure no
hungry.
them t
Ozarks,
rustle th
pecker
trunk o
able si
bird pe

Th
in obs
and ar
in the
coaxin
windo
early f

*Fee*

of firepla
cold wea
Bewick's
session,
over and
every an
microsco
their acti
song, or
sticks fror

I hav
seems to
size. The
a dazzling
red, is on
titmouse
amazeme
bombed
too near
sure the
swallowed
gulp, but
over the
and never

Until
counter w
lies, I char
the part of
some red-
the humm
that I was
preserves
passes per
straighte
hanging in
my nose, h
the speed
moment I f
with a thir
got the me
that the cr

would as soon perch below a branch as upon it. Like the wrens and brown-creepers, he lives on tiny insects, larvae, and insect eggs that are hidden in the crevices and rough bark of trees, searching them out so assiduously that he pays no attention to equilibrium or position. He goes under, over, and around trunk and branch with sharp eyes concentrating so intently on the task at hand that it makes no difference to him whether he is right side up, or upside down, standing on his head or tail! Occasionally nuthatches tire of bugs and swoop down for a sunflower seed to vary their diet, but I consider it small pay for the entertainment (and protection) they provide.

A rustling in the ground litter usually betrays the towhee. Leaves fly as these robin-size birds scratch in the mulch for bugs and worms that make up their diet. I never see them near the feeder and so must assume they are not interested in sunflower seeds. Bluebirds stay with us all winter and spend the cold nights in the nest boxes where they raise their summer broods. But they, too, show no interest in sunflower seeds, preferring cedar berries, weed seeds, and the seeds of last summer's hollyhocks and other flowers. Blue jays and cardinals are frequent visitors that seem to appreciate the plump sunflower seeds, but as spring turns into early summer, they disappear into the denser brush and are heard more often than seen.

Robins are migrants here in the Ozarks. I have never found them nesting. They head north in early spring in flocks of one to two hundred, then return in similar numbers in the fall to feast on cedar berries, holly, and dogwood before going further south. I feared at first that they might linger in spring long enough

*Beautify your landscape with flowering shrubs like shadbushes (*Amelanchier spp.*).*
*Many birds enjoy their blueberry-like fruits.*

for the cherry crop, since a large flock could make short work of my few fruiting trees. But they are gone before cherries ripen and the remaining fruit-eaters—catbirds, brown thrashers, mockingbirds, and jays—are not numerous enough to cause heavy loss. They work the high branches and treetops where I couldn't gather the fruit anyway, and so there is still plenty left for pies and freezer.

Just to be on the safe side, I have a couple of mulberry trees to persuade the birds to go easy on the cherries. It should be remembered that there are white and black varieties of mulberry, and for aesthetic reasons it is wise to choose the white. The birds like them equally well, and you don't have bright purple splashes all over in fruiting season.

## Hardware Cloth Protects Strawberries

I refuse to share strawberries with the birds, and I have found a simple way to protect them with strips of hardware cloth. I use ½-inch mesh that is 2 feet wide, cut into 6-foot lengths for easy handling. Bent lengthwise in a V-trough and inverted over the berry rows, the hardware cloth can be used year after year—and it completely foils the most persistent birds. There are plenty of wild berries in the open spaces of the woods, so I have no compunction in denying them my choice OGALLALAS and OZARK BEAUTIES.

Raspberries, blackberries, currants, and blueberries are sometimes sampled by feathered neighbors, but since we grow them in abundance, no one begrudges the small loss.

Water is probably more important than supplementary food for the birds. In periods of drought, especially, we try to keep water available, not only for drinking and bathing, but for nesting help. Barn swallows and cliff swallows must have mud for their nest-building, and even the phoebe and wood peewee start their nests on a secure foundation of adobe.

On a tree farm there is always the urge to cut out poor stock, weed trees, dead trees, and "wolf" trees in order to grow only a solid phalanx of the favored variety. Perhaps there is an improvement in appearance, but from a wildlife standpoint the practice is questionable. Birds are highly specialized over many centuries and countless generations. Environment that suits one species may not sustain life for another. Occasional open spaces, glades, and savannahs are needed by such birds as quail, larks, and others. Dead trees and branches are vital to woodpeckers. And last year's holes are needed as nesting sites for screech owls, tree swallows, blue jays, and others.

Sharing with birds is far from a one-sided venture. Aside from the pleasure, we are indebted to them for their service in pest and disease control.

*May 1966*

# StingingNettle— Weed of Wonders

## Euell Gibbons

Seldom does the rare, exotic plant prove the most interesting in herbal research. Far more often it is one common, familiar, and despised weed that is discovered to have undreamed-of virtues. The common nettle—a particularly pesty plant of surprisingly uncommon value—is a good illustration.

Nearly everyone who ever ran barefoot as a child knows and hates this plant, but it is only a stinging acquaintance. Nettles are common along roadsides, in waste places, and on vacant lots where barefoot children like to play. When contacted by a bare ankle, the plant causes a painful smarting followed by a red rash. Recently I was picking nettles on a nearby farm, and the puzzled farmer wondered aloud why anyone would want to gather "them damn weeds." I started to explain some of the uses of this wonder plant, but he interrupted and said, "All I want to know about nettles is how to get rid of them." That's the attitude most people have.

And yet, this detested weed is one of the best-tasting and most nutritious foods in the whole plant kingdom, a far better vegetable than many

Surprising, perhaps, but this thoroughly disliked "pest plant" has some completely likable—and valuable—benefits for man and beast.

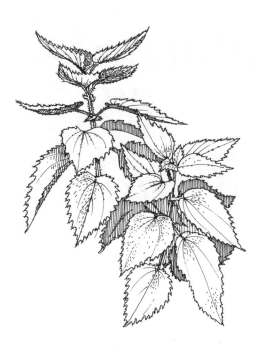

*Underappreciated nettles (*Urtica dioica*) are amazingly versatile plants that have more to offer than painful stings.*

remedies and herbal medicines. (This is probably due to its high content of vitamins and minerals, for I believe that far more sickness is prevented or cured by proper feeding than by drugging.) A lively soft drink can be made of nettles, which is reputed to cure the aches and pains of the aged, but it also makes a pleasant beverage.

Although America has some edible native nettles, the common nettle (*Urtica dioica*) was originally a European plant. It was introduced early into this country, quickly became naturalized, and is now found wherever conditions are suitable for its growth. While usually seen as a small plant, 1 to 2 feet high, it may reach heights of 6 to 8 feet in rich stream valleys. The leaves are opposite, heart-shaped, finely toothed on the margins, and tapering to points. Small green flowers are borne on branched clusters springing from the leaf axils. The whole plant is downy and also covered with stiff, stinging hairs. Each sting is really an exceedingly sharp, hollow spine arising from a slightly swollen base. This swelling contains the venom that is released through the polished spine whenever the plant is brushed. The venom is partly formic acid, which accounts for its sharp sting, closely related to the sting of a bee.

that this same farmer's wife raises in her kitchen garden. People in many parts of the world regularly gather and cook these greens, not because they are healthful, but merely because they like them. However, in addition to their good taste, they are rich in vitamins A and C, amazingly high in protein, filled with chlorophyll, and probably rich in many essential trace minerals.

## Home Remedy, Herbal Tea, and Textile Uses

In addition to these virtues, nettles have also long been used in home

## Cooking Transforms Plant

Eating nettles is not at all the unpleasant experience you might expect it to be. When gathered at the right stage and properly prepared, it is very palatable. A good French cook can make seven delicious dishes of nettle tops. You can do as well, once the general principles of nettle cookery are known.

Like many other vegetables, nettles must be gathered at just the right stage to be good. The common nettle has perennial underground rhizomes, and from these the tender shoots spring up as soon as the weather is warm. It is only these first nettles, gathered when less than a foot high, that are good to eat. Later in the year, gritty particles called *cystoliths* are deposited in the leaves, making them unpalatable. When nettles are cut down, a new crop springs from the base of the cut plants. I thought surely these newly grown plants would be good, but when I tried some in midsummer, they were gritty and gruesome.

Take only the tender tops of young, first-grown nettles, before they begin to bloom. Wear leather or plastic-coated work gloves while gathering nettles, for even these young plants can sting fiercely. Wash the greens by stirring them in water with a long-handled spoon, then use a pair of kitchen tongs to put them directly into a large saucepan with a tight cover. The moisture that clings to the leaves will furnish ample cooking water. Cover and cook gently for 20 minutes, drain, *but save that juice.*

You can chop the greens right in the cooking pot by using a pair of kitchen shears. Season the vegetable with butter and spice to taste, and it is ready to serve—and a more wholesome vegetable never came to the table.

Cooking, incidentally, completely destroys the nettle's stinging propensities and actually converts the venom into wholesome food. Let's return to that juice we drained from the cooked nettles. Just seasoned with a little salt

*When I was a child, we treated nettle stings by rubbing the affected area with juicy leaves of dock (*Rumex crispus*), which brought almost magical relief.*

and pepper and a very little vinegar, it makes a tasty soup that is supposed to help remove unwanted pounds. Mixed with a little honey it is said to relieve asthma, allay a cough, and help cure bronchitis. Taken as hot as you can drink it, after exposure, this juice has a reputation of helping to prevent colds. I know it is a nice, warming drink on a chilly day, giving a warm glow all over. And to top all its uses, when cooled, this same juice is said to be a fine hair tonic, reputed to prevent falling hair, eliminate dandruff, promote a healthy scalp, and help keep the hair neatly combed.

*April 1966*

### Herb Tea for Plants

We had a real problem with damping-off on our tomato and squash seedlings until we began giving them chamomile tea. We make a strong tea with 3 teaspoons of dried chamomile to 6 cups of boiling water. We allow the tea to steep and cool, then water the seedlings two or three times until all signs of damping-off have vanished and the plants are restored to health.

*Marion J. Fear*
*Magog, Quebec*
*November 1984*

# World's Most Important Organic Gardener

## John Y. Beaty

The reason I say that Luther Burbank was the world's most important organic gardener is that he produced more new types of useful plants than any other person before or since. When I worked with him, beginning in 1912, he told me that one of his chief desires was to enable people to produce more food and flowers and forage crops from the soil. To accomplish this ambition, he developed new varieties of fruits, nuts, forage plants, grains, flowers, ornamentals, and vegetables totaling over 1,000 new selections.

The accomplishment that is most difficult to visualize was the growing of 90 tons of a forage plants per acre. The forage crop was his fast-growing spineless cactus. The slabs of this cactus could be planted close together in a field. It grew rapidly, and the weight of the slabs, which was the part of the cactus fed to livestock, was far greater than any other forage crop.

In the 77 fruitful years of his life, Luther Burbank produced more superior varieties of plants than any other man. The author, who worked extensively with Mr. Burbank, reveals some of the happenings that made Burbank the incomparable "plant wizard."

## A Soil-Improvement Story

Perhaps the best way to explain his understanding of the soil needs of crops is to tell the story as he told it to me of how he prepared the soil on his 4 acres in Santa Rosa, California, where he tested thousands of new varieties of plants, including the fast-growing spineless cactus. Here is the story in his own words:

"When I bought this 4-acre place, it was a neglected, run-down plot which had been on the market for years. The land was about as poor as could be found. Many attempts had been made to cultivate it, but a crop had not been grown for a long time. When I bought it, I had a plan in mind that I thought would transform it into a producing garden.

"My first activity was to place tiles under the whole tract at a depth of 4 feet to drain surplus water into a nearby stream. The land at one time had been the bottom of a pond and it had sunk below the level of the surrounding area, so it was necessary to drain it and to level the land as well as fertilize it.

"You may not believe it when I tell you that I used 1,800 loads of barnyard manure on that 4 acres. This manure helped both to put the soil in good condition and also to level off the place. You may wonder how I was able to cover up that much manure. It wasn't easy, I can assure you. A lot of manure was first spread on the surface. Then, as we plowed it, I had two men follow the plow and throw manure into the furrows so that the next furrow slice would bury some of the manure.

"The next spring, after this land was tiled and fertilized, it was planted to fruit trees. The year after that, enough nursery stock was sold from this planting to more than pay for the original purchase price of the 4 acres.

"I had in mind, of course, growing many different kinds of plants on this land, so I modified the soil in different parts of the 4 acres for use of different kinds of plants. Some places I added sand to make it more suitable for raising bulbs. For a few years, the land was used entirely for the production of nursery stock in order to enable me to get money ahead to start my work of developing new varieties."

Mr. Burbank had another 8 acres in Sebastopol, a short distance from Santa Rosa, where he grew plants on a larger scale, but his original testing was on these 4 acres in Santa Rosa. He first planted the seeds he wanted to experiment with in greenhouse flats and kept them in the greenhouse until the seedlings showed well above the surface. He immediately began to make selections among the seedlings, throwing out any that had undesirable characteristics. Then, as soon as those that seemed to be promising were large enough, he transplanted them into his garden outside.

He kept careful records, of course, of the parentage of all these plants and the productiveness they showed. Because his garden was so well-prepared, the plants grew rapidly and he was able to see the results of his experiments more quickly than would have been possible in a less carefully prepared bed.

## 113 New Plum Varieties

At Sebastopol, he had an orchard of plum trees on which he grafted scions from seedling plums started in Santa Rosa. This grafting was done in order that he might see the fruits more quickly. If he waited for the fruit to be produced on the seedling trees, he would have to wait seven or eight years; but, by grafting scions onto the older producing trees, he saw results in one to two years. He then studied the fruits as they appeared on the larger trees and, as soon as he concluded that there was something wrong with the fruit or the scion on which it grew, he would destroy that scion and the seedling tree and start to work with others. He worked on a tremendous scale. It is hard to believe but, actually, he was testing about 30,000 new selections of plums on his plum orchard at Sebastopol every year. As a result of this large-scale work, he eventually produced 113 new varieties of plums and prunes, which have proved to be more useful than those that were available before he started his work.

In telling me about his methods of handling the seedling plants when he transplanted them into the garden from the flats, he said:

"Almost all plants should be set out in the field somewhat deeper than they grow in the greenhouse boxes. When plants have long roots, these should be straightened out and placed as deeply as possible in the soil to give them a good start by the time the dry summer weather commences. Otherwise, these baby plants could not, in some cases, extend their roots fast enough to keep up with the gradually disappearing moisture and so they might die of thirst.

"When the seedlings are removed from the protection of the glass house to the open air, it is best, if possible, to choose a time when there are no severe winds and when the sun is not too hot and the atmosphere neither too dry nor too chilly.

"I have found that, here in California, tender plants will stand moving from the greenhouse to the open air best if I can guess when there is going to be a warm rain. In other words, I like to have the rain do the first watering. However, as you see, I have an irrigation system here with which I sprinkle the soil from those pipes out there that have nozzles along their full length. In other words, I can produce a rain when that is necessary." (The pipes he referred to were supported on stakes about 3 feet above the ground, and the nozzles were so arranged that they sprayed on both sides of the pipes.)

Mr. Burbank's first important introduction of a new plant was made when he was still a young man in Lancaster, Massachusetts, where he was born on March 7, 1849. When he was old enough to make a garden for himself, he raised vegetable crops for sale, and he early learned many of the lessons necessary to produce the best vegetables for sale. For example, in order to have sweet corn ready to sell before others in the community had mature ears, he planted the seeds in boxes in the house a number of days before it was time to plant them outdoors. Then when it was time to plant them outdoors, he set out little plants that had a head start on those of his neighbors.

## Potato Seed Success

One day, he was going through his crop of EARLY ROSE potatoes when he saw a green seed ball on one of the plants. His study of plants told him that each seed in that little green ball would produce a new variety of potato. When the ball was mature, he carefully saved it and the next year planted the 23 seeds that were inside. Twenty-one of the new varieties of potatoes were of no value; they were not as good as those already being grown, but two of the new varieties were better. They had large, smooth tubers with a delicious white flesh. One of these was sold two years later to James J. H. Gregory, a seedsman at Marblehead, Massachusetts.

The seedsman introduced this as the Burbank Seedling, and it rapidly increased in favor and has since traveled entirely across the country. But it all started from the growing of the seeds in this one little potato seed ball in Massachusetts. I recently checked with the experiment stations in those three states and learned that about

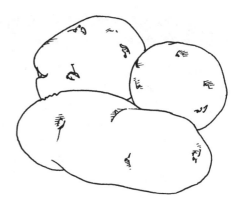

*Burbank's seedling potato grew into a multimillion dollar crop in Oregon, Washington, and Idaho.*

$120 million worth of Burbank potatoes are grown each year.

As was the case with the potato, Burbank grew some of his new varieties by simply planting seeds. When you plant the seeds of those crops that are commonly reproduced by bulbs, tubers, corms, cuttings, or scions, you get a new variety from each seed. Every seed of an apple, an orange, or a plum will produce a new variety. It is true, of course, that most of the new varieties will be of less value than what we already have, but occasionally, there will be one that will be better, and if that is introduced, it may prove of tremendous benefit to mankind.

The second method used by Mr. Burbank was to cross-pollinate varieties and grow the seeds resulting from the cross. He did this when he wished to combine the good qualities of two varieties of plants. He had some astonishing results in that he was able to cross some kinds of plants that the scientists had said could not be hybridized. For example, he crossed the plum and the apricot and produced a new kind of fruit, which he named the plumcot.

## "The Industry of One Man"

In Bulletin 691 of the California Experiment Station issued in March 1945, Professor W. L. Howard writes about Burbank's accomplishments: "Burbank's most lasting fame will always be associated with the long list of plum varieties he introduced. To him belongs the credit for introductions that started huge horticultural industries in all parts of the world where early flowering fruits can be grown.

"Twenty of his varieties (18% of the total introduced) are still widely planted throughout the United States and other countries. Ten of the number are standard shipping varieties wherever Oriental plums are grown for marketing, as in California, South Africa, Argentina, and Australia. In California alone, they form the basis of a major industry. At present (1944), there is in this state a total of about 24,000 acres of Burbank varieties—upwards of 2,000,000 trees. Thousands of carloads of fruit are shipped annually; and the money returns run into the millions—not a bad showing for the industry of one man."

The bulletin just quoted tells about the success of the many varieties Mr.

Burbank introduced and describes the following number of varieties:

- Tree fruits: 177
- Small fruits: 96
- Forage plants: 40
- Grains: 14
- Nut trees: 11
- Herbaceous ornamentals: 399
- Ornamental vines: 12
- Other ornamentals: 9
- Vegetables: 93
- Ornamental shrubs: 22

Considering the tremendous benefit of his work to people around the world (many of his crops are grown in many foreign countries), Luther Burbank was easily the world's most important organic gardener.

*March 1957*

### Soaking Seeds

Instructions for starting some seeds suggest soaking them in warm water for 24 hours. I had trouble keeping the water warm until I thought of using my thermos bottle. I place each kind of seed in its own plastic bag with holes punched in it, put the bags into the thermos, and fill it with warm water. By the next day, the seeds are ready for planting.

*Carol Neff*
*Vichy, Missouri*
*November 1985*

# Throw Away Your Spade and Hoe

*Ruth Stout*

Getting on in years? Well, don't ever think organic gardening must be a wonderful experience of the *past*. You can do it "from a wheelchair, if necessary!"

When someone, not long ago, saw my garden for the first time and heard the method I've worked out, she exclaimed: "Why, you can grow vegetables until you're a hundred! From a wheelchair, if necessary."

I'm now 69 and am not a particularly vigorous woman, but I do all the work in a garden 40 by 60 feet, raising enough vegetables for my husband, my sister, myself, and many guests. I freeze everything, from early asparagus to late turnips. We never buy a vegetable.

I also do my housework, raise quite a few flowers, and rarely do any work after 2 P.M. I'm scarcely ever more than just pleasantly tired. Dinner at night usually requires about half an hour's time, with food from a deep freeze to rely on.

Now I'm not boasting, at least not about what a whiz of an organizer, or something, I am. But I *am* proud of having figured out a way of gardening which brings top results with a minimum of labor. Do you, perhaps, feel you would like to be able to garden until you're really getting along? Well, you can.

Twenty-four years ago, my husband and I moved from New York City to a farm in Connecticut, and I could hardly wait to plant a garden. We had a much too large plot plowed up, and that first summer I struggled with stones and fresh sod in which the spot abounded. And I of course hoed, weeded, and cultivated.

For several summers thereafter, I kept growing more than we could use, foolishly unwilling not to utilize the whole plot, since I had spent so much time getting it in shape. But gradually I did reduce the size of my garden, until, 14 years ago, it was only a third as large as it was originally. However, it was still too much work; I, of course, wasn't quite as full of pep as I had been, and also I was now trying to can all the surplus.

The only jobs in the garden I

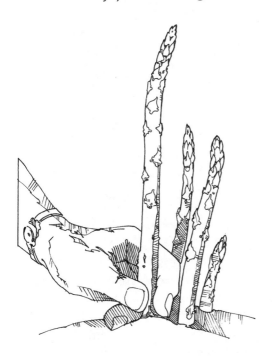

*Asparagus does beautifully on land that is not planted year after year.*

didn't do were the plowing and harrowing; every other thing I had always done myself. And very eager each spring to get started, it seemed that usually everyone had just broken or loaned his plow, or had had some other calamity, when I was rarin' to put in some peas.

## To Heck with Plowing!

About 11 years ago, I was as usual trying to be patient until someone could do some plowing for me, when finally, one day, I used my head. No, not for plowing—for reasoning. My asparagus was doing beautifully and I said to myself: That ground hasn't been plowed for over 10 years; what has asparagus got that peas haven't? To heck with plowing! I'm going to plant.

So a little fearfully, I started to put in peas and spinach, intending to dig a minor trench first to loosen the earth. But I found that the mulch (leaves and hay) that I had dumped on the garden in the fall (to be plowed under in the spring) had kept the earth soft and moist; I merely needed to clear a spot with the rake and drop the seeds.

And having once started to take things into my own hands, I kept on. If I scramble around and get lots of mulch, I thought, and wholly cover the garden with it (6 or 8 inches thick), no weeds can get through and the sun can't bake the soil. Even by the end of June, when I plant the last corn and the second beets, carrots, and so on, the ground will surely still be soft. And it was—but I'm getting ahead of myself.

Our milkman, a farmer, was glad to give me what he called "spoiled hay" and I called wonderful mulch. I spread it thickly over the entire garden, except, of course, on top of the seeds I had just planted. I did, however, put a lot over the asparagus, as I knew that could come up through the mulch. In a couple of years I abandoned all commercial fertilizers.

After putting the hay around, I soon found that the only jobs left were planting, thinning, and the picking. Whenever I wanted to put in some seeds, I raked the mulch back and planted, and later, when the seeds had sprouted, I pulled the mulch close around the little plants, thus keeping the ground around them moist and outwitting the weeds.

Naturally the neighboring farmers at first laughed at me; for a few years they doted on stopping by in the spring to ask if I didn't want some plowing done. But, little by little, they were impressed by my results, and when they finally had to admit that the constantly rotting mulch of leaves and hay was marvelously enriching my soil, they didn't tease anymore. On the contrary, they would stop by to "have one more look" before finally deciding to give up plowing and spading and to mulch their own gardens.

There is much talk nowadays of compost piles, and they are fine, but hard and cumbersome work for a woman.

## One Carrot Feeds Five

My plot has become so rich that I can plant very closely, and I don't even use manure now. The garden is now one-eighth its original size and so luxuriant that in the fall we call it the jungle; one of my carrots, sweet and tender, was large enough to serve five people. My sweet Spanish onions average 1 pound apiece; some weigh 1¼ pound.

I have never liked to transplant (it would be impractical, anyway, from that wheelchair of the future), so I plant such things as cabbage, cauliflower, and so forth, 12 or 15 inches apart and then pull out all but one in each group.

Another item: do you have trouble with bush peas bending over—lying on the ground and rotting in wet weather? All you need do is pull an extra amount of hay up to them on all sides and they stand as straight as tin soldiers, no matter how loaded with peas they are. And they are easy to pick.

I mulch the flowers, too, but with a bow to beauty, I use the leaves and hay from the vegetable garden after it has rotted sufficiently to look almost like earth. Sweet peas, which seem to be difficult to grow hereabout, respond miraculously to my system; I don't dig a trench or use manure, but plant them in the vegetable garden and mulch them. This past dry summer, when even some artesian wells in our locality gave out, didn't faze my sweet peas. I never had more or nicer ones, didn't water them at all, and picked the last lot in mid-September.

I haven't used any poison for bugs in ten years, and I never see a bean beetle, a corn borer, an aphid, or a cutworm. I stopped using poisons because I hated the thought of them, and at first I couldn't understand why the bugs didn't plague me. Was a kind Providence rewarding me for—well, I didn't know what for—*or* were these tales I had heard lately about organic gardening really true? I didn't feel that I knew enough about the subject to argue the point, so I settled for being grateful that some little fairy, organic or otherwise, was keeping the pests out of my garden.

## No Heavy Work

If you have to garden and are not very enthusiastic about it, my method is your answer; you can do the job with minimum time and labor. And if you love such work, it is also the answer; you can keep at it indefinitely.

So get rid of your hoes, spades, and cultivator; the largest digging tool you'll need is a trowel. And when, although you're really getting along in years and you still have a wonderful garden, people marvel and ask who does the heavy work, you can truthfully reply: "There is no heavy work."

*July 1954*

## Wood Ashes Make Bugs Vanish

Here's something we discovered this spring about gardening. The bugs were beginning to get the green beans, and I was hesitating to use poison, when a good neighbor lady said, "Why, child, you needn't put poison on your green beans; just get some plain old wood ashes and sprinkle some on them."

Needless to say, I was skeptical, but since my neighbor lived next door, she would know if I didn't try her suggestion. Well, I sprinkled wood ashes over the whole garden, even the cabbages, and do you know, it worked! Sprinkle the ashes once or twice while the beans are growing, and when it is time to pick them, there won't be a trace of an insect or insect damage. The good lady specified that it had to be wood ashes that had not been wet, and that they can be used on the whole garden.

My husband and I are ready to burst with pride over our organic garden. This fall I am going to deep mulch one garden (we have two gardens) and give Mrs. Stout's method a try. My husband says it can't be done. We are soon about to find out.

*Mrs. Kenneth Carter*
*Warrensburg, Missouri*
*September 1959*

# Rex Stout Tells Ruth How to Garden

## Ruth Stout

Brothers and sisters don't always agree—especially in the Stout family, where one is foremost mystery writer Rex and the other is our mulcher Ruth. Here, brother Rex tells about some gardening experiences, and sister Ruth comments sagely.

When my brother Rex and I were on a radio program together not long ago we got into a tangle, which stopped just short of a hair-pulling match, because he contended that gardening was hard work and that there was no way to get around this. However, we do agree in general, and when I asked him to come over to lunch and talk about flowers, I thought I would probably go along with most of his comments.

To put him in the best possible humor I fed him the Stout national dish: navy beans simmered for hours with a hunk of salt pork. Then we got into comfortable chairs, and he began:

"Of all the activities a man can spend his time on, gardening is about the only one which is certain to present him with a bewildering succession of delight and dismay." So far, so good, but he added: "If, after my 30 years of trying to nurse hundreds of plants into vigor and bloom, I was asked to give useful advice to an aspiring gardener, I would tell him to always expect the dismay; then the delight, when it comes, will be a glorious surprise."

My system (or temperament) is just the opposite; for goodness' sake, expect delight. If dismay is what you get, it will be a jolt, yes, but think of all the wonderful expectant hours you spent! And the dismay needn't last long: In no time at all you find yourself anticipating fresh delights.

Rex went on to say that certainly you must never expect a particular delight to repeat itself, and I had to agree with this. He illustrated: "A few years ago I acquired three plants of a new variety of penstemon, and put them in a likely corner of a border. When they bloomed the following year they were really spectacular, and some weekend guests were so indelibly impressed that the following year, on the proper date, they unexpectedly arrived with a whole gang of their friends, to show them what a genius Stout was with penstemon. What they saw was one or two scraggly, spindling miseries, with neither bud nor bloom nor prospect of any."

## Plants Have Their Own Laws

He went on to say that he was just about convinced that plants have their own laws, and that they dislike, even bitterly resent, man's attempt to devise and establish sets of rules that vegetation is supposed to follow. Even if the man-made laws are empirical, if they're based on long observation of the conditions under which this or that vegetation is supposed to thrive, plants still don't like the idea; they don't want man presuming to tell them where and how to get along.

"To demonstrate this theory," Rex continued, "some 20 years ago, I decided I wanted some edelweiss in the rock garden, so I read up on it: four articles in my collection of magazines and a chapter in each of three books. Then, feeling that I knew all that man had discovered about edelweiss, I selected a spot, prepared it accordingly, got plants from a good grower, and put the little dears in the ground.

"The following spring no sign of edelweiss, and that identical performance was annually repeated for 6 years; I checked over and over with the information, to make sure I wasn't slipping up somewhere. The seventh year, I was finally rewarded: One wretched little sprig of edelweiss showed up. Outraged, I lifted it with a trowel and transplanted it in a wet, poorly drained border that never got much sun, back of some primroses, a place having all of the attributes edelweiss is supposed to hate, and none of those it likes, according to the literature. This was 13 years ago; that spot (about 5 feet square) has gradually become as fine a plantation of healthy and happy edelweiss as you would care to see."

I believed every word of this, and when he went on to say he had had similar experiences with blue gentian, trailing arbutus, hybrid columbine, yellow lady slipper, and so on, I flippantly suggested:

"So the answer is simple enough: the way to grow flowering plants successfully is to read the rules, then carefully violate all of them."

Good to know, if true, but we both had to admit that we had successfully grown a great number of plants by following the rules. Rex said he had decided that each and every individual flower is unique. But he added that you might as well begin by following the rules (some of them, anyway), provided you know how to interpret them.

"Which reminds me of a zinnia story," he said. "Neil and Sara bought a place in the country and proceeded to garden like crazy. They asked me to dinner the Fourth of July and had a list of horticultural questions ready for me. One of their troubles was that their zinnias hadn't come up, and to prove they had bought good seeds they showed me the empty envelope, and also declared they had carefully followed instructions.

"Sara said, 'For instance, it says on the envelope that the distance should be 12 inches, so we dug the trench exactly 12 inches deep, even measuring it with a ruler.' Before you follow any rule, you do have to understand it."

And it doesn't hurt to try figuring out some of your own, I was thinking, but I kept still: Rex would get around to that, I was fairly sure. And he did.

"When the new hybrid petunias began to be available," he said, "all the articles by experts said they should be started in flats, so I did this the first three or four years. And I never had a complete failure, always getting some plants, but never as many as I wanted. The little seedlings took a lot of tending, too.

"Three years ago I decided to try

another way: In August I mulched a spot (12 square feet) with salt hay to keep the dirt mellow and to abolish weeds; in November I removed the mulch, lightly loosened the top $\frac{1}{4}$ inch of soil, and after mixing the petunia seed with granulated sugar, I broadcast them over the 12 square feet. No raking in.

"The following spring, I got a much higher percentage, having about 220 plants left after three thinnings. I now use this routine with all annuals which self-sow in my climate."

I wanted to ask why, if they self-sow, he doesn't just leave them alone—let them do the whole job themselves. It could be he meant those flowers that he was planting for the first time, or there might be some reason why it's better to plant fresh seeds every year, even if the flower is self-sowing. But I didn't ask any questions; if there *is* a reason why these plants should have a fresh sowing every year, I don't want to know it. I am busy enough.

## Two Gardener Types

Now Rex was off on a different angle: "There are two kinds of gardeners— those who insist on trying to master the demand and temperaments of the more difficult flora, and those who refuse to bother with the prima donnas. The latter gardeners, of whom I am one, fill their beds with friendly types that will stand for a lot of give and take.

"For instance, a friend of mine insists on growing Lady Washington geraniums, because they're more difficult to manage, whereas I have zonals, because they're easier to grow—and just as desirable. My favorite geraniums are the scented-leaved ones; they don't flower as exuberantly as zonals, but the great variety of their fragrances more than compensates. The apple geranium is my particular pet, and from October to May, I keep four or five of them here and there around the house, rarely passing one without thumbing a leaf and having a sniff."

Then, with a sidelong glance at me, Rex suggested: "What say we end this with controversy?"

"Sure, why not?" I shrugged, but was alert, wondering what was coming.

"For one thing, you're going to make a religion out of gardening, if you don't watch out," he said. "There's nothing wrong with mulch, but if you, for instance, pile it thick on Virginia bluebells, you won't get any spread. Organic gardening is okay, but if there's too much organic matter in your nasturtium soil, you'll get only

leaves—no flowers. Chemical fertilizers are all right if you know how to use them properly and can afford them. There's nothing wrong with spraying for insects and diseases if your nose can stand the smell and your back and pocketbook can stand the strain." He stopped and grinned. "Your turn."

## Ruth's Response

"You sound like a roomful of garden club women," I began. "About Virginia bluebells: If they won't spread under mulch, skip it.... Plant nasturtiums in poor soil, but put mulch on top to keep moisture in and weeds out.... If you're devoted to chemical fertilizer, enjoy yourself; I don't need it. As to poison spraying, I loathe the job and the odor, and can't get rid of the perhaps fanciful notion that maybe the poisons don't discriminate between good and bad bugs, so I don't spray and I never lose a vegetable crop. I have black leaf spot on my roses, but so do people who spray theirs. I wouldn't advise anyone not to spray—that's his affair—but I'm genuinely sorry for sprayers."

I added: "If you *were* a group of gardeners, I would probably end this way: "Read what the experts say, if you want to, then go ahead and use your own brains, too, not just theirs." You can relax, Rex; I'll never make a religion out of my way of gardening.

*September 1958*

# The Couch
# I Live On

*Ruth Stout*

America's favorite mulcher—now over 80 years young— lets you share her latest "pillow talk" and her easy-does-it garden method!

When I assure a group of gardeners to whom I am giving a talk that my year-round mulch system eliminates nine-tenths of the labor necessary in the time-honored method of plowing, cultivating, and the like, I can sense—by the expressions on the faces before me—that this claim doesn't mean very much. Perhaps that's because it's too nebulous; it sounds too indefinite. So, sometimes I am more explicit, going into detail as to how much time I spend on my gardens during the four seasons. And this, although almost invariably convincing the audience, surprises even those who have read my books about this time-saving idea.

First, I state that I do all of the work in my 45-by-50-foot vegetable garden, besides several flower beds, and someone invariably raises his hand at this point to ask: "What time do you get up?" The answer to that, at any time of year, is "When I feel like it"—which is practically never before sunrise. For some obscure reason, I like to have the sun up and on the job before I start to operate! If I'm up late the night before, which isn't often, it may be eight or nine o'clock before I get up. (Since my husband's death five years ago, I live alone, so no one else is affected by my rising time.)

Let's start with a morning in spring, traditionally the busiest season of the year for a gardener. I may perhaps cover the crocuses with wire (to outwit the rabbits), plant some vegetable seeds, lay some potatoes on the ground and cover them with hay (my method of planting them), gather dandelions for lunch, or dig a few parsnips for dinner. A little later in the season, I may pick and freeze some asparagus. And I'll check to see if there are spots anywhere in the garden that should have more hay laid down on them.

All of that may take an hour or two. Then I'm back into the house, to answer a few letters from gardeners who may want to know how thick to spread the mulch, and so on. And where am I when I write? Well, you won't be too surprised (I hope) to learn that I'm propped up on the couch again; for me it's relaxing to have my feet up when I'm not on them. And that's considered healthful, too, I believe.

Then, if in the mood, I go outdoors again for a short time, then lunch, and I'm through for the day as far as work is concerned—except, since it's spring, I must go to the garden and do some covering if frost threatens. However, with baled hay already lying along each row, this isn't much work. I find it is more satisfactory in every way, in my opinion, than hotcaps or baskets or anything else I've ever used.

## Gardens Need Little Attention in Summer

Now it's summer, and my sister has come out from New York for about five months' stay in her cottage, which is the proverbial stone's throw (or maybe two throws, depending on who's doing it) from me. She likes to do a spot of cleaning in my house once a week, but since she seldom spends more than three or four hours at it, I could, of course, take care of it myself and still stick to my "no-work-after-lunch" routine. My gardens, both vegetable and flower, now need almost no attention, except to pick whatever's ready to eat.

I freeze quite a lot of just about everything I grow and never buy any vegetables except sauerkraut and artichokes. Incidentally, I hope you freeze peppers and tomatoes *raw;* they taste as though they had just been picked when you take them from the freezer. Just cut them up without peeling and put into containers to freeze.

When I said that my garden needs "almost no attention," I meant that there is still some planting to be done in early summer—corn, soybeans, kale, turnips, lettuce, peas, Chinese cabbage—all of which work probably consumes from two to three hours. So, at this time of year, when gardeners who aren't letting mulch do most of their work are weeding, hoeing, watering, and maybe indulging in a bit of swearing at times, we mulchers can do just about as "the spirit moves us"—to be outside if that's our desire, but stay inside if the sun is too hot, and so forth. And our plants won't suffer from lack of attention.

## Starting the Year-Round Mulch System

Let's consider those of you who already have a garden plot (I am speaking of vegetables, but flowers can be handled the same way) that up to now has been plowed once a year. It is spring, and if you are an organic gardener, your patch is covered with last season's refuse, such as squash and pumpkin vines, corn stalks, pea vines, and so on. This year you aren't going to plow, so you just go ahead and put in the very earliest crops, such as lettuce, parsley, spinach, and peas. As soon as the tiny plants appear, put plenty of mulch (hay, leaves, sawdust—any vegetable matter that rots) between the rows and up close around the plants.

Here in my Connecticut garden, for instance, I plant bush peas between the corn rows and pile plenty of hay on both sides of them so that they won't fall over and shade the corn. Also, the hay keeps the vines upright and easy to pick.

Next, some mulch—about 8 inches thick, to discourage all weeds—should be spread over all the rest of the garden before you plant; if you don't do this, the ground will be baked if it doesn't rain. And if it should rain, weeds will get ahead of you.

When you plant in a garden that is already mulched, first mark the row, then pull the hay away from the spot, and plant right in the earth, just as you would if you were gardening the old-fashioned way. I find it a good idea to cover the plantings of small seeds (carrots, for example) with either a narrow board or strip of paper, or with ½ inch of sawdust; this will keep the ground soft and moist. However, if you use a board you must be very sure to remove it just as soon as the seeds germinate and then, of course, pull the mulch up close to the plants.

Larger seeds, such as corn, peas, beans, and squash, may be planted the usual way, them immediately covered with a loose hay mulch, 1 or 2 inches thick. I have found that covering the corn seeds nonpluses the crows; at least I haven't had any trouble with them since I've done this—and I had plenty of crow-worry in former years.

Onion sets may just be scattered around on last year's mulch, then covered with a few inches of loose hay; by this method you can "plant" a pound of them in a few minutes, and you may do it, if you like, before the ground thaws. Also, lettuce seeds will germinate if merely thrown on frozen earth—but not on top of mulch. And this, of course, can't be done if you plow before planting.

Many people have discovered that they can lay seed potatoes on last year's mulch, or on the ground or even on sod, cover them with about 1 foot of loose hay, and later simply pull back the mulch and pick up the new potatoes. In case you haven't noticed, potato plants and their flowers are quite pretty, so you can start this crop in a flower bed if you like. Ours is placed at one end of the bed of iris.

A few weeds may come through your mulch here and there; this will be because you didn't apply it thickly enough to defeat them. They are easy to pull if you want to take the trouble, but the simplest thing is to just toss a bit of hay on top of them. And if a row of something such as turnips or carrots needs thinning, this can be done effectively by simply covering the plants you want to get rid of with a little mulch.

## Autumn Chores and Winter Pleasantries

My garden chores in the fall are much the same as in summer—harvesting and freezing the produce. About the middle of November, I spread hay around and rake leaves. Now is also a good time to carry some hay into the corn patch with a pitchfork, putting chunks all along the rows. Next spring, I will prop up my pea plants with it when this vegetable is planted between the rows of corn. And I can take anywhere from a week to a month for this hay job; there's no reason for it to make me feel pushed. I'll put a few bales on top of the row of carrots and will dig them throughout the winter, whenever I want some.

I order my seeds and arrange the packets alphabetically, make a diagram for the coming season's planting, and write a weekly column—all of which can be termed "work," so I do it in the morning, knocking off at one o'clock. However, since my first garden book was published, more than 2,200 people have called here, morning, afternoon, and evening, to have a firsthand look at my mulch system. But showing them around and answering their questions isn't "work," really.

## Make Up Your Mind

About the hardest work is probably making up your mind to one thing: If you are the only person in your neighborhood who is using this no-plow, no-spade, no-cultivating method, your friends and neighbors will say you are crazy. Ignore them. They will change their tune. Twenty years ago everyone called me crazy, but just the other day, a neighbor said to me, "Doesn't it make you feel good, when you drive around, to see the great piles of hay in so many yards?"

It does. It makes me feel very good—even more relaxed and smiling here on the couch!

*June 1966*

# Organic Gardening's List of Seed Suppliers

What could be easier than planning your garden and shopping for your seeds from the comfort of your home? Here's *Organic Gardening*'s latest list of seed catalogs, complete with asterisks (\*) beside the companies that offer only nontoxic untreated seeds and a "+" sign by the ones that will ship to both the United States and Canada. (Companies with no "+" prefer to ship only within their home country.) Browsing through seed catalogs is a great way to ease the late-winter wearies and to get great ideas for your garden at any time of year.

### Abundant Life Seed Foundation *+
P.O. Box 772
Port Townsend, WA 98368
*Nonprofit foundation dedicated to the preservation of open-pollinated and heirloom seeds. Over 600 varieties of vegetable, herb, flower, wildflower, and tree seeds. Free catalog.*

### Aimers Seeds Co. *+
81 Temperance St.
Aurora, ON
Canada L4G 2R1
*Flower, vegetable, and herb seeds. Also bulbs, roses, and native plants. Catalog $4 U.S.*

### Alberta Nurseries and Seeds Ltd. *+
Box 20
Bowden, AB
Canada T0M 0K0
*Flower and vegetable seeds, ornamental and fruit trees, and perennial flowers suited to short-season and West Coast gardening. Catalog free in Canada, $2 U.S.*

### W. Atlee Burpee Co. *+
300 Park Avenue
Warminster, PA 18974
*Large selection of flowers, vegetables, and fruit and nursery stock. Free catalog.*

### Bountiful Gardens *+
18001 Shafer Ranch Road
Willits, CA 95490
*Nonprofit project offering a wide range of open-pollinated vegetable, herb, and flower seeds. Sole U.S. source for Chase Seeds—European heirloom vegetables—plus many cover crops and grains. Catalog free in U.S., $2 (U.S.) to foreign addresses.*

### Butterbrooke Farm *+
78 Barry Road
Oxford, CT 06483
*Pure line, short-season vegetable seeds at reduced prices.*

### The Cook's Garden *+
P.O. Box 53528
Londonderry, VT 05148
*Vegetable and flower seeds including large selection of salad greens. Free catalog.*

### William Dam Seeds Ltd. *+
P.O. Box 8400
Dundas, ON
Canada L9H 6M1
*Vegetable, field crop, herb, flower, and houseplant seeds. Catalog $2.*

### De Giorgi Seed Co. *+
6011 N Street
Omaha, NE 68117
*Vegetable, flower, herb, grass, wildflower, and perennial seeds and bulbs. Free catalog.*

### Deep Diversity Catalog *+
Box 190
Gila, NM 88038
*One thousand varieties emphasizing biodiversity; food plants, herbs, flowers, fiber plants, heirlooms, medicinals, and plants with no known value. Catalog $4; free seed list.*

### Down on the Farm Seed *+
P.O. Box 184
Hiram, OH 44234
*Vegetable and flower seeds, mainly open-pollinated. Free catalog.*

### Ecogenesis Inc. *+
16 Jedburgh Road
Toronto, ON
Canada M5M 3J6
*Insect- and disease-resistant vegetables. All open-pollinated. Catalog $2.*

### Fedco Seeds *
P.O. Box 520
Waterville, ME 04903
*Vegetable, herb, and flower seeds at low prices. Selected for flavor, productivity, and suitability to northeastern U.S. climate. Catalog $2.*

### Henry Field's Seed & Nursery
415 N. Burnett
Shenandoah, IA 51602
*Vegetables, fruits, trees, shrubs, perennials, bulbs, herb seeds, plants, beneficial insects, and garden supplies. Free catalog.*

### Filaree Productions *
Route 2, Box 162
Okanogan, WA 98840
*More than one hundred strains of certified organic garlic. Free catalog.*

### Garden City Seeds * +
1324 Red Crow Road
Victor, MT 59875
*Hardy varieties; roots and tubers; many heirloom, organic, open-pollinated varieties. Free catalog.*

### Ed Hume Seeds * +
P.O. Box 1450
Kent, WA 98035
*Vegetable, flower, and herb seeds for short-season climates. Dahlia and gladiolus bulbs, safe slug and snail control, bird deterrents, and other garden products. Catalog (U.S.) $1; (Canada) $2.*

### Johnny's Selected Seeds +
310 Foss Hill Road
Albion, ME 04910
*Vegetable, herb, flower, and specialty seeds. Free catalog with detailed cultural information.*

### Mapple Farm *
RR #1
Hillsborough, NB
Canada E0A 1X0
*Certified organic French shallots, Chinese and Jerusalem artichokes (in spring and fall), Egyptian onions (in midsummer), and limited supply of sweet potato slips (early June) to Canadian customers only. Catalog free with SASE.*

### Native Seeds/Search * +
2509 N. Campbell Avenue, #325
Tucson, AZ 85719
*Collects native-crop seed stocks from the greater Southwest. Membership includes discount on seed packets and subscription to the quarterly newsletter. Membership $20 per year. Catalog $1.*

### Nichols Garden Nursery +
1190 N. Pacific Highway
Albany, OR 97321
*New and traditional vegetables for the flavor-conscious gardener. Gourmet and Oriental varieties, herb plants, and herb and flower seeds. Gardening supplies. Free catalog.*

### P & P Seed Co. * +
14050 Route 62
Collins, NY 14034
*Giant vegetable seeds. Free catalog.*

### Park Seed Co. * +
Cokesbury Road
Greenwood, SC 29647
*More than 1,500 varieties of flower seeds, bulbs, flowering vines, roses, and herbs, and 400 varieties of vegetable seeds. Gardening accessories. Free catalog.*

### Peaceable Kingdom School * +
P.O. Box 313
Washington, TX 77880
*Organically grown, open-pollinated, vegetable, ornamental, and herb seeds. Free catalog.*

### Peaceful Valley Farm Supply
P.O. Box 2209
Grass Valley, CA 95945
*Organic, open-pollinated vegetable seeds and bulk cover crops, wildflowers, native grasses, and pasture seeds; bulbs, seed garlic, and potatoes. Free catalog.*

### Pinetree Garden Seeds +
P.O. Box 300, Route 100
New Gloucester, ME 04260
*Specializes in small packets of vegetable, herb, flower, and everlasting seeds at reduced prices; also bulbs, tubers, and plants. Free catalog.*

### Plants of the Southwest
Agua Fria, Route 6, Box 11A
Santa Fe, NM 87501
*Native and drought-tolerant seeds and plants of grasses, flowers, shrubs, trees, and traditional vegetables. Catalog $3.50. For price list, send SASE.*

### Prairie Grown Garden Seeds * +
Jim Ternier, Box 118
Cochin, SK
Canada S0M 0L0
*Seeds for short growing seasons. All seeds open-pollinated, grown without the use of agricultural chemicals. Catalog for two first-class stamps (Canada); $1 (U.S.).*

### Rawlinson Garden Seed +
269 College Road
Truro, NS
Canada B2N 2P6
*Vegetable, herb, and flower seeds. Catalog free (Canada); $1 (U.S.), refundable.*

### Ronniger's Seed Potatoes
Star Route 80
Moyie Springs, ID 83845
*More than 150 varieties of seed potatoes including many heirlooms and European strains, all organically grown. Catalog $1.*

### Salt Spring Seeds * +
Box 33
Ganges, BC
Canada V0S 1E0
*Organically grown seeds. Over one hundred varieties of dried beans. Specializing in high-protein crops. Catalog $2.*

**Saskaberia Seeds** * +
P.O. Box 26
Prairie River, SK
Canada S0E 1J0
*Seventy organically grown
tomato varieties. Catalog $1
cash (U.S.).*

**Seeds of Change** * +
P.O. Box 15700
Santa Fe, NM 87506
*Certified organically grown
seeds. Open-pollinated food
plants, herbs, and flowers.
Traditionals and heirlooms a
specialty. Free catalog.*

**Seeds Trust,
High Altitude Gardens** +
P.O. Box 1048
Hailey, ID 83333
*Vegetable, wildflower, herb,
and native grass seed adapted
to high elevations and cold,
short growing seasons. Catalog
$3 (U.S.); $4 (Canada); price
list free with SASE.*

**Seeds-West
Garden Seeds** * +
P.O. Box 27057
Albuquerque, NM 87125
*Heirloom and hybrid vegetables
and herb and wildflower seeds
chosen for short season and
western growing. Free catalog.*

**Select Seeds—
Antique Flowers** +
180 Stickney Hill Road
Union, CT 06076
*Seeds of old cultivars of garden
flowers with the emphasis on
fragrant, cutting garden varieties. Catalog $3 for two years.*

**Shepherd's Garden Seeds** +
30 Irene St.
Torrington, CT 06793
*Vegetable varieties chosen for
fresh eating, adaptability, and
disease resistance. Also, old-
fashioned, everlasting, and edible flower seeds. Free catalog.*

**R. H. Shumway,
Seedsman** * +
P.O. Box 1
Graniteville, SC 29829
*Vegetable, flower, lawn, and
field seeds. Fruit, roses, bulbs,
and shrubs. Specialize in old-
time and open-pollinated seeds.
Free catalog.*

**Southern Exposure
Seed Exchange** * +
P.O. Box 170
Earlysville, VA 22936
*Specializing in open-pollinated,
disease-resistant vegetable varieties; many heirlooms.
Multiplier onions, garlic, herbs,
sunflowers, and uncommon
vegetables. Catalog and garden
guide $2, refundable.*

**Southern Seeds** +
P.O. Box 2091
Melbourn, FL 32902
*Seeds of vegetables and some
tropical fruits for hot climates.
Free catalog.*

**Stokes Seeds Inc.** +
Box 548
Buffalo, NY 14240
or
Box 10
St. Catharines, ON
Canada L2R 6R6
*More than 2,500 vegetable
and flower varieties. Free cat-
alog contains detailed growing
information.*

**Talavaya Seeds** *
P.O. Box 707
Santa Cruz, NM 87567
*Native open-pollinated seeds,
especially corn, beans, melon,
squash, and chilies. Free
catalog.*

**Terra Edibles** * +
Box 63
Thomasburg, ON
Canada K0K 3H0
*Organically grown vegetable
seeds, including heirlooms and
varieties for small spaces, high
flavor and nutrition, edible landscaping, and attracting bees and
butterflies. Free catalog.*

**Territorial Seed Co.** *
P.O. Box 157
Cottage Grove, OR 97424
*Mainly for gardeners west of the
Cascades. American and Euro-
pean seed selected for short sea-
sons, cool climates. Free catalog.*

**Territorial Seeds Ltd.**
206-8475 Ontario St.
Vancouver, BC
Canada V5X 3E8
*Primarily for gardeners on the
lower mainland and islands of
British Columbia. Seed selected
for short seasons, cool climates.
Free catalog.*

**Thompson &
Morgan Inc.** +
Department PRS
Jackson, NJ 08527
*Free flower and vegetable seed
catalog.*

**Tomato Growers
Supply Co.**
P.O. Box 2237
Fort Myers, FL 33902
*More than 200 tomato and 75
pepper varieties. Free catalog.*

**Totally Tomatoes** * +
P.O. Box 1626
Augusta, GA 30903
*Hundreds of tomato and
pepper varieties. Free catalog.*

**Vermont Bean Seed Co.** *
Garden Lane
Fair Haven, VT 05743
*Hybrid and heirloom seeds.
Free catalog.*

# Index

Note: Page references in *italic* indicate tables. **Boldface** references indicate illustrations.